P9-DWK-024

Picking flowers
ON DUSTY ROADS

Picking Flowers
ON DUSTY ROADS

ODDNY GUMAER

partners
PUBLISHING HOUSE

Partners Publishing House

PICKING FLOWERS ON DUSTY ROADS

Copyright © 2011 by Oddny Gumaer

All rights reserved. Printed in Thailand.

Editor Ed Strauss
Layout & Design Sacha Olson
Front Cover Photo Kris Ryan
All Other Photos Private

Printed by ActsCo Printing

No part of this publication may be reproduced, stored
in a retrieval system, or transmitted in any form or by any
means – electronic, mechanical, photocopy, recording or
any other – except for brief quotations in printed reviews,
without prior permission of the publisher.

Requests for information should be addressed to:
pickingflowers@partnersworld.org

Unless otherwise indicated, all scripture quotations
are taken from the Holy Bible: New International
Version. NIV. Copyright 1973, 1978, 1984. Zondervan
Publishing House.

FOR ELISE, NAOMI & KRISTIN

May you never stop looking for flowers

*All profits from the sale of this book will
be used to help the people of Burma.*

CONTENTS

FOREWORD

Oddny has done it all.

As a child in Norway she collected apples to send to the poor children of Africa. At nine years old she was the founding member of an environmental group that worked for the rights of the animals and against the cutting down of trees. She made her parents eat weeds to save money and be kind to the planet.

Through her teenage years she carried membership in many different activist groups such as No to nuclear weapons, No to the building of dams, Amnesty International, Soviet out of Afghanistan. She was a founding member of Socialistic Youth Forum. Oddny was a featured face of the local newspapers.

Her idealism coupled with an encounter with Christ in 1985, lit a new fire of zeal in her life. She became a vegetarian and attended a small Bible school in Sweden. Plan A was to go to South America or the Philippines after that, but in a twist of divine comedy, Oddny ended up living in Tokyo leading Bible studies for young Japanese students.

That's where I met her in 1987. She was the angel of Ichikawa (Say it to the tune of U2's song, Angel of Harlem, from the album: Rattle and Hum.) Two things Oddny didn't ever want to do: One, live in a capitalist country and two, hang out with an American. Ha, ha, the joke's on her. She moved to Japan and married me, Mr. USA.

We got married in 1990. I wore the tuxedo of a 70's guy that married a lady from Russia and disappeared. Looking at the old photos, I think the velvet bow tie should have been a deal breaker.

After that she survived a two-year culture shock in Las Vegas. She visited Tonga and India, studied for and passed her 6th grade exam in Thai language, and learned to weave through Bangkok traffic on the back of my motorcycle while working for Youth With A Mission (AKA Youth Without Any Money).

In 1994 we met refugees from Burma for the first time. Oddny says this is where she learned what faith is really all about; that refugees showed her what Christianity should really look like.

And that is the subject of this book. It's about meeting the people of Burma, starting Partners Relief & Development, and trying to figure out how to reconcile the deepest desires of the soul together with the daily grind of life on earth.

If you read this book you will fall in love like I did. You will meet an articulate woman with a heart, and hear how her faith informs her experience. She's expressive and sassy; brutally transparent and honest about her shortcomings. This narrative will inspire you. Read on.

Finally, true to her ideals, Oddny dedicates this book and all its earnings to the people of Burma. Just be glad she doesn't make you eat weed soup too!

STEVE GUMAER

Lucky husband to Oddny, CEO and Co-founder of Partners Relief & Development

Introduction

Major Lah Muu died fighting for freedom for his people, the Karen of Burma. His wife is a widow. When I first met her she lived in the only teak house in Mae Saliit Khee village on the Thai-Burma border. I remember looking at her face and wondering if I had ever seen a more beautiful woman before. She was not young, nor did she look like a model from a fashion magazine. She had a serene beauty, like I could have imagined belonging to an Asian Mother Earth.

She was the first Karen person I ever met, her house was the first Karen house I ever entered, and her costumes were the first Karen costumes I ever admired. They were colorful like the lotus flowers around her pond. It looked like she had been created to wear those costumes. She would walk around her property doing her daily chores with a straight back, head lifted high, and steps so soft that the grass hardly bent under her.

The Karen people of Burma wear colorful and ornate costumes like those of Major Lah Muu's widow. Each village and area has different colored shirts and patterns. They all look beautiful to me. For years I have been spending time with the Karen and almost without exception I receive a hand-woven bag or shirt as a parting gift when I leave them. I don't know how many shoulder bags I have. The incredible thing about this is that not one looks the same. They are all unique.

When I first got to know Major Lah Muu's widow, the Karen and their costumes, I noticed strings hanging from different places on their garments. To me they looked like somebody had been in a hurry and hadn't taken the time to fasten the threads when the piece was ready. They were annoyingly messy. Then they told me the meaning of those threads, and I learned to love them.

They would hold the threads in their hands and say, "Try pulling one of them apart!" I did, and it was easy. Then they asked me to take a whole bundle of the threads and try pulling them apart. It was impossible.

"This is a symbol of our people," they explained. "If we stand alone, it's easy to break us, but together we make one strong bunch."

Since then I have never been annoyed with the threads that get tangled with each other after a little bit of use. I just say, "It's the Karen people learning to get along so they cannot be broken."

This book is a bit like the threads on the Karen costumes.

I tried so hard to come up with a theme for this book and to focus on one thing. In fact, trying to decide what to write took me about three years. Actually writing the book only took six months of getting up early in the mornings before the rest of the family woke up. I thought about writing a fictional narrative that would be seasoned with facts so that in the end the main characters got each other and kissed, but the reader would also be left with a good portion of facts about Burma. I just don't know how to write fiction though. It would have been so cheesy that my book would end up on the same shelf as the cheap romance novels.

Then I was going to write a true story with fictional elements about one of the people I know. That wasn't going to work either. I didn't feel that I knew anybody from Burma well enough to write three hundred pages about them. I could have written about my husband, Steve, and filled a few books with interesting stuff, but he's not a refugee or a displaced person.

One day I went for a walk in the rain and it was a really bad day. I'd had an attitude problem most of the day, and my family probably thought it was just as well that I was out of the house. It dawned on me that I needed to think like my art teacher taught me: you cannot create art if you're thinking about making something people will like. That will never be genuine. You need to follow your heart and make what is inside you. I thought about my book and that's what I decided to do—write about what's inside me, write about what's on my heart, and write about what I think is important. It may be that nobody will read it, and while that would be sad, it would be okay.

What you're about to read are some of the things that are on my heart at the moment. You may be surprised after you have plowed through the whole thing, that this isn't even all the story. There is more that I could have written. But I remembered my friend in the refugee camp, Arthur, who said, "It is useless if it is of no use."[1]

This book is a jumble of stories—stories about Burma, Partners (the organization we started), my kids, my faith, people I have met and love, my husband, and myself and all my struggles. It doesn't really have a theme because I realized as I was writing that I'm a person who seldom can focus on one theme. My brain skips from one thing to another like my kids skip from one stone to another on the beach. But I believe that all these stories

---

1   See the story of Arthur, page 58

together, although a little weak on their own—like the threads in a Karen shirt—come together to make one strong story. It's a story about faith, injustice, joy, courage, failure, pain, and a lot more.

You have to realize this: it's not a comprehensive story about anything. If you're looking to understand the whole history of Burma, don't look here, because I left a lot out. I'm not a detail freak, nor do I know all the historical and political facts. (However, I did add a short section on recent history at the end of the book.) I just wrote the things I know and that are fairly indisputable. If you want to know more, I have a few books to recommend.

It's not a comprehensive story about Partners either. It's just a collection of stories that are important to me. I do hope that it will give you somewhat of an idea of this group that comprises crazy and brave (actually, not all of them are crazy, but all of them are brave) people from all over the world. Each member of our Partners family has an amazing story to tell, and I only wrote a few here. If it had been a Partners history book, I would've written about when our leaders got together and played with play dough and came up with our vision that we all love so much—free, full lives for the children of Burma. Or I would've written about Sonya finding a husband at long last, or about Ruth getting bit by a tiger.

It's a small appetizer—something to make you want more. It's certainly not a good theology book, although the word theology is mentioned. It is not a book about how to raise children, because, frankly, I'm still trying to figure that one out.

So, what you have is a book full of loose strings that I hope will make one strong bunch. As I wrote it I felt like I was writing a very long letter to my best friend. Maybe that is how you will choose to read it.

Lotus

HOW IT ALL STARTED AND CONTINUED. IT'S ABOUT HOW
SOME XENOPHOBIC DICTATORS CHANGED THE COURSE OF
MANY LIVES. IT'S CALLED: HOW TWO UNLIKELY-TO-
SUCCEED PEOPLE DECIDED TO MAKE A DIFFERENCE.

ELVES IN THE DARK

It was dark when we arrived at the road's end. For seven long hours we had been on a bus with a suicidal driver then had sat on the back of a truck for an hour. Now all around us was black and wet with tropical rain that drizzled down with the same predictability as the arrival of hungry mosquitoes. The truck stopped, leaving no sound to remind us of the world from where we had come. It was quiet, the way the jungle is quiet—no big noises, just thousands of small ones coming from critters we couldn't see.

I noticed eyes. At the edge of the jungle I saw outlines of people, like dark elves that I could barely distinguish. They were there to meet us and to escort us to their village. Some of them had brought umbrellas which they now held above our heads so that we could stay dry, thinking nothing of the fact that they themselves were getting soaked. In seconds they had picked up all our stuff, which included the toilet and the things we needed to build the village's first bathroom, and all the food we would be eating, including a tray of forty-eight eggs.

I knew I was with people I was going to enjoy when one of the village's young men lifted up the toilet, put it on his head like it was a hat made for occasions like this and trotted on through the jungle as if it was the most natural thing in the world. "Hey, don't you guys ever wear toilets on your heads?"

It was a night I will never forget, a trip that changed my life, and days that God had prepared me for ever since I was a little girl back in Norway.

LIVING IN A CAVE WITH THE
WASHING MACHINE ON THE TOILET

It was going to be a break from my Thai language studies. Anybody who has studied Thai will understand the need for a break every so often. It's an incomprehensible language, which most languages are when you don't know them, but surely, Thai is more incomprehensible than others. It has its own alphabet with letters resembling spaghetti noodles thrown about. Thai is tonal, which means that if you use the wrong tone, you'll call somebody a demon instead of older sister; you'll say you are eating a mountain for dinner instead of rice; and, like some friends of mine have done, you may call God a fat woman instead of saying that God is great.

We were living in Thailand and my husband Steve and I were dirt-poor—at least by some standards. Our mode of transportation was a small moped—maroon-colored, and with a gutless engine—or the overcrowded Bangkok buses that cost us less than fifteen cents a trip. We lived in what we had nicknamed *The Cave*. *The Cave* consisted of two rooms in a dormitory in the middle of Bangkok. It was all we could afford, and we walked the four flights of stairs up and down anytime anybody called us on the pay phone down by the entry of the building. That is where we hung our laundry too.

Our two rooms had only one window between them. It was the size of a hand towel. There were two small bathrooms with walls that only went half way up to the ceiling and no plumbing for the sink. When we brushed our teeth and spat in the sink, it would land on our toes seconds later, like a Colgate-flavored waterfall. Since we had the luxury of two bathrooms, we used one of them as a kitchen and placed a washing machine on top of the toilet.

This plastic washing machine with only one setting and buttons adorned with Korean writing had been one of our biggest investments. To pay for it we had painted greeting cards that we sold at our church. The machine balanced well on the toilet, although it may not have been entirely safe. But who thought about *safe* in those days? We lived in a country where men who liked to live dangerously, did the electric wiring creatively. All over the country you could see wires that looked like thick licorice laces, bundled together and dangling over rooftops and roads.

Our dishes were washed in the plumbingless sink. This would take no time at all since we only owned four plates and seldom got into any lavish cooking. All the cooking was done in a toaster oven which limited our dinner options considerably. The clothes we owned were kept in a trunk.

We had chosen this life and only occasionally minded it. We worked for an organization called YWAM (Youth With a Mission) which we, along with thousands of others, had renamed, "Youth Without Any Money." To be mostly broke had its advantages too. How else would we have experienced having "helmet-head," a hairstyle obtained by wearing a motorbike helmet for hours in hot, humid weather? Or feasting on that yummy food bought for pennies from street vendors? When we got bored of the grilled cheese sandwiches that we made in our toaster oven, there were delicious servings of pickled squid, lemon grass and cilantro-flavored soup, curries made by the world's best spices—all pounded together in a mortar—and mint-flavored meat sauce to be had on the street. No dish would ever cost more than a dollar.

I was pretty confident that God was pleased with my good behavior during those days. I was one of those Christians who memorized Bible verses as well as fasted. The fasting was extremely rare and random, but it was still very spiritual when I did it. I felt a sense of superiority compared to a lot of other Christians. Steve taught me a lot, and together we were quite the theologians. His big thing was to come to terms with the Arminian and Calvinism debate. Were we predestined or not? That was the big question those days. It was a huge deal for him, and, I guess, considering what he thought was at stake, it *was* a big deal. Was our depravity total or was it just kind of? Did Jesus die for all or just for the chosen few? I sure hoped it was for all, or that I would be among the chosen few.

In the evenings we could cuddle up on our bed with a mattress filled with coconut husks and enjoy the ideas of J. I. Packer, Tozer, and other great men of faith. We were getting spiritually fat and jolly.

One day we met a lady from Denmark named Anette. Her husband worked for the UN and we thought they must be incredibly rich, living in a real apartment, driving a car and even having a maid. Anette had a heart for righteousness and a big task that she shared with us. She had met the Karen people from Burma and had fallen in love. She had also encountered their enormous needs. Although she went to see them regularly, she had realized that she couldn't help them alone, especially since she and her husband would be leaving Thailand shortly. Would we like to just go and have a look? Perhaps there was something we could do.

Of course we wanted to go! An adventure was something we rarely declined. To get a break from the Thai spelling rules definitely appealed to me. We got on a bus, took a bunch of Dramamines (for motion sickness) and headed for the Thai-Burma border.

But who *were* the Karen from Burma? We didn't know. The only point of reference we had was a cut-out article a lady in the U.S. had sent us. It had a grainy black and white picture of some savage-looking jungle people in a boat. The article described the people group, but it was so poorly written and the picture was so depressing that we had added it to our paper garbage before we finished reading it. So, we really knew nothing about them.

From Anette we learned that Burma was a country ruled by a military junta and that the Karen, along with other ethnic groups, were victims of the dictators' oppression. Most of the people we'd be meeting would be people who had fled their homes because of the acts of the government army. When she told us this, it didn't mean much more to us than if we had read it in the newspaper. Just facts. Yeah, wars happen. I think I was more intrigued to meet a real refugee (almost like going to Alaska and seeing a real grizzly) than I was broken by the fact that right next to us was a country ruled by fear with millions of people suffering under conditions I was unable to imagine.

It wasn't until I sat face to face with the story that it became real. It wasn't until I realized that suffering had a name that I started feeling the pain. It was when a child who had lost her mother stood in front of me that it dawned on me: this was Jesus. This was when His words really hit me: "Truly I tell you, whatever you did for one of the least of these brothers and sisters of mine, you did for me" (Matthew 25:40 NIV).

It happened on day two of our adventure when we were taken to a refugee camp. Among other life-changing events (with people who didn't turn out to be grainy black and white, nor savage) during those few days, we met people who showed us faith in a new way. I don't think it was their intention because they didn't know us, but they challenged us in a way I don't think we had been challenged before.

Well, actually, that's not true. I'm sure we had been challenged plenty of times. We were just slow of hearing and we had focused our energies on a few wrong places. The Bible was there for us to read and live by, but we had somehow missed some of the main points in it. It was as if God had decided to use a different strategy to get our attention.

In the refugee camp we met men and women and children who had fled a war, who had lost what they loved the most, and who had seen evil acted out in a way that ought to be impossible. They had cried for an end to their suffering, they had prayed, they had begged. Now they attempted to build a life worth living there among the thousands of others who shared similar fates, and they smiled as they welcomed us into their homes. In the afternoon of the second day in the camp we walked past the house of a woman named Rose.

Childhood aspiration or Adult anemia?

I felt like I was saved from the premature death, the death which *Vitezslav Gardavsky*, a Communist atheist, describes as a *death after which we go on living for many years.*

A time came to mind when, as a four-year-old farm girl with freckles and pig-tails, I collected apples in my home country, Norway, to send to the poor. God must have put dreams into my heart already back then. Dreams about something bigger, a calling to not settle for a life lived cautiously, but courageously. Eugene Peterson says in his book, *Run with the horses:* "Some people as they grow up become less. As children they have glorious ideas of who they are and what life has for them. Thirty years later we find that they have settled for something grubby and inane. What accounts for the exchange of childhood aspiration to the adult anemia?"[2]

I didn't want to become an anemic adult who had stopped dreaming as soon as obstacles lined up. I wanted to live for what mattered and for values that would outlast me.

---

2   Run with the Horses, *Eugene Peterson* (InterVarsity Press 1983)

ROSE — CHOOSING TO REALLY SEE

Rose had been waiting for years.

She hadn't been waiting to leave the refugee camp. This, she knew, would be a waste of her time. The barb-wired enclosure with thousands of bamboo houses built on the green hills next to Burma was her home now, and she had accepted that fact. She hadn't been waiting for a new job. What she was doing here was what she was destined for. The children in her care needed her. Many of their parents depended on her for them to make it through their days of idle waiting and yearning. The children whose parents were no longer with them relied on her for their lives. No, she knew, without any doubt, that she needed to be where she was.

There were days when her dreams took her back to a world she had once belonged in, and with the dreams came the longing and the regrets. When those feelings threatened to take control, she would brush them away the way she brushed flies off the children's faces when they were sleeping. *It will accomplish nothing to live in the past*, she told herself. She had long ago stopped asking the question, *Why?* These days she was more concerned with another question: *How?*

So her waiting wasn't so much for herself as it was for her people. What she had been waiting for was an end to the war. She was waiting for the day when the world would put her people on the headlines of their newspapers and broadcasts. She was waiting for the day when politicians would say that they were done talking, done using big words she didn't even understand. She was waiting for the day when the welfare of her people would mean more than policies, economics, investments, power, and influence. She was waiting for the day when her people could freely walk back to their villages and homes. She wondered if her waiting would ever end. "Unlikely," she sighed.

Long ago her life had different concerns. Her life had felt so busy back then, but now she smiled at the trivial matters she had concerned herself with: How to cook the best curry for her family or guests? Where to buy the brightest-colored sarong? She let her thoughts take her back to her Rangoon from time to time, and she remembered the tall trees lining the streets where she had lived, the ladies walking to and fro, carrying their market goods on their heads, in baskets, or in plastic basins. Their backs were so straight that it seemed like a bamboo pole was fastened inside their shirts. With their *longyis* tied tightly around their slender bodies they reminded her of the sunflowers in her garden.

The days hadn't been carefree. Nobody who lives in a country oppressed by military dictators is carefree, not even the rich. Fear lingered in the air, impacting every decision, whether it was to invite friends to a birthday party or to laugh at a comedian's show. Trust was a rare feeling those days. To guess who was a tool of the regime was like solving murder mysteries; it could be the street sweeper, the taxi driver, or the person reading the newspaper at the teashop on the corner. One would only find out who it was if one's tongue slipped and spoke a negative sentiment about the government. Such an unfortunate mistake would most likely result in being arrested, sentenced to prison, humiliated, and tortured. It was as important to learn to be quiet and not make any comments that could be judged as negative as it was to learn to fetch water at the well or how to greet an elder.

Still, it was the happy days she often went back to when she let her thoughts wander. How strange that was, she mused. There had been endless trials and heartbreaks, yet, when she reflected on her life, she felt like her days had more laughter than sorrow. She thought of her children playing games with the other kids on the street. She remembered the early morning walks on the trail around Lake Inya with the women from her neighborhood. It used to be something she looked forward to every day. The artificial lake was a meeting point for many. The large body of water was a refreshing sight in the middle of the polluted city.

She was so ignorant in those days, just living her life and caring only for the tasks right in front of her: going to the market, making *samosas*, attending church, making sure her kids had their needs met and her husband was happy. *Had she chosen to be ignorant?* she wondered. Surely the signs all around her had been obvious enough for her to know that she lived in a bubble that could burst at any moment.

Of course she knew that she had been living under some kind of house arrest. The whole country did. But they could never speak of it. They walked around, doing their duties with a smile on their faces—all of them. But if they moved their glance up from the smiling mouth, they saw the fearful eyes. The eyes spoke of bondage, resignation, fear, anger, pain, hunger, and great sorrow. She had seen this every day, but chosen not to really see.

She had seen it in the hungry faces of children and mothers, in the squatters on the outskirts of the city. She had seen it in the faces of the rickshaw drivers who were resting under the trees by the street, waiting for customers. She had seen their fear and their desperation. She had seen it in the frustrated college-aged youth who kicked up dust as they walked down the streets, weary and restless, waiting for a chance to study. She had seen it while watching the news every night. Why did they never get to see any other news than the regime's leaders in their starched uniforms, dark glasses and rows upon rows of medals, doing their duties—dedicating a Buddhist temple, overseeing a new building project, clapping at dancing and singing competitions? Like lobsters that were boiled alive the people accepted that this was how it was, and asked no questions. *Create no waves in the still water.* That was the unspoken command.

She thought of her husband during those years: young, enthusiastic, and so full of ideas and dreams—his wiry hair always moving in all directions, just like his spirit did. In his tanned face were pale freckles, almost invisible, unless one was very close. *One freckle for every new thought,* she would muse. She had fallen in love with his boyish enthusiasm and zealousness. She still loved this part about him. It was also what drove her crazy. His passion and energy was what kept him away from her most of the time.

He spent his days at the medical school. But when her friends' husbands would come home from school or work, her husband was somewhere else. She never knew where. When she asked him he just smiled and said, "I was out doing some important business pretty girls like you shouldn't worry about." At first he would be gone in the evenings, but come back before she fell asleep. He would smell of tobacco and exhaust from cars, but would never say anything about where he had been. Then, as time passed, he wouldn't come home until the middle of the night. Many times she had not even noticed him laying down beside her on the mat on the floor. She had been sleeping soundly.

Finally he would be gone for a day at a time, then for many days. She got used to it, and started being surprised when he came home rather than being gone. She stopped asking him where he had been. She knew he wouldn't tell her. She thought about following him secretly to see where he went, but she was afraid of what she might find. She lived in a country where she had learned that questions were better left un-asked, so she practiced this discipline with her husband.

Then one day he started talking. He told her about their people in other parts of the country who were on the run from the military. He told her of villages destroyed, children killed, of women raped, and of innocent people being treated worse than some of the animals she had seen at the market.

Why had she never heard about this? The news was full of all the favors the generals were doing for the nation, but never a word had been said about driving innocent people out of their homes. As with a lot of other issues, she had chosen not to learn more, she had chosen not to ask, she had chosen not to care. Now, as her husband spoke, she felt that the attitude she had been nursing was indifference, and that it was an attitude as wrong as the gravest sin. Indifference was worse than jealousy and hatred, because indifference left one resigned to doing nothing.

·   ·   ·

It was an idea so unheard of that she had just shrugged at it at first. He could have asked her to get into one of those airplanes she saw in the sky from time to time and it would have been about as crazy. She didn't say much and hoped the thought would pass like the common cold did a few times a year. But it didn't. Every day he would bring it up, and little by little she knew that they needed to do this.

It wasn't so much that she was worried about what it would be like as she was worried about what everybody would say. *Take your children where? To do what? You do this willingly?* She could already hear the voices of accusation from her mother and sisters. They thought she was the most fortunate of them, married to a kind and clever man who was going to become a doctor. She would be living the life they had only dreamed of. Now she was going to give it up? They wouldn't understand. They wouldn't approve.

When Rose and her husband told their family that they wanted to leave Rangoon for a while to go and live with refugees in Thailand it caused a bigger uproar than if the *Swedagon* pagoda had fallen over. It didn't help to explain that they were going to help their own Karen people; maybe some would even be distant relatives. The only thing that anybody heard was that they were leaving comfort and safety to go to discomfort and unsafe conditions. Nobody in their right mind would do that. And nobody in this family had ever *not* been in their right mind.

It took them days to get there on foot. They slept in the houses of relatives on the way. Rose remembered thinking that it felt like all the Karen were related. *We are the Karen*, they said. *We are one family*. They arrived at the village at dusk. She still remembered walking up the steep hill and then overlooking it from the top. It didn't look like she had envisioned it— destitute, gloomy, and desperate. These were people who had fled their homes after all. Instead she saw children playing, women busy doing the chores that women did everywhere—carrying water, wood, and food, washing clothes, cooking, and nursing babies. The men carried bamboo logs or were busy building. They were so far from her home, yet she felt strangely at home while she watched the activity below her. They entered the village and made a temporary home.

It was when they started hearing the stories that she understood why they had come. On the floor of their newly-erected bamboo hut she was told of the horrors of a war that she hadn't known existed. She had thought that her life was like a mild house arrest, but the people she talked to spoke of lives of abuse and violence. *Can humans do these atrocities to other humans?* she wondered. She concluded that men who did the things they had done to these women had long ago ceased to be human. They had turned into monsters like the ones she had read about in the ancient fairytales, the evil demons with green faces often referred to as *yakshas* by her Burmese neighbors—man-eating monsters with only one goal in mind: *power and dominance*.

In the weeks and months to come Rose was busier than she had ever been. She took care of their own kids and other kids. She soon understood that many of the children in the camp were neglected and in need of attention. She realized that the village only looked idyllic on the outside. The longer she stayed there, the more she saw that behind the thin bamboo walls were despair and rampant thoughts of revenge, violence, and death. Not only that, but at night she'd lay awake, hearing the sobs of the women whose husbands let their frustration and pain out by hurting the person closest to them. She heard children cry in the night and knew that she'd never know all the reasons they were crying.

When not caring for children of all ages, Rose would help at the clinic where her husband worked. There was no end to all the sickness. She was glad that there was now a clinic in their area, no matter how small and primitive. She would shudder and think about all the villages with no access to medical care. How many suffered unnecessarily from the lack of medical help? She remembered the big, shiny cars of the generals and the fancy costumes their wives were wearing, and spat on the ground.

In the afternoons she would sit by the river doing their laundry while watching her children play. They were catching bugs and little fish, climbing the trees and swinging from vines. They were turning into jungle kids who were happy and content, but who were not learning to read, write, or do the most basic math. In the mornings she would try to teach them herself, but it only took a few weeks for her to understand that this was not a sustainable solution. Her husband was even more concerned. "A proper education is the best gift we can give our children," he would say. "If they are going to have a good life in the future, they need to go to school."

The problem was that there were no schools where they were living. They would have to leave if the kids were to study. She knew her husband would be reluctant to leave his work in the village. He seemed to have found his dream job and his dream place.

She had an idea then and launched it one evening when he was in a good mood—full from a satisfying dinner, smoking one of the locally-made cigars called *cheroots*. "I could go alone," she said quickly, as if saying it quickly would make him agree quickly. "I can travel alone—with the kids, of course." At first he looked at her as if she had just suggested that she join the resistance army. Then he thought more of it and smiled. She could tell that he loved her and was proud of her courage. He had often praised her for giving up her comfort and wealth to come here and live at the village. Now she was suggesting a perilous trip back to the capital alone with their children. As he digested the idea, he seemed to think that if anyone could make that trip alone, it would be her.

As soon as he agreed she started making plans. She had to act quickly before he changed his mind and told her she was crazy. The trip would be long and dangerous, not to mention uncomfortable. But she was excited. Soon she'd meet her family and her kids would meet their cousins. Soon she'd be strolling down the market aisles, looking for her favorite food stall. Soon she'd be sharing her stories with all her friends.

The trip back was as hard as she had imagined, and harder. Crossing the *Daw Na Mountain* was almost as painful as giving birth. Along the way she traveled with others who were on the way back to their villages or other places. Many took turns helping her with the children and shared their food with them. She appreciated the hospitality and the generosity of her people. A guest was a guest, even while traveling together. If she had learned nothing else the years they had been with the people in the village, she had learned that hospitality didn't depend on a person's wealth, but on a person's heart. But even with a lot of helpers and new friends, the responsibility of traveling so far with small children was a lot more than she had anticipated. She told herself that surviving the trip was the goal. The condition she would be in when she arrived was not as important.

Finally they were there, at the outskirts of her home city. She could see the pagodas from afar. But something didn't seem right. It was as if even the pagodas warned her not to enter the city. Like omens of what was to come, ominous clouds gathered above the ancient buildings, letting go of their weight as the water fell over the city like many thunderous waterfalls. It was the monsoon season, so the rain shouldn't have surprised her. Yet the darkness that came with the rainfall filled her with a feeling of foreboding. It wasn't good to be back.

Rangoon welcomed her like a sick sister. Nothing was like it had been when she had left.

She walked into her former life, met her former friends and neighbors and heard the stories of a regime that had gone mad, of people who were tired of waiting for a change, and who, like wild animals let loose after being in a cage for too long, had vented their frustrations in ways nobody had thought was possible. "We have waited for twenty-three years," they said, "and what have we gotten? Now we hear on BBC radio that our country has 'least developed country' status. What status is that? It's a status for losers."

"We're desperate," her former neighbor told her. They were whispering even though they were inside her house. But these days even the walls had ears, and nobody knew who would be the next victim of the police's random arrests. "We have lost all our money. It's worth less than the paper napkins on the dinner table. It's worth less than lizard poop. All the money we had saved is gone. We can use it to start a fire." As her friend talked, tears rolled down the tired face. Rose had heard the story from many others, but she wanted to hear it again. The general had gone completely crazy now; there was no question about that. His lucky number was nine, so one morning the people woke up and found that all their bank notes were no longer worth anything. Instead, new money was issued, all with numbers divisible by the number nine. All other paper currency was of no value. None at all. Gone were their savings for their children's educations. Gone was the money to pay for rent. Gone was the money to buy food at the market. Gone was their money.

Rose was letting her thoughts take her on the journey she had been on so many times before. The thoughts had almost arrived at that fateful day. The day she lost all hope in goodness and love. The day it felt like God had left her.

Her nephew had always reminded her of her husband. He had the same kind of relentless zeal and way of getting people to follow him into almost anything. She had a feeling that he was up to something when he hardly ever came home to sleep in the evenings and seemed to be gone a lot during the days too. Remembering her husband's activities from years ago, she assumed her nephew was up to something not totally legal. She knew better than to ask.

She found out soon enough. The explosion could be heard in much of the city. Smoke bellowed out of the government radio station as her nephew came panting into the house where she was staying. "I have to leave before they find me," he whispered, afraid they might already be on his heels. Within minutes he had gathered a few belongings and was on the run. She had no idea where he was going, and again, she knew it was better not to ask. She didn't want to know in case they came asking for him.

She had the feeling that evil was coming after her that night when she went to bed. It arrived soon after midnight. It came for her in the dark. No explanation was given for her arrest, just an accusation that she was associated with the resistance. "You think we don't know who you are?" they snarled. "You who went to the black zone[3] without permission! You, a teacher of foreign ideas! You who are married to that slimy doctor that everybody talks about! And you want us to think you are innocent?" She begged and pleaded, she screamed and cursed. All to no avail. They couldn't find her nephew, so they arrested her instead.

Even after her release, she couldn't allow her mind to dwell on those months in prison. As soon as her mind would take her there, she would get up and get busy. She would think of something that she needed to do.

When she slept, however, she couldn't control where her mind took her. That's when the dreams became real and she relived what happened in the dark cell in Insein Prison. "Leave me alone!" she would scream. "Get off of me! I didn't do it!" she would sob, keeping her arms in front of her. The people who had been sleeping close to her would try to calm her. She would wake up, shaking, sweaty, and afraid. She would look into the dark and ask, as she had done many times before, "Where were You when I needed You the most during those months?" And as she had so many times before, she would hear the calm voice saying, *I was there. I was there and I cried with you.* She didn't understand why He, or anybody else, didn't do anything more. One day, when she met Him, she would be told the answer to that difficult question … the *second* most difficult question.

She remembered the day she was let out. Eight months later. It was a warm and sunny day. Her relatives and her children welcomed her—her daughter five, her son a year younger, making their best efforts to help her adjust to life outside the prison walls. All she knew was that she had to get back to the place she belonged—to the arms of her husband, in the village where they had found their destiny.

And then she received the message. It was a message she hadn't anticipated. Not in her darkest nights in the prison cell had she thought that she would hear this: "He's dead. He grieved for you more than anybody had seen a person grieve. Night and day he cried like a child. 'Why did I let her go?' he would bellow and take another sip of alcohol.

---

3   The government divides the country into three zones: the black zone, which is controlled by the opposition, the brown zones which are contested, and the white areas, which are controlled by the government.

Then he got the deadliest disease of all: malaria. The sickness filled his body with a raging fever, making it look like the enemy had sent him a final greeting. When he started hallucinating they decided he needed to go to a hospital. Resourceful villagers were able to get a truck to come and pick him up and take him to the hospital in the nearest town. Not long after he was admitted, however, most of his friends and enemies knew where he was. He was a famous doctor in the area now, having gone from village to village treating the sick. He was loved by his own people, but the enemy detested him, because where they wanted to bring death, he had brought life.

He struggled through nights bathed in sweat. IVs were in his arms and the hospital's sarong was his only clothing.

Then, one morning when a friend came to visit him, he was dead. He had died during the night, alone and desperate. When his friend alerted the hospital staff they looked at the dead man in disbelief. "How could this be?" they marveled. "He was starting to get better last night and we were sure he was through the worst of it. Now was not the time for him to die."

The hospital released his body. His friends arranged a funeral and buried him. But they never found out who had killed him. They knew that it wasn't the malaria, but one of his many enemies who had killed him. That was as certain as the fact that moths fly towards the light at night.

Rose sighed. How she would have wanted to feel his skin against hers one more time, to hear his voice whisper her name. How she would have wanted to feel his fingers in her hair. Instead she remained in Rangoon. There wasn't anything for her to go back to in the village now, just memories. The children went to school in the city. She worked for the rich foreign diplomats and ambassadors in the city. They thought she worked there to earn money, which she did. But she also learned their language. This, she knew, would be a valuable tool in the future. Sooner than she had anticipated she got to use her skills. She was hired to teach at one of the high schools in town.

Meanwhile her country was falling into deeper and deeper desperation. It was as if they were hanging in the air like an insect caught in a spider's web. There had been intense struggles and it looked like they might manage to break loose. But then the spider spun its web once more and the struggle started all over again, some days with a little more

Within a system which denies the existence...

"Within a system which denies the existence of basic human rights, fear tends to be the order of the day. Fear of imprisonment, fear of torture, fear of death, fear of losing friends, family, property or means of livelihood, fear of poverty, fear of isolation, fear of failure. A most insidious form of fear is that which masquerades as common sense or even wisdom, condemning as foolish, reckless, insignificant or futile the small, daily acts of courage which help to preserve man's self-respect and inherent human dignity. It is not easy for a people conditioned by fear under the iron rule of the principle that might is right to free themselves from the enervating miasma of fear. Yet even under the most crushing state machinery courage rises up again and again, for fear is not the natural state of civilized man."

— Aung San Suu Kyi (*Freedom from Fear and Other Writings*) Penguin, 1996 strength, other days with less. They heard whispers that The Lady was back. Some of Rose's neighbors had seen her speak at the Pagoda. A hope that they scarcely dared believe began to rise. Perhaps, perhaps The Lady would bring them to freedom. The generals couldn't oppose the daughter of the great, former leader Aung San, could they? But they dared not speak of it.

Rose had felt slightly guilty for her lack of involvement, but she had no desire to demonstrate on the streets, carrying banners or guns. What she wanted was to live her life in freedom and peace.

Pretending to be going for an errand, Rose and her former neighbor and good friend had walked over to Inya Lake one hot April afternoon. After seeing it, the bloodstains on the bridge haunted her at night. The bridge she had walked across so many times as a young girl now stood there as a witness to the brutal death of innocent youth. It was no longer called White Bridge. Its new name would forever be Red Bridge. Over and over again in her mind she saw the young students—brave youth, courageous, and full of righteous zeal. The leaders in the front were carrying the symbol of Burma: a flag with a peacock—proud and colorful like the people. They were singing songs of victory and of freedom. One song led to another. Then they halted.

The barbwire and the soldiers lined up in combat position by the bridge brought the songs to an end. The students begged to pass, but were not heard. Instead soldiers surrounded them front and back. They were trapped. Within minutes the songs turned into screams of terror as the soldiers shot, clubbed, and beat the youth to death. The students who ran were tracked down, dragged to the lake and held under water until they were no longer breathing. The girls were gang-raped while others continued the killing. They lost more than a hundred youth that day.

The next day the bridge was quiet. The bridge was hosed down with water as government officials frantically tried to hide the evidence against Sein Lwin, the man who now was called the Butcher of Rangoon. He was one of the generals Rose had seen on TV many times. Always slick, always on Ne Win's side. Sein Lwin was a butcher of innocent people. Sein Lwin had ordered the massacre on the bridge. He would strike again.

The auspicious morning arrived with a cool breeze and the promise of a day with no rain. It was August 8, 1988—8.8.88. It was a date to remember. They took to the streets, the ochre-robed monks, children, students, housewives, as well as doctors. Change was all they asked for. Their lives were what they were willing to risk. *That* is what the army took away from them as they rolled out the tanks and shot at the peaceful demonstrators. Automatic rifle fire sprayed bullets into the crowds. Blood was flowing on the streets, the screams were heard all over the city—the screams from the dying, and the screams from the mothers and fathers who lost their beloved children on that day. "Three thousand dead," some said. "Five thousand," said others. They would never know the exact numbers. Nor would they know how many died in the prisons later, hidden in dark cells, tortured beyond recognition.

When the commotion finally died down, the streets were quieter than ever. The only sounds heard were the tanks moving away in the dusk. Then there was the eerie silence. The sound of death. The sound of power becoming an evil machine that strangles and clubs down any who dare to rise up against it.

In the dead silence that followed 8.8.88 Rose felt like she could not breathe. "They are taking everything from me," she thought, "even my ability to breathe." As government officials scrubbed the blood stains off the streets and posted press releases that said that the people filling the prisons were rebels (not the innocent young men and women that they were), they also took the opportunity to close down all schools. All colleges and universities—even elementary schools—were shut down. No statements were made about when they would open again.

Again her children were playing on the street with no school scheduled for the foreseeable future. "This is not what my husband would have wanted for them," she resolved. "It's not what I want either." "The government may try to crush us, but they can't crush me so easily. I will get my children an education at whatever cost." That same night she had phoned her aunt who was living in a village in Karen State. "Can they come and stay with you and go to school there?" she had asked. She promised to pay well and assured her aunt that her children were well behaved and helpful. "I will try to go to Singapore," she promised, not knowing how she was going to get there. "They pay maids really well there."

Leaving her kids with her aunt was hard. She missed them already as she walked away from the village. But she knew she was doing what was best for them, and that they were in good hands.

There was a nagging thought that she had not been able to shake off during the years since her imprisonment and her husband's death. She was not sure he was actually dead. She had not seen his body before the funeral. She had not sat at his wake together with the others, watching over his spirit. She had not seen his grave. How could she be sure that he was dead? What if he had been waiting for her all this time? What if he thought *she* was dead?

As if God had seen her worry, one day she met a lady who told her that refugee camps had been established on the Thai-Burma border. Thousands had fled since the 8.8.88 uprising. There were so many children, but not enough people capable of teaching them. Would she like to come and help? There would be very little money, but a free place to stay and enough food to eat every month.

Like a magnet the camp drew her to itself. She thought it was her husband whispering in the night. Singapore stopped calling her. The thought of doing something meaningful with her life, the thought of her children going to school in the camp and living with her, the thought of being with others who she knew in the village, and the thought of maybe seeing her husband again, made the decision easy. She got her children and went.

He was not there. His grave was, however. Maybe she had known it all along, but had not wanted to admit it. Seeing his grave enabled her to move on. She made a home for the three of them and started her life as a refugee.

Rose had been waiting for many years. Waiting, she thought, was a way of life. It was not a waste of life. It was a rich time of pondering and reflecting, of planning and dreaming. Waiting, she thought, was an art she'd learned after she became a refugee.

She heard voices and the language spoken was neither Burmese nor Karen. She heard English. She smiled. She loved to speak English and to get to know new people. Perhaps today she'd make some new friends. She stood up and walked outside.[4]

---

4   The story of Rose is based on several talks with her and with her daughter, June Rose. The historical facts are true; some of the reflections around it are imagined. I do, for example, know that she lived in Rangoon, but not if she actually took a walk to see the Red bridge. What happened on that bridge, however, is true. I did the best I could trying to imagine her thoughts, but, of course, nobody will ever know if I succeeded.

HER STORY BECAME A DEVOTION FOR US

Rose stuck her smiling face out of the door when she heard us walk by her house and asked if we wanted to come inside for coffee.

Her house was similar to all the others—built with bamboo and nothing else. On her front porch, however, she had flowers thriving in tin cans and other containers. It seemed that vegetable oil cans were the best pots to use for flowers in a refugee camp, those and the boxes used for cookies with pineapple filling. Her plants made her home look inviting and non-refugee-like. So did her happiness.

While drinking the coffee she prepared for us we heard parts of her story. We were sitting on the floor, wiping sweat from our faces and nodding to all the passersby who pretended not to be staring, but who couldn't really help themselves. Among other items in Rose's house we noticed a white leather-bound album. It looked so out of place that we had to comment on it.

"That's my wedding album," she said and brought the book to us. She opened it and pointed. "This is my husband." Then she laughed, putting her hands in front of the mouth. We didn't know what was so funny, nor did we see her husband anywhere in her home. "He's dead," she explained and then we heard the rest of the story. (I have since learned that the Karen, like many other Asians, laugh when something is very sad or embarrassing. It's confusing at first, but after a while one gets used to it.)

Her English was excellent and she was a great cook as well. She could make the most scrumptious meals from only the basic ingredients available to her in the camp. She was a perfect refugee friend. Steve and I spent hours with her talking about her life and whatever else was on our minds.

We looked through her wedding album and it seemed like a fairytale far away from the world we were in now. We never did talk much about her husband though. During the years of knowing the Karen, I've also learned that they don't often speak in expressive terms like we do in the West— especially not about their feelings. It seemed like Rose had accepted the fact that her husband was gone, and that she was now a widow, a refugee, and a single mother. Those were the facts. What was the use of wallowing in the painful feelings and analyzing them time and time again? She much preferred to talk about the future, about her children's accomplishments, about her neighbors, and other foreigners she had met.

I thought about how I would have felt if I had been Rose. If I had given up my safe life to go and help poor people and instead of being blessed with peace and happiness, I had only experienced sorrow and pain. I think I would have blamed God. I would have labeled Him unfair, to say the least. I mentioned this to Rose.

"Well, I'm not going to become bitter and I'm not going to give up," is what she told us. "I believe that there is a bigger purpose with me being here, and I have asked God to show me that. This is why I have started a small school for young children and an orphanage." This was theology I hadn't found in books. This was actually theology that made me look down on myself because I felt dirty. I was in the presence of a saint and the spiritual bodybuilding I had been doing seemed like a joke when compared to the life of worship this lady lived. With all my self-righteousness and all my assumed skills, I quickly admitted to myself that I didn't have the character it took to face what Rose had faced and not become bitter. I thought that if what had happened to Rose had happened to Oddny, people would have met a grouchy, mean, bitter, and hunched-backed woman. I would have thrown rocks after children and cursed while spitting.

Rose's story became a devotion for us. The humble service of so many others we met in the camp challenged us to take a closer look at our values and rethink some of our priorities. In the camp that should have been a place of sorrow, we found inspiration, dedication and commitment. On our first trip there, God used the refugees to show us what books couldn't. He woke us up.

There were two verses that we had somehow missed all those years in Christian service. They were verses that I have never heard a sermon about. They are verses that are so easy to understand and so hard to live. We discovered it some time after our first visit, read it, and felt like God had pinched us. We said, *Ouch! That hurt!* The verses were 1 John 3:17–18 NIV: "If anyone has material possessions and sees a brother or sister in need but has no pity on them, how can the love of God be in that person? Dear children, let us not love with words or speech but with actions and in truth."

Our love had to be shown with action and in truth, John said. We knew deep down in our hearts that this was God speaking to us.

WHEN PEOPLE NEED MORE THAN SYMPATHY

Soon after our first trip to the refugees, we went again. The journey there was always somewhat of an event. We spent hours on prehistoric buses driven by men who were in a hurry to get home for dinner or who wanted to test their good karma by doing acrobatic moves on the narrow roads. We prayed a lot on those buses. The prayers may have been something like this: "Oh, God! Oh, no! I'm closing my eyes!"

The buses rarely had air-conditioning, but were instead equipped with television sets that played the most hideous and gory horror movies or shows featuring made-up ladies or pretty transvestites in bright-colored outfits, singing Thai pop songs. If the windows hadn't fallen out, we could actually open them, thus allowing tepid air to flow through the aisles of vinyl-covered seats. The air felt good, but did nothing for our thighs that were glued to the vinyl seats with sweat. Then there were more hours spent on the back of trucks together with lots of tribal people who always made the trip entertaining. We sat next to cute little women with toothless smiles who squatted on the floor holding dirty, see-through plastic bags which they threw up in every twenty minutes or so. Sometimes the truck had to pull over, and the same ladies jumped off to pee on the side of the road, under some bushes. To the other passengers this didn't seem any stranger than pulling off at a gas station is for us. All people have to pee sometimes, right? We thought the *hill-tribers* were cute and got used to all the detours into this or that village where somebody's aunt lived. Once a passenger truck didn't show up, but a Coca Cola truck stopped and offered us a ride. We got to sit on top of hundreds of Coke boxes on the truck bed all the way to the nearest town. This may have been the closest I had ever been to heaven.

The verses from 1 John, along with so many other words of Jesus, were bothering me. My feelings were a motley mix of: "I'm so privileged to have been introduced to the people of Burma," and "I kind of wish I hadn't met them because now I have to do something for them." I, like many others I have encountered, could speak about solidarity with the poor with great ease. I had no problem sympathizing with them, and even giving them some of my money. But what to do when I'm face to face with them and the people I'm looking at need more than just sympathy? What to do when I realize that the time has come to step into the lives of others, and it's going to mean some sacrifices on my end?

When we met Rose again she had a new story to tell.

THE GIRL WITH NO NAME

It was getting late. Peter's legs were tired and his stomach was grumbling. He and his companions had been walking since dawn and he was looking forward to a rest. Only a few more minutes of walking and they would get to a clearing in the jungle. A creek was close by so they would be able to take a bath too. A bath would rejuvenate him. Then came food. As always, they would make a small fire on the ground and boil the rice in their steel cups. They didn't have much to eat with the rice any longer, but if they were lucky there would be some herbs and roots near their campsite. They still had some salt left too. Food was almost as exciting to think about as sleep. He would fall asleep as soon as he laid his weary body on the hammock that he strung between a couple trees.

None of the men were talking. They had been together every hour of the day for weeks now, and, while they still had more to talk about, the silence between them bore witness to a team so at ease with each other that words were not necessary at all hours of the day. Peter enjoyed the solitude.

He thought about the past weeks. In his head they seemed like one long march, broken only by the occasional gunfire when the enemy had been so close they could hear their voices and see the remains of their cigarettes, or the days they had spent helping civilians flee from the government troops, and the hours they had spent treating the sick and the wounded. Yet other days had been so quiet it seemed like they heard nothing but the snapping of the branches they walked over and the songs of the birds in the tall trees. There had been days when they could allow themselves to sing too. Those were the rare days when he almost forgot that he was walking on enemy territory, and that he was one of the people the government had labeled as a terrorist, a threat to the peace of the nation, a Communist and a violent monster.

Why am I in my own country, walking on the land that my forefathers have walked on, but still considered an intruder? Peter wondered. He knew the answer, of course, but he still had to ask the question ever so often. The question made him angry, and the anger made him walk faster, more determined to not stop until he, his people and his unborn children again could live on this land in peace and build their houses, till their land, grow their crops, and dance in the moonlight the way they always had.

It wasn't until he joined the resistance that he understood what the government used as an excuse to destroy their homes and kill their people. Until then he had thought that all the junta's attacks were random acts of evil. Since it had always been that way, it would always stay that way, and his main goal in life would be to stay away from the bullets. But when he joined the resistance, his leader had explained the government's policy to him in simple terms. "Peter, they call it the Four Cuts," he had said while he vigorously chewed on his betel nut. Every few minutes he spit red saliva over the rock he was sitting on. Peter thought that if he could aim as well with his gun as he aimed his spit then no enemy soldier would be safe.

"This policy is the regime's way of cutting insurgents—which, you understand, is us—off from four items: food, funds, intelligence, and recruits. If I have an enemy and I want to make it impossible for him or her to hurt me, I make sure that they have nothing to eat, no money, no way to get information about me, and that nobody else will take their side. Then my enemy will be harmless and will say that I'm a nice person just to get something to eat."

Peter nodded. It seemed straightforward enough, but still didn't explain why the army felt justified in burning his village, and his relatives' villages—over and over again. It didn't explain why they had killed the farmer they'd found in the jungle, and why they had killed him in such a grotesque way. Peter would never forget the mutilated body and the face with the eyes missing. Surely that farmer had not been a soldier with the resistance.

"No, he was not a soldier," explained his leader. "But the Burma Army may have accused him of giving water to a resistance soldier, or of having given him rice and of having hosted him at his house. That could have been reason enough to kill him. When the ones in power suffer from chronic paranoia—which it appears the regime that rules our country does— and think that pretty much the whole world is their enemy, then the Four Cuts-policy becomes a ghastly justification to kill people. It becomes an excuse to attack civilians, destroy their homes, kill their livestock, and think of the most heinous things you can do to human beings and then do them."

His leader looked into the fire that was slowly burning down. It was dark all around them and in the trees the cicadas were playing their songs.

He felt close to this man. He was a fighter, he liked women and alcohol too much, but he would die for his friends if he needed to. And when a heinous injustice was being committed, he was not afraid to attack the perpetrators, fight them, and give his life to combat them. Inside the rough exterior, Peter knew that there was a soft heart that believed in beauty and willingly gave love.

This was many years ago, and his leader was on a different mission now. But Peter remembered that night well. He had thought, *I am the soldier the Four Cuts-policy was designed for. I am the man that they want to starve to death.* He hadn't really thought of himself as a brave and vicious soldier, but as a young man who didn't want to see his mother, his younger siblings, and his other relatives tormented. He had no desire to kill and fight. He just wanted freedom for his people. The way things had turned out, it seemed like he would be spending his life fighting. Fighting for what was his right, fighting to defend the innocent, fighting to save lives that were of no value to the regime that ruled them from so far away.[5]

When they got to the clearing they threw their packs on the ground. The weight of the bags became a part of who they were during the long treks through the jungle. When the day came to an end and the pack could be removed, they all felt strangely light. They divided the tasks—two men made the fire, the rest hung their hammocks, and started preparing the rice. And before it got too cold and too dark, they went down to the creek for the daily bath.

Peter heard the sound on the trail to the creek. At first he thought it was an injured animal. If that had been the case they would likely have been able to eat meat for dinner. But the longer he listened, the less the sound reminded him of an animal. It was a person crying. It was a child.

He followed the sound. It didn't take very long. A child was huddled under a blanket under some bushes. She stared at him with eyes like an animal's, filled with fear. Peter squatted down and spoke with a soft voice: "Hi there, little one. Pha Doh (Uncle) Peter is here to help you. Are you hungry?" At first the child just tried to disappear under the blanket. But the thought of food seemed to be hard to resist. Slowly she moved closer.

---

5   Many people have difficulty with the concept of an armed resistance movement, so I've included 'A very brief history lesson on Burma' in the Appendix. However, if you'd rather have a good cry right about now, keep reading Peter's story.

After a few minutes he was able to pick her up and carry her out from under the bush.

He had forgotten about the bath. Instead he walked back up to the campsite. The other men looked at him bewildered. Where had he gotten a child? Soon they were all busy wrapping her up in blankets and trying to get her to eat. One of them had a sweet candy in his pocket and he gave it to her. She took it, held it in her hands, but didn't put it in her mouth. She wouldn't speak. She just looked at them with dark, sad eyes. They compared her size to that of other children they knew—some of them were fathers themselves—and guessed she must be about three years old. She probably knew how to talk, but was shy. Or something terrible had happened that had left her unable to speak.

As they sat around the fire, eating their rice with very little else, they tried to guess what had happened to the little girl. Their first guess was the most likely one. They knew that not far away some villages had recently been attacked. They had met some of the survivors who had fled with what they could carry on their backs. The villagers had told them of burned homes, broken tools, destroyed rice crops, and the deliberate planting of landmines where people were likely to walk. They had heard of a rape of a girl who was alone in the house when the soldiers came. They had heard stories of familiar atrocities, but that didn't make them any less shocking. It seemed that everything was allowed in the name of the Four Cuts-policy.

Most likely this girl had been living in one of the attacked villages. Perhaps she had fled with her family some days ago. But if she had fled with her family, then where were they now? They had met nobody on their patrol today. And the villagers they'd talked to had said nothing about a lost child.

It was perplexing. The Karen loved their children—not only their own children, but all children. If a child were orphaned, there would almost always be neighbors or relatives who would take care of the child and raise it as their own. In fact, Peter knew many families whose houses were full of children, but only a couple of which were their own. So even if this little girl had lost her parents in the attacks, surely there would have been others there to care for her.

They went to their hammocks that night, still wondering why a child had been left alone in the jungle. Peter volunteered to sleep on the ground, next to the fire so that the child wouldn't have to be alone. After she had eaten a bowl of rice, she had curled up under the blanket and fallen asleep. Still she hadn't spoken a word. But Peter thought that she looked less afraid than she had when he first found her. His last thought before sleep won him over was his hope that they would find the girl's family the next day.

·　·　·

Some days later they were still looking. Nobody knew who the child was and why she was in the jungle alone. They met some villagers who guessed that the parents of the child had either felt like they couldn't take care of her and had left her, hoping that somebody would find her and give her the care they couldn't give. Others suggested that the parents had been killed, or thought they were about to be killed, so had hid their child while they were being pursued.

As the days went by, she started speaking some and laughed at the uncles who took care of her. "Pah Doh!" she called all of them. They took turns carrying her on their shoulders as they walked. As she warmed up to them, they tried to get her to talk about what had happened. When they questioned her, however, she became serious and only said a few words: "Mommy gone. Daddy gone." Then she'd turn around and point to something she had seen in the jungle.

We're men who carry guns and whose duty is to protect innocent people who are being attacked, thought Peter. *We're here to protect what is ours. I can kill a tiger if I need to, and I will fight the enemy's soldiers, but I don't know how to get a three-year-old child to tell me something I want to know.* To raise this child was not for him, nor for the rest of his team. Resistance soldiers had different duties.

As they approached the end of their mission, they also approached Thailand and the Mae La refugee camp. They would be entering Mae La Refugee camp shortly. The last night before they arrived at the camp, they were sitting by the campfire, warm, clean, but not very full. The last few days they'd had to ration the rice pretty strictly. The only person who had eaten until she was full was the girl. "I know somebody who may be able to take care of her," said Peter's friend. "Her name is Rose and she already takes care of lots of children. She's like a mother to them. Let's walk to her home and ask if she has room for one more person in her house."

They all had grown fond of the little girl, but the next day they told her that they were going to take her to a new mommy. They didn't know if Rose would take her, and only one of them even knew who Rose was. But they dared not let the girl see their hesitation. They made it sound like it had all been planned as well as the new moon celebrations in their villages.[6]

---

6   This story is based on facts we received from Rose. A girl, three years old had been found in the jungle by resistance soldiers. The fate of her family was unknown. The character of Peter is fictional, but the setting is realistic, based on my own experience walking through the jungle with soldiers. The Four Cuts-policy is very much a reality, so is finding a tortured corpse (FBR report January 11, 2008). I have often wondered what the story of this girl actually was. We may never find out.

STARTING AN AID ORGANIZATION WITH 30 DOLLARS

"The soldiers gave me a baby to care for," Rose said. The baby was a three-year-old girl, but Rose may not have known the word *toddler*. "The soldiers found her under some bushes in the jungle. The fate of the parents is unknown."

"I want to take care of her, but I can't afford it," Rose told us. "I have so many children already." The two *Youth-Without-Any-Money* looked at each other and at her. An orphaned child needed help. Could we tell her and Rose that we were sure Jesus loved her, and that probably He would find a way to provide for her, and then pick up our shoulder bags full of the Bible and good Christian books and walk out of the camp? Could we say that we didn't know whether she was predestined to eternal life or not?

The answer was so simple when we sat there with Rose, hearing her tell the story of the little girl. We had to be Jesus' love. "How much will it cost to care for her?" we asked in a wimpy voice, knowing the limits of our income. "About a thousand baht a year," Rose said. One thousand baht? That's thirty U.S. dollars. And that was all she needed to provide for the child! Well, now the answer was really easy. Of course we could help her. We pulled out the bank note with the spaghetti scribbles. It didn't feel like much. It wasn't much. But for that little girl, it was a lot. It was life itself. And it was then that a new kind of adventure started for us. Without really knowing that's what we were doing, we started our organization, Partners Relief & Development, that day.

SOMETIMES PEOPLE QUESTION IF
WE REALLY KNOW WHAT WE'RE DOING

Most people start their organizations with a budget, a PhD and a board. That would be the logical way to do things. Steve and I started at the complete opposite end. Logic has never been our forte. We had no money, no degrees, we didn't know the meaning of a board, and since we had almost never had much money to speak of, a budget seemed like a complete waste of time. "We have money, we spend it; we don't, we pray," was more our way of living.

Over the last few months Partners has been running a campaign on our website that I really like. It's just called *Help and Hope*. Because really, when you think of it, it all boils down to that.

In the early days of Partners we'd count our money and always be short. The few *bahts* we had left when the rent and gas for our motorbike was paid, wasn't enough for much of a relief effort. Once, not knowing what else to do to produce some cash, I asked my mother back in Norway to help us. Although my mom has always been a woman of meager means, she believed in our cause. She conducted a raffle together with her friends and raised a whopping thousand dollars! We were beside ourselves with excitement. With that money we were able to pay for the building of Sarah's malaria clinic. Sarah was the wife of Shwea Mya, a pastor whom we had befriended. She was a nurse and wanted to have a way to treat all the people in her village, and the area around, for malaria.

We gave her the money and the next time we went for a visit to drink sweet instant coffee at their house, they proudly showed us their little clinic. You may not have thought it was much of a clinic if you judged it by our standards in the West. It was the shape of a giant shoebox, which meant that it only had three walls. The front was open like a stage, allowing anybody who wanted to have a peek, to enjoy the view.

The clinic was built with uneven teak boards, cut and planed by the villagers themselves. On the inside of the walls were rough shelves, put there to store medicines and other equipment. Two wooden benches, adorned with nylon mosquito nets, were on the floor. These were the clinic's two hospital beds. If they needed to treat more people than they had space for at the clinic, Sarah would put them in her house. She had lots of floor space, and with just a few mats, she could have several sick people lay down in her living room. A small table was used for a desk and she had purchased all the basic essentials for doing medical checks and treating simple diseases. Sarah beamed with pride and nurse-enthusiasm. For her and the people in her village, this was better medical care than they'd ever had.

Steve and I were proud of our first real project. We were proud of the fact that things had come together, and here we were looking at a simple structure that could help save lives. Not only would the clinic save lives, we had enabled Sarah and her husband to do what they had been dreaming of doing for so long. We felt unnaturally kind.

And with the malaria clinic built, we still had a bit of money left. Not long after, at six in the morning, we were sitting with Pastor Karol outside his house. Morning mist still covered parts of our world—a simple village by the river, surrounded by August mountains, with banana and palm trees lining the trails. A short swim across the river and we'd be in Burma. The villagers were mostly refugees who had fled their homeland and settled here. It was cold and we were huddling around the fire.

Pastor Karol was an important man in his village, a strong leader and the pastor of the small village church. When we asked him what the needs of his village were, he answered, "Oh, we have everything we need." He pulled out a bottle of his own homemade rice whisky and gave it to Steve. "This will keep you warm," he said. He smiled while using a bamboo stick to poke the fire. "We Karen always drink this early in the morning. It gets us warm." Steve knew it was a test that he didn't want to fail, so he took a slurp and said he felt really warm now. Karol nodded approvingly.

Karol then admitted that they did indeed have a small need. They needed a water hose. With it they could more easily get water from the well, making life a lot simpler for the villagers and the students at the school. A hose! *We* could help get a hose! While he told us about the time he had gone hunting and happened upon a boa constrictor that had just swallowed a deer, we counted up the money needed to buy the best water hose available at Mae Ra Maat market.

·   ·   ·

Sometimes people question if we really know what we're doing, running a charity that helps displaced people. To answer that question is quite easy: "Not really." It's like having kids. Not many of us knew what we were doing when we were handed that little bundle. We all *thought* we knew, but I doubt that a single person actually did. A PhD in early childhood development may be helpful, but you'll need more than that to handle a three year old, not to mention a teenager. When it comes to changing the world, Burma in particular, I've concluded that none of us really know what we're doing either. But I have found that no qualities are better to have than these: a willingness to learn and take risks, and the guts to never give up.

Over the years I've talked to lots of journalists. They're always looking for an original story, something kind of wacko, and we fit the bill. I love talking to them. The reason is, of course, that I get to do all the talking and seldom get interrupted. The journalists write and the ink splashes around their tense fingers; I preach my message for as long as they're willing to listen. Later I find that many have messed up the facts, and sometimes they write that I said things I never actually said. One journalist, for example, quoted me as saying that I wasn't interested in curtains. This wasn't true, and how he got that idea is beyond me. But all journalists want to know this: What got you to think that you could start an organization without any money or skills to run it?

That's an honest question that begs for an honest answer. What I usually tell the sincere interviewer is that we didn't, in fact, plan to start an organization. What we did was to respond to the call we felt God had given us, and that was to step into the lives of the displaced people of Burma and show them His love, by our actions, not only by our words. We felt that to ignore that call would have been a sin, and that we most likely wouldn't have been able to live with ourselves if we hadn't acted on what we knew was right. After all, the Bible says, "If anyone, then, knows the good they ought to do and doesn't do it, it is sin for them" (James 4:17 NIV). We would have been hypocrites in the very worst meaning of the word.

Did we know what we were doing? Heavens, no! I can think of two words that describe my first endeavors as an aid worker: naïve and ignorant. For instance, I thought that all poor people were kind and honest, just because they were poor. It didn't take long to find out that people in refugee camps are sinners as well. People lie, gossip, steal, and commit adultery there as they do anywhere else. There is rivalry galore. To realize this proved that I had a few things to learn, but I don't think it proved that I should quit. If we only reach out to people who have their lives figured out and who mostly act like bleached and starched pew-warmers, then I'm in big trouble myself. That's not the box I belong in. So we kept working on the projects we started and learned as we went. One important lesson, for example, was to ask for receipts.

Another surprise was on meeting other aid workers in the area. The surprise was not that they were there, but the way many acted when they met us: like sales people on commission. I'm serious. So many of the charities we encountered were more territorial than red-bellied lemurs in Madagascar. In my innocent stage I'd thought that all aid workers would work together as one big happy family, saving the world together. But what I found was that they had a lot in common with Wall Street or some other place where people are trying to get their piece of the cake. For many, the goal was not first and foremost to help people, but to build their own kingdoms and climb the career ladder up to the high priesthood of charities.

Not all were this way, mind you. Some opened their arms wide to the newly-hatched aid workers that we were. They shared their experiences and told us what they knew. They acted as if it was just fine to be a little ignorant, because all people have been ignorant at some point. Those are the people who helped us to not give up, but to remember what Jesus had said.

It's not the Garden of Eden. The people who are poor and oppressed also have issues. The people who are there to help have even greater issues. Human nature is inane here like anywhere else.

But there are flowers. We have met people who are full of courage and love, who have taught us what it means to be a hero in the truest sense of the word. They are the ones who have made it worth not giving up, and who are the real reason that my faith in human beings is still intact. There are many saints, people the world may never hear about, who have followed their hearts and convictions to the battlefields where they held the sword of righteousness high. They have taught me by their examples that we have been chosen for something important and that it's worth dying for.

I have learned a few valuable lessons since the first malaria clinic and the water hose. I have learned how to make a budget in Excel and how to market our cause. I have learned the importance of delegation and that soya beans are a good source of vitamins and protein for malnourished people. I have learned about weaving textiles and emergency relief. This is great and has come in handy. But it is falling deeply in love with people, trusting them, and working with them that have changed me the most. I started out lacking in skills, and that's probably how I will end too. But more and more I am convinced that God doesn't look for skills, but for a heart that's not afraid to try, not afraid to fail, not afraid to say, "Help!"

And that's where you find me: still unable to do so much that I know I ought to be able to do, but surrounded by people who can carry me when I fail. My own shaky voice frequently calls out, "Help me! I don't know what I'm doing, but I'm not going to let that stop me if this is where You want me."

AND WHEN WE ARE DEAD,
OUR BLOOD WILL TURN INTO HEAT

A refugee camp is like a huge waiting room. The main difference is you don't know if the doctor will ever say it's your turn or if the train will ever leave. Many wait in the waiting room their whole lives.

The first time we went to a camp it was exotic and fascinating. I felt like it was hard-core, something only people living on the edge got to experience. It wasn't particularly hard-core, of course—just different. And just like you notice everything unfamiliar when you go to a new country, I noticed a lot of differences in the camp. It was not like my living room.

It would be nice if I said that the thing I noticed first in the camp was the courage, the love, and the generosity. There is a lot of that in the camps. Or that I noticed the hundreds of dirty children running around like little puppies, playing with toys made from sticks and other artifacts the kids in my home would call rubbish.

But, no, I didn't notice all that until later. The first things I noticed, and that I always struggle with, were: *heat and dirt*. It's so hot that the air feels like liquid, like we're being boiled alive. And it's dirty—like a dust mine. A while back our family spent a day waiting at the house of Karen friends, and in order to not go crazy by letting the April heat overwhelm our brains, we tried to describe the heat. It was scary.

Steve always gets more creative under pressure and he let it rip: *Sweltering, blistering, and scorching heat. Heat as hot as the devil's snot. If heat could be tasted, it would taste like ten chili peppers. Heat steals creativity, creates listlessness, and laziness—like the very air you breathe has a bad case of constipation.*

Elise had more to add: *Sweat dripping down my fingers as I try to inhale. Instead of fresh air I choke on a million degrees of burning oil. Even though I stand still, not moving an inch, I feel small particles of doom. I try to laugh, but the air tastes like boiled salamander excrements. The water is so hot it burns my stomach as it goes through my digestive system. The roof above radiates oppression. The solar panels collect too much power. It makes me feel angry, grumpy, sad, and mad.*

Now Kristin had something to say about the heat: *It's hot like the fire that burns your house down.* And it was true. We were in a fire.

With sweat dripping down her forehead, Naomi continued the horrid description: *It's as hot as the Burma Army shooting someone. And when Elise reads to me, the words are as hot as boiling water. And when we're dead, our blood will turn into heat. When I see a dog it looks like a ball of heat, and when a dog slobbers all over me, I feel sweaty. And when I see a bug, I feel creepy like sweating heat.*

As if speaking on behalf of humanity in a case against heat, Steve continued (although he'd had his turn already, but he was unstoppable): *I'm like a cauldron of boiling soup, as hot as an asphalt road in Death Valley. I'm as hot as a volcano about to erupt. It's a breezeless day like black jello.*

Imagine living in that every day! The sad truth is that Westerners like us are real wimps when it comes to bodily discomforts—heat in particular. When we feel like we're going to perish in a cauldron of boiling soup, the Karen are playing soccer. When we think that we can't possibly walk another meter without a bucket of water to drink, the refugees run up and down the hills carrying their wood and other supplies on their heads and backs. It takes no genius to see that in the setting of sweltering equatorial heat, we are the inferior species. Inferior or not, it takes my attention away at times. I walk among victims of war whose stories are so many and so tragic that it will make heaven cry, and all I can think of is that small waterfalls are falling down my face and neck and body.

The dirt in a camp is unavoidable. How, exactly, *do* you keep anything clean in an enclosed area with thirty thousand others and no running water? Have you ever tried to keep your floors polished when the only two seasons in your world are the dust season and the mud season? Six months of monsoon rain and all these thousands of people walking to and fro in a small place makes really slushy mud.

Somebody who went to visit a camp a while ago came back disgusted. "I don't mind so much how primitive it was," he said to me. "I just don't understand why they can't stay cleaner." I wanted to say, "I don't mind your tucked-in and starched shirt so much, but I mind how stupid you are."

The wheres, whys, and whens of my refugee camp visits are all a blur. There have been so many visits, so when people ask me how many times

I've gone to the camps, I answer the same way refugees answer when we ask them how many times their homes have been destroyed by the Burma Army: *More times than I can remember.*

Our visits to the camps usually have some purpose, like delivering supplies or interviewing people. What I like the most though is to go there without any other purpose than, "Hi, I was in the area. Do you mind if I pop in for a cup of tea?"

Visiting Rose and her children was always a combination of fun, work, and, of course, a lesson in Christian living. Never did we leave her house without a solid devotion tucked into our hearts. She never preached or sat us down to give us a lesson. No, she simply lived and we observed.

There was usually a new project in the makings when we arrived. One time she had made a library for mothers; another time she was making a playground for the children in the camp who had no access to school or daycare. Then there was the music school and the sewing classes and the mothers' club. We were always inspired by her endless ideas and initiative.

You could read this last paragraph and think that we were talking about a person who was going to be running for governor in some big city with lots of private and government funding, as well as lots of fame, but that wasn't the case. This was a refugee, a widow, a poor person, a person who was living in a dusty refugee camp where everybody was destitute, and where there was no money for these kinds of endeavors, where, strictly speaking, there was not even any space for these kinds of buildings. *Library for women? What kind of nonsense is that? We need the space to squeeze more people into the camp.* But Rose was an overcomer, and the library was built as well as the playground. We were there the day they started using the slide. True joy was redefined that day!

Then one day when we came to visit she had a Burma Army soldier staying with her. That shocked us a little. For a Karen to have a Burma government soldier at her house was like inviting a Nazi for coffee during WWII in Norway. You could lose your head for less.

"He defected from the Army," Rose told us while we were standing on the floor looking like dumbfounded cartoon characters.

"When he came to the camp he was injured and broken. He went to many people asking for help, but nobody wanted to help him," Rose explained while laughing the way she usually did when she told intense stories. This man was the embodiment of all that was evil and bad for the refugees in the camp. He was from the Army that killed their children and stole their land. He had been wearing the uniform of the men who burned down homes and raped women. I don't think I would have invited him in for a plate of rice either. "They wanted nothing to do with him," Rose explained. "He's from the enemy and people didn't trust him. They hate the Burmese. But I thought about what Jesus would have done and told him that he could move into my house as long as he helped keep the orphanage going by doing practical things around here. He was happy to do that, and, guess what, now he has become a Christian and the community is slowly accepting and trusting him."

Easy as that. Invite the enemy into your house because that is what Jesus would have done.

Rose challenged us. I would sometimes groan, *Why, oh, why, did she have to challenge us so much?* I thought about who my worst enemy was and asked myself if I would have been as gracious. Then I thought about all my *friends* and realized that there are times that I'm not even willing to do for my friends what Rose did for her enemy. It didn't make me feel real great. Rather, it made me feel more like a parenthesis in a book of real heroes.

We would play with the children on the floor and hug them and hold them because so many of them just needed some affection. They were serious, mischievous, cute, dirty and full of lice at times. Some of them peed on us—more than once. Being with children like that brings out a lot of feelings in a person like me. I love it and hate it at the same time. In the part of myself that is my core, the authentic me, so to speak, I know that this is life in its truest form. You can't fake-hug orphans who have lice and who pee on you. You're either in or not. You need to decide to embrace this child all the way or not at all. And you need to decide that if you wake up with lice the next day that's okay too. But then there is the other part of me, the part that is a little further away from the core that gets all worried about the smell and the dirt and the germs and the boogers in the noses.

When we started having children of our own we would bring them to visit the orphans and the other refugees too. We brought Naomi the first time when she was just ten months and Elise was two. "I like it here in Norway," Elise exclaimed, thinking that she might find Grandma in one of the bamboo shacks. When you have kids things all of a sudden get more serious. At least they did for me. Now I exposed them to unknown dangers such as bamboo ladders.

All Karen houses are built on stilts, and we always have to climb up a ladder to get into the houses. Imagine trying to keep a ten-month-old away from the ladder and the hole that would suck her straight down to the hard and dusty ground! While I chased after my baby who was very interested in exploring the great unknown, I wondered how Karen babies survived all these centuries of bamboo ladders. What I learned was that they had indeed survived, and if their babies could stay in a Karen house, so could mine. And, guess what? She did.

I learned to love all those times when we took our girls to the camps and they were whisked away to some place with lots of Karen loving them. They looked like white marshmallows in a sea of licorice. Usually by the time they were brought back to us, they looked a little more Karen and a little less like a Gumaer. They had been decorated with Tanaka powder in their faces, making them look like they were white tribal people. Their hair had been styled in Karen fashion (not always vogue, but definitely a unique style), and instead of the T-shirts they had been wearing they were now dressed in Karen costumes. They rarely walked because somebody always wanted to give them a ride on their shoulders or back. They were happy with all the love and attention, and when it was time to leave they often cried because they were leaving their best friends.

There are bright moments and there are laughs, there are flowers in tin cans and shiny tinsel on the beams of the churches in June, but the fact remains: the camp is a waiting room. Waiting to go home. Waiting for a change. Waiting to be able to work and study. Waiting to walk away from the barb-wired fence and to run as far as one wants. Waiting to be free.

But as the waiting is happening, life also unfolds for the thousands who have made it their home for the time being. I have met many of them and they have put a mark on my life in a way much different than the dirt and the heat do. I can easily wash the dust off my feet, but the stories of the people I have talked to in the different camps stay with me like permanent splashes of color that I needed to add to my outfit.

Not wanting to fit into molds

Naomi has always been the more outspoken of our girls. She has never wanted to fit into any mold, and especially not the molds she thinks her parents have made for her. She came out rebellious. As soon as she was out of my warm and cozy womb she put up a fight, and was going to roll over on the table. This isn't a lie, because Steve saw it with his own eyes. His eyes may have been a little blurry, but he saw what he saw, and that was that we had gotten ourselves a challenge.

So when we spend time in villages or refugee camps, Naomi doesn't automatically say that she loves this kind of life. She rather says the opposite. This has put us in a few embarrassing situations. While visiting Rose and her children once, we brought a couple whom we really wanted to impress. We wanted them to think we were a family who had it all together. If that's what we wanted to portray, we probably ought not to have brought Naomi.

Rose's staff had cooked lunch for us. I have to admit that there are times that I don't particularly like the food the refugees serve us. I can say this because I know that they don't like our food so much either. They hate pizza, for example. But we eat what we get served. That is the rule and always will be. Seventy orphans were sitting there quiet as kangaroos. (Have you ever heard a kangaroo make a sound?) They were eating their lunch without complaints or messes. Not a single spoon was dropped, and these were toddlers! We observed in awe as we waited for our noodles to be served. Our girls waited and I felt proud to have such perfect children. Naomi's blond hair was in pigtails and her bangs were a tad too long, covering some of her big, brown eyes. She looked at the food in front of her, put her spoon down in defiance and declared loudly, for the whole house to hear, "I do not eat orphan food!"

The couple we had brought still liked us — Naomi in particular.

GOING HOME

She's on a mat on the floor, surrounded by the people who love her and depend on her for their lives. Into her nose goes a plastic tube that pumps snake oil into her frail body (This is not a metaphor. It was actual snake oil). Seventy children stare. In the background are the sounds of the camp: children playing, mothers nagging, rice being pounded in a wooden mortar, and an occasional grunt from the neighborhood pig. But nobody pays any attention to the sounds outside the building. They can only stare.

On the walls around them are photos from years of Christmas performances and other big events. Little three-year-olds dressed up like sheep and the older boys dressed like wise men. There are photos of visitors who have come and gone, most of them from other countries. Many of them are wearing the Karen costumes they were given as a thank-you-for-coming gift. In one corner sit the sewing machines. The new costumes for all the children are in the making. The color this year is blue. They will be proud and beautiful when they dress up in their finest outfits for church, for school performances, for when the special visitors come. Some of the costumes hang on wire-hangers on the bamboo walls; others have been folded neatly and put in recycled bags. They smell of mothballs.

There are several calendars on the walls as well, calendars from the church associations with circular Karen writing on them and a picture of handsome, young couples dressed in Karen traditional costumes—the men in red, the women in white. There are calendars from other countries as well, whose photos give a taste of the world outside the camp.

Below them is the kitchen, equipped now with low tables and stools for seventy. The floor is luxurious compared to other floors. Instead of mud, this one has cement. In the back of the room the helpers spend hours washing, cutting, pounding, frying or boiling the ingredients that have been made available to them that day. Some days they must use all their creative energies to think of how to make the food enough to feed so many, and make it tasty as well. Other days are pure cooking joy. Those are the days when they have meat available and an abundance of fresh produce. Today nobody is cooking. It's as if they forgot that people need to eat. Eating won't be a priority today. The cooks, the caretakers, and the substitute mothers are also staring.

There is nothing to do but to wait. The adults place some of the youngest children on their laps and start singing softly. Others join and soon there is a choir singing hymns of heaven, of Jesus, of the peace He will give.

Rose takes a deep breath and she leaves them. She goes home to be with Jesus, to meet her husband and to be free at last. She is only fifty-two and so many still need her.[7]

---

7   This is a true event, based on Steve's account and my own observations. Rose died surrounded by all her children. She was buried across the Moi river, inside Burma.

MY TRUCK COULD HAVE FLOWN
LIKE CHITTY CHITTY BANG BANG

There are so many things in this world that I don't understand, and one of the issues I don't understand the most is why the best people die and the bad ones don't. This is not an absolute rule, of course, but I have seen it happen too many times, and if I were God, I wouldn't let it happen this way. Does it make any sense to you that the old generals in Burma who drink whisky and massacre people at the same time as they hoard all the nation's natural resources would outlive strokes, floods, and car crashes, but heroes like Rose and others of our Karen friends who have given their lives to serve, don't?

Rose didn't take particularly good care of herself. She didn't sleep enough and she worried too much. She had seventy kids to provide for and I'm not so sure I would have slept much either if that had been me. One day she had a massive heart attack and died. I wasn't there when it happened, but Steve was. He came back with red eyes and so much pain in his heart. He was sad for losing Rose, because she had meant so much to us, but he knew where she was now. She was with Jesus. It was her kids that broke him. "They lost their parents once," he cried. "Now I watched them lose the only person they knew as their mother once again. Those kids were sobbing on the floor and I didn't know what to do for them."

We managed to get a new mother for the children. Most of them moved to another home where they were loved and cared for. Steve and I helped move them and it was a day I'll never forget.

When it rains it really rains. That is how it is in Asia. They don't do namby-pamby rain in these areas of the world. It's as if heaven has a surplus and opens the sluices. The day we moved Rose's children, it was like that. The rain mixed with the dirt, and we were left with roads that had mud a foot deep. We had all these kids that needed to get from one end of the camp to another. They had all dressed up in their finest. It was looking like a resplendent task.

I will remember Naw Muk Kapaw forever. She was the little girl that had been found sleeping with the pigs after her village had been attacked and no people were left in it. For a couple of years we thought that she was mentally challenged because she acted very peculiar and she didn't speak. But little by little some of the emotional wounds healed and she became a chatterbox, cute as a bug's ear, as they say in Texas. She had always had a special place in my heart because her story was so tragic and because I had seen her go from being a closed pupa to a beautiful butterfly.

Now Naw Mu Kapaw was standing in the field of refugee mud wearing a dress as white as a bride's gown. Her short hair was combed flat and on her face was a smile of great anticipation. She was only going to move from one part of the camp to another, but for an orphaned five-year-old that was a big event, considering she hardly ever left the compounds of the orphanage. I lifted her up and put her in the front of my truck. Immediately she started telling me stories. She had so many stories to tell that I could have driven all the way to Indonesia before she stopped. It was extraordinarily interesting although I only understood a word here and there.

I had filled my truck to the brim with orphans. They were inside the truck and practically overflowing on the bed. It's not easy to think of what to compare the vision from my rear view window to, except that I saw miniature refugees everywhere. The anticipation in the air had enough energy for my truck to just take off and fly like Chitty Chitty Bang Bang. It didn't, however. Instead it ploughed its way through the wet and sticky mud to the other side of the camp. There we got all the kids out and started to ascend to the top of the camp where their new home was going to be. They skipped and jumped and fell and tumbled up the steep and slippery hill, and when we arrived, we had seventy mud pies to offer to Pae Luu who was going to become their new mother.

When she just laughed and welcomed them inside where cookies and special treats waited, we knew they would be well taken care of.

This kind of closed a chapter of our lives. Of course we stayed in touch and still supported the orphans and Pae Luu, but she had other relationships and support from elsewhere, so as the kids grew up we moved on to other places and people.

AT THE VERY LEAST, THE HOST COUNTRY
SHOULD BE ABLE TO MAKE SOME MONEY FROM THEM

There's no shortage of interesting people in *Kawthoolei*—which is the Karen name for Karen State. (It means Land With No Evil. Ironic, isn't it?) This also holds true for the camps that hold all the *boganyong* (While I'm at it, showing off my language skills, *boganyong*, of course, means Karen. How we've gotten Karen from this word is a mystery.)

Mae La refugee camp is the biggest. Every time I go there it seems the number of inhabitants has increased. Last I heard, it held thirty thousand people. I've been there more times than I can remember, but every time I get lost and need a guide to escort me to my destination. The camp is an elaborate maze of small streets and alleyways going in every which direction—not unlike London. It's divided into zones and sections, and all people living there seem to know how to get from one section to another. I think that takes some supernatural skills, because to me it all looks as confusing as algebra.

While walking through the different streets and paths, I notice that life goes on with remarkable normality among the people I see. It doesn't surprise me much any more, but it never fails to impress my guests if I happen to bring any. I guess we, who are not refugees, have an image of a refugee camp as a place where people sit still, overcome by despair and depression, waiting for the next ration of rice and for tomorrow to come. This may be how it is in some refugee camps in other countries, but it's not at all that way where I've been.

First off, you notice that people laugh. Of the thousands of refugees I have walked past, I only have befriended a few handfuls, so I am in no position to say how they *all* feel and why they laugh. But just like the Gallup people who do surveys among a few hundred people and from that determine how the whole world feels about their love life or political views, for example, I too have some ideas about the Karen, based on the lives of the few people I know.

Life is hard, our future is uncertain. We don't know if our people will survive and we have suffered more than you may care to imagine, but here we are and we need to make the best out of it.

They may not use these exact words, but this is the general consensus. When something is funny, they have to laugh even though yesterday was sad. Although they have no possessions or land, not even a birth certificate to show off, they won't let themselves lose their dignity to an idle pity party. Their initiative is as remarkable as their sense of humor.

You know, legally, if you're a refugee, you're not allowed to work at all. A refugee is actually supposed to sit still and receive charity. That is the only way the host country will allow refugee camps to exist—because if the refugees do nothing to provide for their own livelihood then they will depend on the host country for their carrots, for example, or their pork. The money that relief organizations give them is used to buy food from the host country's farmers. The idea is that since they live for free in a camp in a foreign country, at the very least, the host country should be able to make some money from them. This won't happen to the same extent if the exile tries to provide for some of his or her needs. So you can say that laziness is handed to them on a gold platter and I think it must be very hard to refuse and to think of ways to keep oneself busy when they're not allowed to be busy.

Don't be fooled into thinking that life is grand inside this barb-wired enclosure. The life handed to them for free is a tiny spot of land to build a bamboo shack and a certain amount of rice and fish paste once a month, paid for by charities. (Fish paste is a Karen staple food. It's a grey-colored soup that has been made from fermented raw fish, salt, and chili peppers. On good days I have great admiration for the Karen for being able to stomach this gruel—let alone enjoy it. Other times I question their sanity, because, surely nobody in their right mind *likes* this grey, smelly stuff. Then I'm reminded of how hotdogs are made and I shut up.)

I have visited families in the camps who have nothing more than that, literally—a shack, rice, and fish paste. So it's not a life of luxury, and for many, settling in a refugee camp is their very last resort. Some 1.5 million have chosen rather to live in the jungle, constantly running from the soldiers, instead of being stuck in a camp with nothing to do. The freedom from soldiers may be tempting, and it's what brings most people there, but for many the *loss* of freedom is a bigger sacrifice.

This is why I respect and admire all those who manage to get themselves out of bed every day. And not only out of bed, but who manage to find something meaningful to do with their days. Personally, I work a lot better under pressure and if I don't have anything pressing to do, I quickly become very bored and the boredom turns into depression, and if I don't get myself outside to go for a long run very fast, the atmosphere around me becomes toxic. I would have made a very bad refugee.

EDUCATION ORPHANS ON THE TOP OF THE HILL

Two of my best examples of first class refugees are Arthur and Clasper. They get an "A" in refugeeship. They have been parts of our lives for years, and the more I see of them, the more I admire them. Their house is on top of one of the many hills in Mae La. As with all other places in the camp, I need help to find which hill it is every time I go there. And every time we go to visit, a student who lives at Arthur and Clasper's dorm escorts us. We spend the time helping him practice his English while trekking up the steep path.

When we get to their compound Clasper, who is tall and beautiful, welcomes us. She is always wearing a brightly-colored and patterned Karen shirt. She smiles and sits down to speak with us in perfect English. She will tell you that her English is very limited, but it has never limited our conversation. Some of the students living with them will bring a tray with clear glass cups filled with very sweet coffee and then Arthur will walk in. He will have a sarong tied around his slim waist, his hair is combed back, and he smiles without showing his teeth because his mouth is always full of betel nut.

Arthur and Clasper take care of kids. Most of them are not orphaned kids, but children who have come to the camp to go to school because there are none in their villages. This is a common and sad problem in Burma, another result of the government's frivolous politics. When 40–60% of the GNP is spent on the army and less than 1% is allotted to education and healthcare, it takes no genius to figure that money for schools and hospitals is scarce.

Microscopic amounts of money are given to build schools in the villages. The quality of the government-run schools is about as good as the quality of the made-in-China toys you can buy at a Dollar Store. The army also uses the schools as target practice. So the parents decide that in order to give their children an education and a better life than they've had, to send them to a refugee camp where there are schools. And most of the kids at Arthur and Clasper's house are those kinds of kids: education orphans.

It's easy to know the Karen for years without ever hearing their stories. When you think of it, it's easy meeting *anybody* for years without hearing his or her story. We go through life talking with our neighbors about the horrid gas prices and the abominable politics of the poor guy who happens to be the president at the time, but never really ask them to share their story. Or, like me: I have coffee with one of my many best friends, and after we've sat together for an hour or so, it dawns on me that I've done all the talking and the talking was exclusively about me and my own problems. I hate realizing that, and it bugs me that now weeks may pass before we'll get another chance to talk, and for all I know, my friend may have been nominated for an Oscar, and I wouldn't know because I was too busy talking about my boring self.

It took me a long time to hear Arthur and Clasper's story too. I went there with my family and friends lots of times. We talked about the dorm, heard them sing, talked about our kids, and drank gallons of coffee, but it wasn't until recently that I heard more about who they were and why they were in Mae La.

ARTHUR: ALL PEOPLE THAT COME
TO ME ARE WORTHY OF HOSPITALITY

I come from Khia Thia village. You may not know where it is and the exact location is not so important unless you are walking from another village. Just remember that it is in *Kawthoolei*, the Land With No Evil, as we call it. As a young man I went to Bible school. I wanted to learn more about the Lord I serve and I wanted to learn how to serve Him better. My joy, then like now, was to fellowship with other believers. As a young man all those years ago, I would arrange meetings with people from different villages and ethnic groups to come together. They would walk for days just to get to our gatherings, and I thought that our songs surely reached up to heaven. We would stand in our simple village church and sing in many harmonies, the voices blended together like the colors of all of our different costumes. Some were pink, others red, blue, black, and purple.

We Karen are hospitable people. A guest may be an angel, after all, and we need to treat him as such. When a stranger comes to our house, we invite him inside with a smile, and give him a glass of water. The guest may be weary from a long journey and a cup of water will be like rain on a dry rice field. Later, it is our custom to invite our guest to eat with us, no matter how humble our food may be. This I observed my own parents and grandparents do, and this was something I practiced too. It was as natural as cutting bamboo for the fire.

I was sleeping in my house one night when I heard knocking on my door. I got up and peeked through one of the cracks in the bamboo wall. My heart made a small jump when I noticed a man wearing a uniform outside my house. I knew these men often came at night to take their enemies away, but I didn't think I deserved to be arrested for anything I had done. I had paid my taxes, I never criticized the regime, and I tried to follow all the rules they gave us to live by. It was not an easy task since it seemed like each new moon came with a new set of rules. Nevertheless, I was surprised to see the soldier there by my door.

I walked out and asked what the matter was. "You have friends among the resistance movement," the soldier informed me, as if I didn't know who my own friends were. "For this we must arrest you."

I looked the soldier in the eye and said, "I'm going to accept all people who come to me and show them hospitality." I had never gone into the world looking for friends or trouble, but people would come to my house to share news, to hear news, to discuss a topic, or for other reasons that only I and the lizards on my wall knew. None of the people who had come to my door had ever been turned away. I told the soldier this. I don't know why the soldier didn't arrest me then, but he didn't. He looked at me with sad eyes and I turned around and went back to sleep.

During the following days I continued to invite all the people who came to my house inside. I gave them water, and sometimes I gave them food. We never plotted to overthrow the regime. This, we knew, was a task too ambitious for us. Instead we talked about how to build our churches, and how to help our people. In my heart I knew that the days I could sit peacefully on my floor chatting with my guests while we chewed our betel nuts were coming to an end. And they did.

Some days later, there was a knock on my wall again. This time it didn't startle me as much. I had been prepared for what was coming. When I went to meet them, I thought they had come to take me away the same way I had heard they had taken so many other pastors away.

It was the same soldier and he looked distressed. "I am only coming to you this one time," he whispered. "But if you don't pack up and leave this village now, they will surely come and arrest you."

I took my few belongings and walked away. I walked to the refugee camp where many of my brothers and sisters had gone already. I heard of the death and abuse of many of my Christian brothers and sisters after I left my village. They are men and women who serve the Lord with courage and integrity. But the enemy picks these brave men and women and abuses them because of the influence they have in their villages and in the villages beyond their own. I often think that it could have been me tied to a bamboo pole while they jabbed me with sticks, burned me with their cigarette butts, or hit me with their guns before they finally shot me. I often ask why God chose to save me from such humiliation, suffering, and death. He has not given an answer, but I will serve Him for the rest of my days as a sign of my gratitude.

Had I not gone to that camp, I would not have met *her*. She was beautiful then like she is now. I could see her smile from across the camp, and when she looked at me with that smile, I knew that I was lost in love. It was God's plan to send me to that camp to meet her. If that had been the only reason, it would have been a good enough reason.

We married and settled in the camp. Life took on the normal routines like it had in my village. The barbed-wired fences and the guards making sure we didn't leave, and unwanted guests didn't enter, were constant reminders that we were refugees without a land, living in a camp where nothing belonged to us. But other than that we managed well. Like children who pretend they are something much greater than they are in reality, we too pretended that our lives were the best they could be.

I didn't try to become a leader, nor did I want to have a crowd following me. But I refused to be quiet about what I believed was right, so I would speak my mind. My wife, and others, often admonished me, telling me to keep my opinions to myself. But this is against my convictions. If things are not according to the will of God, I will speak on His behalf, even if it costs me my life.

I guess my words flew across the camp and into the enemy's camps just like a bird. I have never bothered finding out who told on me and what exactly I had said that was such a threat to them. But one night, while I was sleeping, they came for me again. They were cowards, these soldiers, and didn't even dare to confront me like real men. Instead, they stuck the barrels of their guns through the walls of my house, and tried to shoot me while I was sleeping. But God must have sent his angels to protect me again, because when I woke up, I was still alive. Maybe they had lost their courage, or maybe God stopped them. I don't know. All I know is that they never did pull the trigger and fire at me. Deep was my sorrow when I found out later that morning that they had killed two other men. These men were as innocent as the children playing beside my house. My heart was heavy with sadness as I thought that they might have died in my place.

We lived in peace for some months after that, but then they came again. I wondered why we had guards watching who came in and who went out of the camp, because, surely, they must have known that these men intended to kill when they allowed them entry. It made me realize that a refugee camp is no safer than a village. The only safe place to be is in the Lord's will.

The soldiers who came for us the next time were intent on killing us. They aimed their guns at us and we started running. The bullets fell all around us like the monsoon rain and we ran between the falling rains. It was a miracle because none of us got hit. After we were safe and had gotten over our fear, we laughed at the soldiers who were so bad at shooting that they couldn't even hit a single one of us. When I went to bed that night, I thanked the Lord for saving my life again. The life of the weakest one of us, however, had not been saved. A ninety-year-old auntie was not able to run fast enough and they grabbed her frail body while she begged them to spare her. "I am of no use to you," she cried. With malice in their eyes they carried her over to a ditch and threw her in. Then, with speed and skill they made a fire and lit the old woman on fire. She had no way to escape the flames or the sound of the laughter coming from her captors. I would lay awake many nights and hear the weak sound of her pleading to be let free in my mind. I asked God to forgive me for not trying harder to save her.

This was many years ago. I sometimes thought that they had forgotten about me. I was becoming an old man, and I was of no use to them. I was living in this camp, unable to do much to harm them. But not long ago, they came into the camp looking for me again. They surrounded my house in the middle of the night. My neighbors told me this because they saw them. Me, I was sound asleep. The next morning they were gone. Nobody knows where they went and why they didn't just come inside my house and get me.

Something else happened some years ago that I will never forget. I had heard about a village that was besieged by the Army. The villagers were running out of food since they were surrounded on all sides. The soldiers were going to force them to either surrender or starve to death. I couldn't stop thinking of the villagers who were prisoners in their own homes. "Let's go help them," I told the students who were staying with us at that time. I wasn't as brave as I tried to sound, but I knew we needed to do this to help our sisters and brothers.

Clasper and others were praying for us at home. This was a mission so dangerous that only with prayer did we have a chance to succeed. I'm a soldier for Christ, but I'm not a soldier trained in how to combat the enemy with weapons. Ambush and military strategy are skills as foreign to me as the skills women have in the kitchen. It was my heart that compelled me, not my intellect. Had I listened to the voice of reason, I would never have gone on such a perilous trip.

We saw them as soon as we approached the village. The soldiers were waiting on the trail. As soon as I saw them I felt like a dead man. We were in the open, and a quick glance in our direction would have been enough for them to know that there were intruders on the path. We knew that none of us would survive if we were seen. Like a cat killing a mouse, they would play with us and kill us slowly. I was shaking while saying the name of Jesus.

It was seven in the morning when we saw them. We had been walking since dawn. We tried not to move. None of us spoke.

Then it happened. It got dark. It was as if the night had changed its mind and come back. Darkness covered the whole valley we were in. We were too surprised to say anything or to figure out what was happening. What we all knew, however, was that the darkness was so thick that we could quite easily get past the soldiers without being seen. And that is what we did. We made it to the village with the supplies and stayed there until it got dark again that evening. Then we took a secret path out of the village and weren't seen by the soldiers. Twice that day we got away right in front of their noses.

I think there is only one explanation for the darkness that fell on that day: they were praying for us back home. This is the power of prayer. It turns light to darkness and darkness to light.

My faith in God is very simple. At Bible school we studied theology and philosophy, but I always thought that the main thing is to keep our hearts clean and God will do the rest. My will and God's haven't always been the same. But I have always experienced God's love and mercy on my life. I have many friends here in the camp and everything I need. My life is so much better than the lives of my brothers and sisters in Burma.

We have had several opportunities to go to a country in the West. I guess it would be a good opportunity for our children, but even all the privileges in the West are useless unless they are useful. In my opinion character is the most important thing. It's more important than skills. What we are doing here in the camp by taking care of all these kids—giving them a home—is what I believe we need to do. We love doing it and we get to form these children into something important. We wouldn't have been able to do that anywhere else. We love what we're doing, so why should we leave?[8]

---

8 Based on an interview with Arthur and Clasper, January 2010. All the facts are accurate, just as they told them to me.

MY FAITH IN GOD IS SIMPLE

The cups have been refilled a few times. There are Karen pastries on the table, along with fat, red bananas that I have only ever seen in Burma. A fly buzzes around, too lazy to do much harm. Outside the walls of the building I'm sitting in are thousands of refugees making a life for themselves. A few have shared their stories with me, but most of them are unknown. I wonder: How many books worth of stories are within the boundaries of this camp? How many men and women have the potential to change the world, but will likely never get a chance to do so? I look over at a faded photo from Arthur and Clasper's wedding. It has been laminated and taped to the wall. Above it is a calendar with a photo of Karen leaders all dressed in their traditional costumes.

I think about the words Arthur said: "My faith in God is simple." It's a paradox that we often encounter with faith, because a simple faith is often the most challenging. How many of us have a faith so simple that we're willing to walk straight on the enemy's path, risking our lives in order to save others? Our complex theology generally won't get us very far. It often only gets us from the parking lot to the sanctuary of the church.

Soren Kierkegaard says it so well: *"The matter is quite simple. The Bible is very easy to understand. But we Christians are a bunch of scheming swindlers. We pretend to be unable to understand it because we know very well that the minute we understand, we are obliged to act accordingly. Take any words in the New Testament and forget everything except pledging yourself to act accordingly. My God, you will say, if I do that my whole life will be ruined. How would I ever get on in the world? Herein lies the real place of Christian scholarship. Christian scholarship is the Church's prodigious invention to defend itself against the Bible, to ensure that we can continue to be good Christians without the Bible coming too close. Oh, priceless scholarship, what would we do without you? Dreadful it is to fall into the hands of the living God. Yes, it is even dreadful to be alone in the New Testament."*[9]

---

9   Provocations: Spiritual Writings of Kierkegaard, compiled and edited by Charles Moore, *Orbis books, Maryknoll, New York 10545*

I think that Arthur and Clasper have grasped this. I don't need to be a theologian to understand what the Bible says. Just take any part of the New Testament and start doing it. Then maybe I too will experience complete darkness after the sun has already risen.

Arthur skillfully mixes some of the betel nut concoction, places it in the back of his mouth and chews. His eyes sparkle and I can tell that he has a lot more on his heart. "Character is more important than skills," he repeats. "Whether we are poor or rich doesn't really matter," he says, as if talking to himself. "What matters is that we are satisfied. Some people are never satisfied."

IT'S JUST TALK

Imagine living in a camp and sharing your bathroom with so many people! Imagine living with thousands of others and never getting the luxury of being alone. Imagine never being able to plan a vacation for anywhere but right there, within a barbwire enclosure. Even though they make the most of it and try to have overcomers' attitudes, life as a refugee must really suck.

There is a life that sucks worse still. That is life as an IDP. IDP is short for Internally Displaced Person and is the term used around the world for all people who have had to flee their homes, but who haven't crossed an international boundary to become "legal" refugees. It's common knowledge that these are the most vulnerable people in the world.

There are approximately 1.5 million people in eastern Burma who have been allotted the glum destiny of IDPs. That means my family times 300,000. Or, it's as if all the people in Philadelphia were wandering around in the forests of America, with no security, only the food they could carry in their baskets, no medicine, and no social services whatsoever. These people are like gypsies, except that they do their wanderings involuntarily. Their villages are attacked and they run into the jungle and hide. Then their hiding site gets discovered or they run out of food to eat, so they move again. Some people, when asked how many times they have had to move, will answer, "I can't remember. I've stopped counting."

You would think that discouragement would be as rampant as dysentery or malaria in those areas. And, of course it *is* discouraging to always be on the run, never knowing if they will live the next day, never knowing if there will be food, never knowing if tomorrow they will have to run again. But something other than discouragement fills the air among many Karen IDP populations. That is faith.

Once we were at our home in Chiang Mai having a leisurely Sunday afternoon when we got a phone call from a friend who, at that very moment, was at a hiding site in the jungle somewhere in Burma. He called from a satellite phone, and getting a phone call from a satellite phone made it feel like a reverent moment. Nobody would call from the jungles of Burma on a satellite phone unless they wanted to share something so important that they were willing to pay the huge amount of dollars per minute it cost to call.

The girls and I were sitting in solemn silence while dad talked. He became quiet. His eyes became watery. When he finally spoke again, it was with a voice that crackled a little as if the sound we heard coming from him had also gone through a satellite first.

When he hung up he told us that his friend had called to share the story of a village that had been attacked and burned the previous night. Now he was together with the homeless villagers at their hiding site in the jungle. They were destitute. They had very little food, no medicine and it was cold. But it was Sunday, and on Sundays Karen Christians always get together to worship. What Steve got to hear through the satellite phone was a group of newly-displaced people worshipping Jesus in the middle of the jungle, with the enemy in the proximity.

We say that all people are of equal value, and politicians, church leaders, housewives, students, and business leaders all agree: we are of equal value. Some even add that since we were created in God's image, we are all valuable—none less, none more. It means mighty little to make claims like that, however, and not do anything about it. It's like when my daughters say that, yes, they're going to clean their room or do their homework, but they make no moves to leave the computer or the fascinating book they happen to be reading. I know then that they have no real intention of actually cleaning the room or finishing the homework. It's just talk.

I walked through the jungle for a day with a man who has been an IDP many times. He shared his rice with me and told me about his wife and baby son back at his home in the refugee camp. His name was Raykaw.

RAYKAW: I FEEL IN MY HEART THAT
WE ARE ALL HUMANS—EVEN SOLDIERS

Raykaw is running faster than he has ever run. When he plays football with his friends in his village, he runs fast, but not this fast. When his friends and he are running down to the secret frog-catching spot at night after it's been raining, he runs fast, but not this fast. When he chases his friends on the narrow paths through the rice fields, he runs fast, but not this fast. He can remember only once when he maybe ran this fast. It was when the bear chased him.

It happened some seasons ago when his legs were a little shorter than they are now. He still remembers his uncle telling him he could go hunting with him the next morning, but only if he got up before the sun rose, and only if he thought he could keep up with his uncle. Raykaw had been so excited that he hardly got to sleep that evening. He kept tossing and turning, causing the bamboo floor to make squeaky noises, like the sounds of the wood-eating insects in the jungle— *keewup, keewup.* When his uncle shook him awake early the next morning, it felt as if he had just closed his eyes. But it was time for the day to begin. While the rest of the house was sleeping, Raykaw and his uncle ate some rice. Then they wrapped some of it in green banana leaves. It would be their lunch that day.

They walked through the jungle on light feet, the uncle first, Raykaw behind him. He made sure his uncle didn't have to slow his pace down, and although his legs were aching from all the walking, he said nothing. He would rather have died than for his uncle to think he was a wimp who couldn't keep up with a real hunter. All around him the jungle was speaking. The sounds were as familiar to Raykaw as the sounds of his mother cooking in the kitchen. His senses came alive in a way they only did when he was hunting. He kept listening for unfamiliar sounds—the sound of a big animal.

They came to a creek where the water swirled in the sunlight, skipping over rocks like a playful kitten. They stopped and filled their cupped palms with water, drank it thirstily, and washed their sweaty faces in the refreshing liquid. Then they walked on, carefree but alert. Raykaw felt strangely safe as they walked. He felt like the jungle had tucked him in. On his left was the creek, provider of water and life; on his right was a steep mountain, imposing and protective. He didn't feel trapped, just sheltered.

Then he noticed that his uncle had bent over and was moving forward like a panther closing in on its prey, his gun held at the ready. Raykaw didn't see what he was aiming at, but imagined a deer. Without losing sight of what he was aiming for, Raykaw's uncle signaled for him to follow close. Raykaw's heart beat a little faster. Suddenly he was unsure. What had the signal meant? To stop or to move? To stay back off to follow close? He really couldn't remember, and decided his uncle had meant for him to stop. He didn't make a sound. A mouse would have been louder. For some seconds it was as if the jungle had stopped speaking too. No frogs were croaking, no beetle strumming its instrument, no birds chirping. Just the sound of his own heart beating.

Then the gunshot: *Baamtsh!* But what was *that*? The deer hadn't been killed by the bullet! And the deer was no deer, but a bear! Now the bear was coming towards him faster than the fastest man could run. It all happened so fast; Raykaw didn't remember even having the time to think. In fact, he didn't remember anything from the second he saw the bear until he found himself on the top of a rock that was impossible to climb. His body was shaking with fear as he looked down from the rock and saw the bear dead on the ground. His uncle hadn't missed with the second bullet. But how had he gotten up on top of the rock and how had he run through the brush full of long and painful thorns? He had no idea. He picked some of the thorns out from his skin, gritting his teeth like a man. *Perhaps God put me up here*, he thought, since that was the only explanation he could think of. *He is the God they teach about at my school and the God that I think I want to follow when I grow up. Did He save me so that I could do something great with my life?*

The hunting trip was a success for his uncle. He carried the dead bear back to the village and they ate a meal rich with meat and spices that evening. They laughed when the uncle spoke of Raykaw getting to the top of the rock that nobody had ever climbed. His relatives playfully checked under his arms to see if he had wings.

But now he is not running away from a bear. He is running from soldiers who are shooting at him. And his uncle is not with him to shoot at them. He is all alone. The men's bullets have not yet hit him. He is quite a bit ahead of them, but how much further will he be able to run at this speed? Anxiously he turns his head just long enough to see the soldiers. One of them is shooting his way. He runs along a creek, skipping on rocks and using the vines for balance. The jungle is his friend and seems to give way to him as he comes speeding through. He hopes the jungle will have mercy and make the going hard for the men who are following. Suddenly he comes to a halt. He is at a spot in the jungle where the trail splits in two directions. He can't hesitate. There's no time for that. But he also can't choose the wrong way. That could be his death. He goes to the right and follows the valley for what seems like the longest run he has ever made. His uncle would have been proud if he had seen him.

After a while he looks back again and sees nobody—only the green, tall trees and the vines hanging down like bamboo rope. He looks again. Still there is only the green silence. He smiles and thanks the jungle for confusing the soldiers. It could have been that they went left at the junction where he went right. But he doesn't feel safe yet, so he continues to run until he sees the roofs of the houses in his village. The familiar sight makes him so relieved that tears come to his eyes. He slows his pace down and is almost walking as he enters the village. His friends ask him where he has been and he tells them, matter-of-factly, that he was being chased by soldiers from the Burma Army, but he got away. His friends look at him in admiration for some seconds then they get back to the game they were playing. Raykaw joins them.

Some months later the din of the monsoon season gives way to clear, cool skies and crisp air. It happens at the same time as the rice is ready for harvest. He is running again. This time he's not running alone. They are all running. There is no excited anticipation in his steps like when he goes hunting or looking for treasures with his friends. There is just the loathsome feeling he always gets when they are forced on a journey like this one. Every year it happens, and every year he hopes that this will be the last time. But now he is starting to wonder. The arrival of soldiers at his village seems to be as predictable as the coming of the malaria mosquito during the rainy season. They come and behave the way they want. Raykaw wonders who their mothers were who taught them such bad manners. From the hilltop they see the smoke of their village burning. He hears the dying screams of the animals and sees his home disappear in a cloud of black smoke. It looks like the smoke is a being that slithers around his house like a snake, and the burning bamboo sounds like a morbid laugh—*mwhee-hee-hee.*

He has packed for this kind of journey before and knew what he needed to bring with him for the weeks or months ahead. In the basket he carries on his back are a blanket, a change of clothes, some rice and his schoolbooks. The rice takes the most space and weighs the most, but he knows they will be happy for every grain they brought with them when the food supplies decrease and their meals consist of more water than rice.

Ahead of him are other villagers. Some of the children are crying. He isn't sure why they cry. It could be because they are tired, because they are hungry, because they are scared, because they are sick, because they have a blister, or for all those reasons. He has learned, a long time ago, that there is no use crying. Nobody will stop for you anyway, and crying just takes energy that will be needed for the long walk.

As the sun sets they stop at a small clearing by a creek that is so small Raykaw thinks that only the babies will find enough water to take a bath there. There is no cheerful chatting among the villagers, only a tired, solemn silence. It's as if everybody is fighting their own battle in their hearts. All of them know that their village is gone. Again. Gone are the houses they painstakingly built just a year ago. Gone are the animals they spent all their savings to buy. Gone is the rice that was going to feed them for the coming year. Gone are the school and the church. Gone are the clothes and cooking utensils they weren't able to bring with them. Gone is their livelihood. Again.

The adults divide the tasks of setting up camp without having to speak much. They have done this before too. It has become a routine. The children know the rules: no loud voices, no laughing, no running around, no climbing trees, no splashing in the water, no making fires. There are so many things that they can't do that they just sit down on the ground looking at the darkness approaching. Sleep comes because the body is weary, but the sleep is not restful like it ought to be. In their dreams they see brown uniforms, guns, and flames. In their dreams they hear cries and gunshots. When they wake up they're not sure if they dreamed it or if it happened for real.

They killed two of our men. One of the villagers knows this. He came late and told them what had happened. He says that the men had been in their houses when the soldiers arrived. They had been trying to hide what they could of their food and belongings, but were just a little too late in getting away. As they tried to escape across the field the soldiers aimed at them and shot. They died. One of the men was the father of Raykaw's friend. Again Raykaw wonders if the soldiers' parents hadn't taught them that it's wrong to steal and kill.

As the days pass, life gets more and more miserable for Raykaw. The first few days they had eaten rice that had been cooked before they left. Now that rice is gone and they're only able to cook on some days. Most days they can't make any fires for fear of soldiers who might smell it or see it, and find their hiding spot. They spend the days looking for food, but are always hungry. Raykaw reads his book together with his friends and passes some time that way. Their teacher must have gone in another direction when they fled, because he's not with them. Last year the teacher had been with them, and that was the best thing that could have happened. During the idle hours of sitting and waiting he had taught them just like he did at their school in the village.

The worst is when the children start getting sick. This also happens every time. They catch colds and the colds turn into bigger diseases. Every night they hear children sob quietly, and the parents hushing them. The Army has not only taken away the right to have medicines and doctors for their sick children; they have even robbed them of the right to cry when they are miserable. Worried parents don't know what concerns them most—that their child is sick, or that the child will reveal their hiding place by coughing or crying. It feels like death lingers in the bushes, ready to invade their space as soon as the opportunity arises. This time nobody dies, but there have been times when they lost some of the children. Those are the times when the days also feel like a dark night.

The nights are long. It is cold and some nights Raykaw is sure the blanket is filled with cold rather than with warmth. He isn't able to sleep much. Then he lies awake and stares at the darkness, wondering who is hiding behind the black shroud that's enveloping the world. He doesn't feel any comfort or safety from the jungle these days. He only thinks of it as the hiding place for evil men.

More than two moons later they reluctantly return to their destroyed village. The men have taken turns walking back to the village to see if it's safe to return. Finally the enemy soldiers are gone and they can pack up their few belongings and walk home. But home is gone. There is no joy in their return. A message is waiting for them in the form of destroyed houses, broken pots and the carcasses of their animals: *Nothing belongs to you. You have no rights on this land. We will be back again and you don't know when. You are of less value to us than the flies on the dead animals.*

Like so many times before, the villagers start by cutting down the bamboo. Little by little a village is erected again. After some days it starts to look almost like it had before the soldiers came and destroyed it. The only difference is that there are more ashes and burn marks than before. Raykaw's father oversees the building of the school like always. "The children need to study," he repeats again and again. For years he has been saying that. The teacher comes back from his hiding place and resumes the lessons. They continue where they left off all those months ago.

Life takes on its normal routine again. But nobody knows for how long.

•   •   •

Many years later I am sitting with Raykaw in the jungle. He is twenty-eight now and one of the best medics in all of Karen State. "I like to help people who are fleeing," he says. "I know what it's like to be an IDP, so it's nice to help them. Also, in my village there were no nurses or health workers. I want to help my people."

On his walks with relief teams through the jungle he gets plenty of opportunities to diagnose and treat the sick.

"You know," he says, "I could have gone to America if I had wanted to. I had refugee status while I lived in the refugee camp." Instead, he chose to go back to serve his people in Burma. When he left the camp, he left the opportunity for money and security. "I didn't want it. I want to stay here, with my family and my people," he says with confidence.

"This is the year I am going to become a Christian," he tells me with the same confidence. "My wife will become a Christian too. My village was animist, but we always learned about the Bible from our teachers. I decided already as a little boy that when I grew up, I was going to become a Christian. My parents have encouraged me to become a Christian too even though they themselves have chosen to stay animist because of the other villagers. But my father has read the Bible and knows all about it. He is a very wise man. He was a teacher and the school coordinator."

It's getting dark around us as we talk. He's looking at his new Casio watch and reminds me that he needs to go soon. He's attending a class for medics. I wonder if he actually has more to learn. He should be the teacher.

"Do I hate the Burma Army soldiers?" he repeats my question as if that was his answer. "I cannot say if they are bad or good. They just follow the orders they are given. They want to control us Karen and if they end up controlling us, that is bad for us. We won't be able to live like we have. We won't be able to speak our language. Nothing. They would control us. But for me, I'm a medic, and that means I will treat all people who need help. I will treat a Burma Army soldier too, even if he is my enemy, and even if he will kill me. I feel in my heart that we are all human, even the soldiers."

Our talk is coming to an end. I stand up and am getting ready to let him go. "What do you want to do in the future?" I ask. I should know by now that this is a question that most people in Burma can't give an answer to. "It's hard to plan my future. Our lives are not like your lives in the West. I always ask God to show me the way. For me, the jungle is my home. I wouldn't survive in a city because I don't belong there. But in the jungle I can do everything."

He walks off into the dark of the jungle. For now he is not hunting bears or tigers, but knowledge on how to better treat the sick.[10]

---

10   Based on an interview with Raykaw at Tha U Wah Camp, Karen State, Burma. All the facts are correct, just like Raykaw told them to me.

How would you feel if you had to wear only shorts to school?

I often speak to children and youth at schools. They make me feel popular and loved, and some of them say the funniest things when I ask them questions. The younger, the better, in my opinion. Most of them seem to have a slight touch of ADHD, skipping from one theme to another while I try to get them to focus on Burma. Just one thought or sentence will trigger a jump to another world, another time, and another life in their fast-moving brains. For example, they will say, "Once, when I was four, I fell off the swing and then my dad bought a new car." One time after I had spoken to a class of second-graders, one of the boys came up to me and said, "I think you should become the queen of Burma." That warmed my heart, and I decided that I wanted him to become a prince, marrying one of my daughters.

Sometimes in Norway, in the middle of winter, I will ask silly questions about wearing only shorts to school. The kids will roll on the floor laughing. It's so stupid that they can't believe I asked it. I will also ask them if any of them were refused breakfast that morning and if any of their mothers told them that not only would they not get any breakfast, but they might not get lunch or dinner either. This, of course, leads to them telling me what they did have for breakfast, and what their favorite food in the world is.

The reason I ask them all these doltish questions is, obviously, that I want them to try to imagine what it's like to be living in the jungles of Burma, in the coldest season. After seeing what they wore to school and hearing about what they have eaten in the last forty-eight hours, I tell them about what life is like in the jungles for children on the run from the Burma Army. While I talk, the children are wide-eyed and outraged. They give me a lot of ideas of how to combat the bad guys. Most of the ideas involve massive violence and some fairly frightening bombs. Bombs with poop have been mentioned.

Sometimes I have been approached by parents who have told me that their kids have come home from school angry, and haven't stopped talking about the injustice that is happening to children in Burma. They will be sitting around the kitchen table eating dinner, and mom and dad will be challenged by their preschooler: "What if you didn't get any dinner and had to go to work wearing only your shorts?" Some parents have been forced out of their complacencies by their children, who have told them it's high time that they do something about Burma. To me, hearing this fills me with joy. I am part of raising a new generation of world changers.

RISKING YOUR LIFE IS A RELATIVE EXPRESSION

At Partners we had to do some soul-searching and ask ourselves if IDPs *really* mattered as much as, for example, our own kids. No matter how we looked at it, we came to the conclusion, that, yes, these people are indeed as valuable and important as our children are. It turns out that they *are* created in God's image and that He loves them as much as He loves our kids. It somehow felt wrong to say that just because they live in hard-to-access areas, they shouldn't be helped. We felt that we needed to take a step further, and reach out to the IDPs.

Enter the FBR, The Free Burma Rangers. It so happened that they felt exactly like we did about most issues—except they don't appreciate lattes as much as we do, and they have strange work hours. (They will come to work at about 12.30 p.m. and work until 4.00 a.m.) They too thought that the IDPs' lives mattered, and that if they did matter, that we should help them. To put it simply, we worked out a work relationship that was something like this: "If you (Partners) pay the bills, we (FBR) will do the job." Depending on what kind of person you are you will think that we (a) got a great deal or (b) got a crappy deal.

I'm not going to get into too many details here because details are boring. But I must spend some time explaining FBR and our marriage to them.

FBR trains teams of local (ethnic) people in frontline medical treatment and reconnaissance techniques. They also document the abuses done by the military and get that information published in reports that travel all over the world. Actually, their mission statement says it well, better than me trying to explain it: *To bring help, hope and love to people of all faiths and ethnicities in the war zones of Burma, to shine a light on the actions of the dictators' army, to stand with the oppressed, and to support leaders and organizations committed to liberty, justice, and service.*

So while big, fat charities and government agencies are saying that helping the IDPs can't be done—so they must put lots of money elsewhere in Burma—the FBR relief teams are out saving lives, and risking their own in the process. I feel proud that Partners (and therefore I) is a part of this amazing work. Hundreds and thousands of people are getting medical help and other assistance because the ethnic teams are bringing them help, hope, and love.

At first we were satisfied by just paying the bills. We knew that the money got to the people who needed it the most. But then some of us wanted to get more involved with the training of the teams, as well as with the IDPs. It's no surprise that my husband was one of them. He would say that he wanted to meet the people we were helping and that he wanted to see the situation with his own eyes. Until then I had been quite okay with having others risk their lives to help and us just bringing in the bacon. Now I had to decide if I thought it was fine if Steve became one of the life-riskers and left me at home.

Steve asked what we would like people to do for us if we were the IDPs? I wasn't sure if I would have wanted a visit from me if I had been an IDP. I wouldn't have been of much help except that I'm a good hugger and smiler. But I could see that Steve would be a welcome addition to any group of people.

To make a long story short, he went on a few trips with the FBR and came back a little skinnier, a little wiser, and a little more determined to keep striving for free, full lives for the children in Burma.

Risking your life is a relative expression. To live is to risk one's life. It's totally possible to get killed driving to work, or when going grocery shopping. One can die from swimming or from eating too many jelly beans. There are, of course some things in life that are more dangerous than other things, and crossing into Burma illegally, for example, may be one of those things that are a little riskier than going for a walk in the neighborhood. To let Steve take the steps that would take him to Burma wasn't an easy decision. We knew that it wasn't safe. But we had to come back to this simple question: *Was it right?* If the answer was *yes*, then it would be worth the risk.

The decisions we make in our lives often involve risk. But should that stop us from doing the right thing? Ponder this, and turn your answer into a devotion.

We had this burden for the children and that was an area where FBR said they needed help. Whenever I thought about children the same age as mine being on the run through the jungle without shoes, warm clothes, food, or even adults to protect them at times, I really felt like crying. I think

I actually did cry. I got a book that explained what happens to children who experience trauma, especially the ones who are victims of war. Then I was alarmed.

It's easy to see what happens to a person who doesn't get enough to eat. They get bloated stomachs, their growth is stunted, they may develop slower mentally, their immune system gets weakened, and they die. Physical injuries are also somewhat easy to diagnose and treat, if one has the skills and medication. But what happens to a person's soul is so much harder to see and to treat. There are no antibiotics that can take away emotional infections. And the more I read about what causes trauma, the more it was clear to me that there's probably not a single child in Burma who hasn't been traumatized in some way—by seeing violence, by experiencing violence, by losing loved ones, by fleeing their homes, by fear, by lack of routines, by insecurities, by lack of trust. You name it! The children of Burma have experienced trauma of all types.

Steve, being an experienced Insider (Here is some inside information: we're on a clandestine mission to Burma, so we can't actually say that is where we're going. So we have come up with an almost impossible-to-crack code for Burma: *Inside*.) himself, agreed that the children's emotional needs were substantial and maybe we could do something to help. The FBR were doing a program for children, but gave us the freedom to develop it into something bigger. This was our chance to do more for the IDP children than we had done until now. We still helped with all the relief efforts and a whole range of other things, but I was particularly excited about the trauma care.

There are some good child psychologists around the globe, but we didn't manage to get any of them to join our staff, making no money and going places that were almost inaccessible, where the working conditions could be both hazardous and extremely uncomfortable. So Steve and I, with the help of other people's material and expertise, put together a manual for healing the children of war. Then, all of a sudden, it was my turn to go *Inside*.

It's a well-known mathematical fact that if you multiply stuff (greater numbers, for example) you get more done. In practical life that means that it would be better for us to train many people to do the things we're good at than for just one of us to try to do all the work ourselves. It seemed absurd for me to go and try to minister to the children myself, but training the ethnic leaders so that *they* could better help, made perfect sense. Since we didn't have anybody more qualified than me to do the training, I went.

So here this is what happened on my first mission.

WE CROSSED TWO MOUNTAINS,
AND THE MOUNTAINS HAD NO MERCY

You'd think that after so many years and so many travels, I'd be used to it the way we're used to getting out of bed in the morning. But every single time I'm going on any trip by myself, I try to get out of it. I have a stomachache and think of all the wonderful things I could be doing at home if I didn't go on this particular trip—the laundry for example, or polishing the silver. I get weird anxiety symptoms and start thinking of how nice it is to sleep in my own bed. I wonder if my children will grow up with bonding issues and a lack of self-esteem because they felt like I abandoned them. If I'm going on longer trips, Steve has to help me pack and he always tells me that I'll be fine and to stop whining like a baby.

As soon as I'm out of the house, however, I'm okay. It's like I become a new person. The world of new adventures is mine, and I think I'm up for all kinds of challenges.

Now I was going to get inaugurated into the club of *Insiders*, and the pressure to succeed was immense. Not so much from others, but from my own ego. It wouldn't be my first time to Burma, but it would be the longest and most challenging one. Ever since I'd heard that it was like some kind of an ultra marathon, my main thing was to get in the best shape possible. I didn't want to fall apart a few miles into the race.

I diligently walked and ran up and down the mountain in our city many times a week. When I could do that without difficulty, I filled my backpack with weights to make the challenge more realistic. As soon as I thought my condition was impressive, all I had to do was to invite some of the FBR staff to come with me. They set me straight. With them on the trail I was like a five-year-old trying to keep up with my older siblings. Still, I often thought to myself that I was lucky to be able to do this kind of workout as part of my job description.

I felt like I could conquer most mountains by the time we were getting ready to leave. Among a million other things, Steve helped me by selecting only necessary items for my backpack. When you're going to carry all your stuff in a backpack for a few days, you want to be a careful selector. First you get rid of the hairdryer.

After a few rounds of getting rid of more unnecessary earthly goods, I was left with a small pile of: two pairs of underwear, two pairs of socks, two pairs of pants, two T-shirts, two bras, one jacket, one long-sleeved shirt, a hammock, a sleeping bag, a small mirror, toiletries (Here I took some liberties. Strictly speaking, you don't need mascara or eyeliner in the jungle, but I feel ugly without them. I knew that the guys I'd be walking with would be bringing knives and other manly gadgets that they thought they needed to fight or kill an animal if one attacked. I opted for a very small knife and justified the mascara that way.), two sarongs, a pair of shorts, a titanium cup, my journal, mosquito repellent, a Petzl headlamp, some Tylenol, a pen, packs of ORS, a light tarp, a small recorder (I was already then thinking about writing this book, so I was going to interview people.), flip-flops, iodine tablets (to make dirty water drinkable), a New Testament (the small ones that the Gideons give out for free in all hotels) and a tiny, but weighty devotional called *The Way of Love* by Anthony de Mello.

I would, of course, be wearing one of the pairs of socks, underwear, pants, and shirts, so when everything was in the backpack I was impressed that I had brought so little. It didn't weigh much at all. Then we put the water bottles in and I felt like I was going to tip over backwards. For the kind of walk we would be doing, water was vitally important. And it wouldn't be easy to refill the bottles, so I needed to bring as much as I could carry. Boy, did I wish that water was weightless!

It's not a bad idea to be forced to carry all your belongings. That really narrows the definitions of "need" down. Maybe we should all be forced to do that. It would get rid of a lot of clutter. What I brought with me turned out to be perfect. If I could have brought one more thing it would have been my iPod. I am serious. I missed listening to the Eels for so long. No Citizen Cope, no Indigo Girls.

We have to drive forever to get to where the hiking started. First a few hours on roads, then we spent four hours squeezed inside a truck, driving on roads that may never have been there. What I mean is that we were transported through the jungle in the backseat of a truck so small that we had to fold our bodies like they were sheets in order to fit. There may have been a trail, but the way it felt sitting inside the truck was that the trail certainly was not meant for motor vehicles. We climbed boulders, drove through rivers and snaked from side to side in mud, on rocks, and in sand. The engine sputtered, the wheels splattered, sometimes we slowed way down as if the truck was fighting its desire to simply die right then and there. I often looked at the driver who seemed to think that this road was as fine as any, and wondered what it would be like for him to actually drive on a highway. He might find it amazingly unchallenging.

I had been an emotional mess before leaving. I'm sure that if I'd found some Valium in a drawer, I would've popped one in my mouth just to stop shaking. I was going to be away from my kids and Steve for almost three weeks, the longest I had ever been away, and I was really concerned about what Steve would feed the kids for dinner all those days. Not to mention if they would remember to shower. My other big worry was that I was going on this trip as the only female, together with four men whom I had never met before. I wasn't worried about getting sexually harassed. I was just worried that they would be incredibly fit. What if it turned out that I was actually not in shape at all and they just zoomed past me in the jungle, leaving me alone to fight the tigers and snakes with my Swiss Army knife? I was scared to find out.

It turned out that my traveling companions couldn't have been better. (Well, Steve would have been a better buddy, for obvious reasons.) They had a perfect balance of the kind of fitness that was able to fight off dangers while I watched, yet not leave me behind because they were so incredibly fast. They treated me with the utmost courtesy, making me feel both valued and respected. They shared chocolate and other snacks with me, which is a sign of true spiritual maturity when you're on the trail and know that when the snack is gone, it is really gone. The next available snack may be deep-fried grasshoppers.

When our drive was over, it felt good to unfold my body. We were joined by several Karen who were going to escort us and help carry some of the supplies that we had brought. They were examining us with great fascination while they smoked their cheroots and pipes. To the untrained eye they may have looked like jungle people from Papua New Guinea, but these were men from Burma. Their jaws were set, their clothes a bit unmatched. They smelled like a mixture of smoke, tobacco, and earth. We were all squatting together. (This is a skill I have learned well while in Asia. One who knows the art of squatting never needs a chair.) I hadn't seen any of them look at their watch yet, and we had been sitting there for two hours. Nobody knew what was happening or when we would start moving, but it seemed to bother no one. Time was coming to us—slowly. It reminded me of squatting on the side of the road with Steve some years ago, waiting for a bus or some other mode of transportation. Many Karen squatted next to us, but none could tell us when the bus would arrive. And it didn't matter at all for them. The bus would come before sundown. That was all they knew. In the meantime, they were content sitting by the road, chewing betel nuts and spitting.

I ate half of a Luna Bar while nobody was watching. You see, this proved my spiritual immaturity because I didn't share. All I thought about was that I only had two Luna Bars in my pack and that when I get too hungry I start feeling like jiggley jello and I'm useless to anybody. From Steve I learned that although you only have two Luna Bars and you don't know when you'll eat next, you should still always share. After all, the others may be just as hungry as you and they may not have any Luna Bars at all. He told me this later, after I came back from my adventure. For me this was a big deal because a small act revealed what was in my heart—to look out for myself first. Do you know how much harder it is to share something you really like, feel you need, and don't know if you will get more of? It is harder than walking in the jungle after dark.

When the sun had set and it was dark we were finally walking. I had no idea where we were, except somewhere between Thailand and Burma. We trotted along by the light of the moon, mostly through rivers, and up and down hills. I loved it and thought about singing. It was a breeze. Doug, one of my teammates, let me use one of his expensive aluminum walking sticks and I was grateful beyond words. The walking stick was going to become my closest friend over the next few days, and while walking I thought about turning this into a sermon. It would be about sharing walking sticks with each other if you have more than one. It doesn't sound very inspired now, but back then I had it all clear in my head and it was a great sermon. I would not mention sharing Luna Bars.

Hours later when the world was sleeping we arrived at a distant camp where we got to sleep and rest. The next day we traveled upriver and arrived at a small village where a bamboo house was hidden behind hills and leafy trees. Here we were told to try to sleep and rest too. The night was going to be long and hard. We were, of course, too excited to sleep much, but lay on the bamboo floors staring at the ceiling. Somebody had used white paint and written: *Do unto others*. I wasn't sure if they had run out of paint or if they just didn't realize that the verse had a part two.

It was finally dark again. We spent some time under a stuffy tarp in a long and narrow boat that had its propeller perched on the end of a long steel shaft—long-tail boats they call them—going even further up the river. Now we were ready for the big trial of strength. More Karen had joined us, both to help porter supplies and to be guards on the trail. As I looked around in the dark it seemed like a whole village would follow us, there were so many people. The porters would be carrying all the sacks of supplies in baskets on their backs. Each basket would weigh about fifteen kilos. They tied the baskets around their heads with strings of cloth and tackled all the hills wearing flip-flops, or barefoot. There was no way I could have kept up with them if they had put themselves in fourth gear.

Perhaps this is weird, unnecessarily personal, but as I looked at the forty or so men that would be walking with me through the night, my biggest worry was not so much the walk. My big concern was where to pee. There were so many men, and I was so visible, being the only female (and a white person besides), that anything I did would be noticed by somebody. I hurried behind a hill before we started walking. Then I trusted that there would be a way for me to go potty on the trail.

The night was long and the walk was the hardest one I have ever done. We crossed two mountains, and the mountains had no mercy. It was steep and difficult and we panted and sweated and climbed and crawled. It was pitch-black all around us and we heard all kinds of strange sounds from bugs and who knows what else. It was a cool night and my headlamp fought with the walking stick for the role as my best companion. A Petzl headlight is worth more than gold, than diamonds, than anything I can think of. I fell in love with my headlight that night. Rocks rolled casually down the trail as we clambered for the top. Roots and fallen logs became enemies that appeared at the most unfortunate moments, like when we were so tired that lifting our feet one more inch into the air seemed like an unbearable challenge. At one point John fell over, exhausted. "I knew it!" he groaned. "I shouldn't have put that chess game in my backpack."

When walking in the night you have the advantage, and disadvantage, of not seeing what lies ahead. I remember one particular place that night, after we had been climbing up for what seemed like three weeks. I had a feeling that we had reached the level of Mt. Everest and that just around the corner was the down slope. I looked up, and the most surreal sight caught my eye. In front of me, going up in an almost vertical line was a string of headlamps. It took me a few seconds to realize that I was looking at yet another steep hill, and the lights were the porters walking in front of us. They looked like pearls on black velvet. Wiping my sweaty forehead, I absorbed the sight, the air, the smell, and the sounds, and felt like a very lucky person. How many get to do this?

We stumbled into the village where we'd be resting at dawn the next morning. We strung our hammocks and had a few well-deserved hours of sleep before finishing up the walk the next day.

You may think that I'm bragging, but the honest truth is that when we finally arrived at the training camp I felt sad. I would have liked to continue walking. I did, of course, not mention this to any of my traveling friends. They seemed all too happy about taking a break and some of us needed a shower desperately. But the strenuous hike just made me feel alive and strong. Since we hadn't seen any creepy crawlers to brag about, I also loved the nightlife of the jungle. Don't for a second think that it's quiet, because an orchestra entertains you all night long. It's therapy. The enchanting sounds, mixed with the cool tropical wind, had blended well with my feeling of mastery over my body. Like never before I had understood that most actions happen in our heads. At least, I was able to make my body obey to a much larger degree than I thought I would be able to. When my body had protested like a spoiled three year old, saying that it couldn't possibly take another step, I had taken control over it.

Now here we were. And here to meet us was *Tha U Wah A Pa*, the father of the white monkey. He was dressed in his black running shorts, wearing a green FBR T-shirt, and a baseball hat. He wore Salomon running shoes and expensive socks. We had arrived at the *Tha U Wah camp* and *Tha U Wah A Pa* looked exactly the way he had looked when I met him in Chiang Mai.

INSTEAD OF A CROWN HE WORE A
BASEBALL HAT WITH AN ALASKA LOGO

Tha U Wah A Pa is the father of *Tha U Wah*, which means White Monkey. In Karen tradition parents get named after their children, thus Tha U Wah's dad was named *Tha U Wah A Pa* (father of the White Monkey). His mom is, of course, *Tha U Wah A Mo* (Mother of the White Monkey). Simple as Thai spelling rules. In English *Tha U Wah A Pa's* name is so much less exotic: *Dave*. The reason this camp was named *Tha U Wah Camp* should be pretty obvious by now: it was White Monkey Camp.

Dave (*Tha U Wah A Pa*) started the FBR when he understood the urgency and complexity of the situation among the ethnic peoples of Burma, and realized that he, in fact, had a lot of the skills needed to bring about change in the country. Together with a handful of Karen he has criss-crossed many of the ethnic states on foot, helping, training, documenting, and being a great friend to his team of guys that we now refer to as the Animals. Each of the Animals has an animal name that goes along with their personality and skills. Once an Animal name has been given, it can't be changed. Such are the rules set by *Tha U Wah A Pa*. My good friend was named Slug. Another one Crazy Chicken. But there is also Mad Dog, Koala, and Monkey. I got the flattering name Lady Fox although I had secretly hoped for *Gazelle*.

Dave likes to lead as a team, and includes as many as possible in all the major decisions he has to make. At times he even denies that he's a leader, but don't let him kid you. He is the leader with a big L and without him a lot of what is happening with the FBR teams—and I dare say, in Burma—wouldn't have happened. But, and this is equally true, a lot of what Dave has done, wouldn't have happened without his wife, Karen's support.

Dave is an easy candidate for hero status among all of us who inter-act with him. He's so talented and well-spoken that we just stare in awe as he tackles most obstacles, such as some of the tallest mountains in the world or articulate leaders. He has a photographic memory, which means he remembers everything. This is a huge disadvantage if you happen to disagree with him and, like me, are facts-challenged. He is funny and fast. He can talk a hole in your head. His best quality, though, in my opinion, is that he encourages all of us to do things we don't think we can do. This has happened to me more than once. And now *Tha U Wah A Pa* was here, in Tha U Wah Camp, welcoming us. I got the feeling that we had arrived at his kingdom and he was proud to show us his place. He didn't have a castle, but a cute bamboo house. And instead of a crown he wore a baseball hat with an Alaska logo on it.

"I CAN'T EVEN TAKE A BATH GRACEFULLY"

After a thorough bath and some rest, life took on a routine in the camp. I tried to fit in and do things right, but, frankly, not everything was easy. To say I was out of my element is an understatement. This is what I wrote in my journal one of those days:

"This morning I woke up feeling grumpy. There is something disheartening about realizing that you're not as good as you thought you were. It's not that I think I'm perfect, but I want to imagine that I at least am a nice person with certain talents. Here at the bamboo scout camp I have decided that the best thing I can compare myself to is a Norwegian cow in the jungle, when what I need to be is a tiger.

"Take the walk here, for example. For months I have been running, biking, and swimming to get in the best shape I can be. My muscles are well-defined. My body looks fine. I can wear tight pants and don't worry about them looking like they shrank in the dryer. I have my good shoes; I have my nice backpack full of high-tech gear. Then, when we started walking up the mountain in the dark, the truth was revealed: there was an army of people barefoot or in flip flops with fifteen-kilo rice bags on their backs who could, and would, outrun me any day. As I stumbled and fumbled up and down the mountains in the dark, using my walking stick like a blind person would, giving praises to Petzl for inventing such bright headlamps, the army of rice sack-carriers moved up and down the slopes like panthers in pursuit of their prey.

"I may get some mileage out of my story when sharing it with those illiterate in jungleology. Surely there are people in the world who will think of my trip as a brave adventure. But I am quite sure that if you ask the parade of porters who followed us, their descriptions of me and the team of similar creatures of no grace, will be full of laughs and giggles.

"I can't even take a bath gracefully. While I know, in theory, how to wash my body jungle style, I still can't make myself look like the Karen women who resemble slender nymphs dressed in sarongs that cling to their bodies like designer dresses from Armani. Me, I have a hard enough time getting the sarong to stay on while I pour water over me. And although I try my hardest to pretend that ice-cold river water poured over my body only feels refreshing, I still gasp for air at least once every scoop. I usually manage to get out of the river without too much effort, but I'm still trying to become proficient at taking my wet sarong off while putting a dry one on without disclosing any of my skin above my ankles or below my underarms. I'm not even going to describe the way I try to get my underwear on under the sarong that must not fall off. There is a good reason why I try to go to the river to take my bath before all the rest. I'm an introvert who treasures my time alone, and I'm afraid to be seen naked on the day the sarong falls off like a shower curtain loose from its hinges. Knowing me, it's bound to happen one day soon.

"I guess it has something to do with the world we were brought up in, and how we learned to see ourselves. I can use that as an excuse for my shortcomings here. *Oh, they should just see me in the kitchen of my own home,* I may think as I watch them make fires from nothing and cooking three-course meals in the kitchen with dirt floors and machetes. *The way I elegantly switch on the burner of my stove is really something. They should see me chop the onions for the salsa. Who said I have no grace? Could they use the computer the way I'm able to, or maneuver in the traffic the way only I can on a Friday afternoon? Did I mention that I can ride a bicycle and knit complicated patterns?*

"I'm not sure that this is the real issue though. Obviously, we are from different worlds: the Western world with all its trinkets, and the jungle world with all its jungle gadgets. It's only natural that we behave like clumsy amateurs in a world that's not our own. I can keep wishing that they could see me in my element, with my hair a different style than the mop-look I have been forced to adopt during these weeks. But I can also decide to give up my pride and let myself go.

"I have no problem being totally honest and sincere while I'm uttering my silent prayers to the only One whom I believe knows me just the way I am while here. Often it goes like this: 'Help me, help me, help me.' 'Please, please.' 'Say something, will You?' My prayers aren't any more eloquent or impressive than the clumsy climbing moves I've had to make as I crawled up steep hills to get here. But they're all I have. I can't make them any better. If I did, I'd be a liar. Maybe I've come here to learn not to be too impressed by myself, but instead to see that I am weak and dependent. In the convenience of my own world, I often don't see this, because I can do so much, and the rest I can fake. It's a humbling feeling, but also freeing. In a way, it's like the sarong has fallen off and here I am in my imperfection. You can take it or leave it, but this really is who I am.

"If I keep being honest with myself, I see that it was actually never an issue of other people rejecting me. I seriously doubt that a single person here at the camp would send me home because of my slow pace, lack of language skills, or hopeless hair. When they watch me cross a narrow bamboo bridge like a blind person would cross the street, they neither laugh nor yawn. The person who rejects the imperfect me is … me. It feels good to be in control and to manage well. To see one's limitations and shortcomings hurts. But I think that the blessing is hidden just there. The blessing comes when we stop striving and pretending. The blessing comes when I stop trying to impress and say, 'I'll give it a go, but I may fall. And if I fall, I'm going to believe that it doesn't change my value and worth. It just means that I'm a person in need of grace and a good blend of all that Jesus has promised.'"

What is the blessing? It could be a lot of things. But perhaps it's to make myself a cup of coffee, sit down on my hammock with a good book and feel at ease with who I am and the fact that I'll never be 100% Karen, 100% jungle queen, or 100% intellectual athlete. But I can be 100% me, and content with that. Because one thing I am good at is drinking a good cup of sweet and creamy instant coffee in my hammock without spilling it.

STRANGE THINGS HAPPENED TO ME WHEN I WAS THERE

It is odd how humans react when we're out of our element. There's a lot of talk about comfort zones these days. It's a trendy word to use, and it seems we're all encouraged to get out of them. I have moved my resistant self out of this zone more times than I can recall, and it never gets any easier. The best way I can describe it is that it feels like getting out of a hot bath into a cold, cold bathroom, with only a damp towel to dry off.

Not that this is a new theory. JRR Tolkien thought of it forever ago, and encouraged us, through Bilbo, and later Frodo, to get out of our Hobbit holes. It's easy to depend on our own skills and abilities in the safe hole where things are cozy and predictable. Alasdair A. K. White says it this way in his book *From Comfort Zone to Performance Management* (I haven't read the book. Those kind of books tend to bore me so I just get the summaries from Steve who happens to read a lot of them, and remembers what they say. Most of what I know about management I have learned from raising kids. One cannot micromanage either toddlers or teenagers.). Anyway, Alasdair A. K. White says: "The comfort zone is a behavioral state within which a person operates in an anxiety-neutral condition, using a limited set of behaviors to deliver a steady level of performance, usually without a sense of risk."[11] In Tha U Wah Camp there was no question that I had moved out of that zone.

Strange things happened to me when I was there in the jungle camp. It was an amazing place. The beautiful surroundings with mountains encircling the compound and a lively river rushing right past were alluring. There were butterflies as big as bats, with colors I hadn't known existed. Cute bamboo houses looked like Asian gingerbread houses and were filled with about seventy young men and women who had experienced the worst of war and who were there to make the world a better place. They were welcoming, kind, generous, and fun. I should have felt at ease the way an orange feels in its peel. But I felt more like a potato trying to get into a banana peel.

---

11   Alasdair A.K. White. From Comfort Zone to Performance Management. *(2008 White & MacLean Publishing)*

While there, I did my job and other chores. (Remember the teaching manual I had written? I thought that would be the main reason I was there.) As the days progressed, however, I realized that I was there not so much for what I could do to help and give, but because of what God needed to do in me. Oh, *brother!* All that work and such a long walk just for *that!* Now my girls were at home eating frozen pizza and hotdogs for two weeks and I was here in the jungle learning things from God. To my rational—or as some would point out, irrational—mind it seemed like a waste of precious time. But, just like the Karen squatting in the jungle, worrying nothing about time, God too was more concerned about doing a work in me than about the time it would take. He knew the kids were in good hands, and that Steve knew how to cook spaghetti too.

The training camp was just like a school where the students learned useful skills for the job that was ahead of them. For most it meant knowing how to treat the sick, how to deliver babies, how to amputate a leg, how to locate a village, how to conduct interviews, and such. Then there were physical challenges in abundance. You've never seen so many pushups in your life—I guarantee it.

They also needed to be prepared to die. One of the first things we got to see when we arrived was the Wall of Heroes. Here were photos of all the rangers who had died while serving their people. One of them was a person whom I had cried over before: Saw Lee Ray. I had never met him, but Steve had. In fact, Steve had taken the photo that was posted on the wall. In the photo, he's standing in the middle of the river with a big smile. His hair is wet and he looks as alive as any other young man in his early twenties. Just a couple of years ago he was in a village in Karenni State treating sick people there. Since there seldom are any hospitals or other medical facilities in the area, the needs for medical attention are immense. You would think that treating the sick wouldn't be seen as a crime worthy of death. But it was. He was found, captured, tortured for two days, and then killed. The day I heard about this I felt like I had a rock in my stomach. Now, looking at his picture and all the others who had died needlessly, the same rock came back.

Watching the young men and women bustling around the compound like diligent ants made me think of a happy village rather than of an army of men and women who would soon face a deadly enemy. They laughed and played soccer. Some of them slept through their lessons. In the afternoons they took baths in the river and washed their clothes. As always in an area with more than one Karen, there was the sound of a guitar and singing. In fact, only occasionally did I remember that we were in a country at war and that it was not impossible that we'd encounter the enemy. One of the times I was reminded of the reality of Burma was when we had a surprise mock attack. It was like a fire-drill at school, when you have to act as if there's a fire, although you know there isn't. This drill was quite a lot scarier than the fire drills. We were sneaking down a steep trail with roots and branches, unexpected drops, and a few slippery parts—in the dark without using any light and without speaking—pretending that at any point we could be ambushed. Let's just say that this kind of role play made my heart thump a little louder and faster.

At all mealtimes the students did their FBR chant: *Love each other. Unite for freedom, justice, and peace. Forgive and don't hate each other. Pray with faith, act with courage. Never surrender.* Don't you think that if the world only followed this mantra, said it before each meal, and kept each other accountable to do what it said, that we'd all live in a better world? I think we would. I think we could cut the military budgets way down and probably need fewer psychologists too.

From my own bamboo hut, which I shared with Amy and Kiryn, I had a first-class view of the daily soccer games. The Karen are fabulous and passionate soccer players. It's a tradition that, as I understand it, has been handed down through generations, ever since Sir George Scott introduced the game to Burma in the 1800s. They play with intensity and skill, but without the proper outfits. You won't ever see a shin guard or cleats. I was regularly invited to play and I politely answered, "No, thank you." Some of the other Westerners who were much braver and not as worried about their appearance as I was, joined in chasing the ball. But, honestly, I felt like if I had joined the game, it would've turned into something like a circus where I was the resident clown.

Instead I would go running. My goal was to stay in good enough shape to get back home. No less, no more. So I would run laps around the compound every afternoon. It's just under one kilometer around, and you may find this an interesting bit of trivia: I hold the lap record. One day I did twelve laps, and that had never been done before. So there you go. I may not be the soccer star, but I am sure good at running around in circles.

YOU SEE, WATER HAS NO BRAIN

Journal entry:

"Lying in my hammock at night looking at a cockroach walking on the beam, coming my direction, didn't scare me much. I switched off the flashlight and went to sleep. Earlier in the day though, I was really scared. It had been the FBR swim day.

"All the students have to learn to swim before they graduate. This is not just so they can have fun, but it could be a matter of life and death. Many of them come from areas with no ocean or rivers, so they have never learned. Others have a superstitious attitude towards water, believing that it's full of spirits. But if they are chased by the army and get to a river, they need to know how to cross it.

"I've always had a tense relationship to water. I'm not sure why. Perhaps it stems from growing up in Norway without a lot of water encounters. Swimming in the North Sea is not for wimps, and I'm a wimp when it comes to cold water. Also, some summers in Norway only last for three days. But the swim-day was an event I had to be a part of even though I grew up in the north of the world. It was one of those times when I knew deep in my heart that to try to get out of it would be wrong. I was worried that I'd have to help rescue somebody from drowning, and I knew that the result would probably be that we both drowned. I can swim in a straight line in a calm swimming pool, but don't make me do anything acrobatic like jumping in at the deep end, for example.

"I tried to stay calm on the hike there. I kept telling myself that it wouldn't be worse than giving birth. I did that three times and survived. I tried to focus on things other than my anxiety, and not to think of the benefits of Valium. We saw the river after about an hour or so. To me it looked like a miniature Amazon—dramatic, powerful and magnificent—a body you do not want to mess with, because this one knows its strength. (The reality was that I'd probably have had to be the size of Barbie for the river to be compared to the Amazon!) We climbed on rocks and under brush that seemed to be the home of many millions of ants. Although it looked like it was a stroll in the park to all the others, I kept looking down at the mini Amazon while silently praying that I wouldn't slip, because it didn't look like a good place to fall in.

"'Here we are,' they said and threw their backpacks off. Here? Holy cow! This was worse than I'd imagined. It looked like suicide to me. Way down there was the river, still confident in its strength. 'Right down there the water is eighty feet deep,' Dave said proudly. 'We will swim across it.' What I had worried about was swimming in a calm and mellow river, a little wider than the pool we go to, but about the same temperament. This was a hundred times worse than that. I didn't worry about rescuing people anymore. I was thinking that if I got into that river, it would be the last thing I ever did. 'Is there anywhere that it's not as deep as eighty feet?' I managed to squeak out, hoping that it didn't sound like, 'I'm afraid.' 'Nope,' said Dave. 'You're going to make it. I'll help you over. Come on.'

"I knew there was no way out of it. He promised to swim with me and keep me from drowning. We prayed and he pushed me into the water that spun around like it was in a blender. I probably lasted fifteen seconds and had no idea what I was doing or where I was going. I really thought it was the end of me. So Dave grabbed me and swam with me to the rope. He said I was really great and that he'd never seen anybody drown so calmly. I was just amazing in my failure. I managed to get out by climbing up on the slippery rope.

"Then I sat for as long as I could talking to Doug about Bach or whatever, hoping Dave would forget about me. Of course he didn't. 'Oddny, I found a much better place for you,' he said after half an hour. 'Oh, I hoped you had forgotten me. Do I have to?" I knew the answer, not just from Dave, but something deep down and far back in my heart. Dave had a long speech about the theories of rapids and strong water, which meant nothing to me, because I knew I was going to die.

"We did a rock climb down to some new cliffs. Here the water was not just in a blender. Here it was practically at a full boil with white foam and all the other accessories. 'Okay, this looks a lot worse, but it's not. You see, water has no brain. It only does what it always does. You have a brain and what you need to do is to make it to the other side by swimming as fast as you can.' 'Yes, but I'm so scared that I don't think I've ever been this afraid before. I'm not as confident as you are and I'll only do this because

I know you'll save my life if I start to drown. You will, right?' 'Yes. You're allowed to be afraid, but you're not allowed to let fear control you. Now, go. The sooner you do it, the better. I'll hold your hand and send you in. You may end up with your feet in the air, but then you just turn around and keep swimming.'

"Then I went. This time, as if by a miracle, I made it to the other side, because, according to Dave's calculations, we started higher up. It was a big deal and everybody cheered. But now I was on the other side and knew I'd have to go back. Five minutes later Dave was ready. We climbed barefoot up and down some cliffs. Down by the river he found the perfect spot for me, his project. 'Okay, here you can jump in and start further out or I'll help you slide in.' 'I can't jump in either. Remember, I've only ever swum in a pool, and Steve taught me to swim.' 'Okay, I'll send you out, and I'll be right behind you.'

So I swam again, and this time I thought I did well. But the current was so strong going this way so I drifted down the river. Suddenly I had absolutely no strength left. I knew I would sink. So I was rescued by Dave, the rope, and the boat, and humbly swam back to the cliffs. Then I was done. The rest of the day I watched as about seventy of the students plunged into the river. Some of them swam like otters. Others braved their fear, and like me, struggled through every second of their crossing.

"In the late afternoon we walked home. We took a shortcut. This involved scampering along the side of the cliffs, finding handholds so that we didn't fall into the river of death. The others saw absolutely no challenge in this easy hike. I pretended like it was a piece of cake too, like this was the way I walked to work every day. Then we found the trail and walked home.

"I'm not sure how I feel about the day. While I'm glad I made it, somehow, it's also a humbling feeling. Everybody was watching me, and it would've felt a lot better if I had just crossed the river like an Olympic champion. There is always a desire in me to impress people, and I didn't feel very impressive. But in a strange way I was also proud. I could have just decided not to do it, and it would just have been a bit awkward. In a very concrete way I chose to walk (or swim) right into my fear and in that way conquer it—at least a little.

"While I wanted Dave to just forget about me, I'm glad he didn't. He was right when he said that it's okay to feel afraid, but that fear can't control our actions. Then we're ruled by fear and not by what is right. I think that fear can be so strong, and it certainly takes different shapes in different people. For me it was the water and all its strength. For others it may be the cockroach walking on the beam. I know that fear can be overcome. It's just that it's so dang uncomfortable!

"Then I was reminded of how much we all need the Daves in our lives, the ones who won't let us fail, and who, even when we *do* kind of fail, still make us feel like champions because we didn't give up. I hope that next time it will be my turn to make somebody face their fear and help them overcome it. But it's very likely that it will be me at the fear-end again, holding onto somebody's hand while they tell me that I can do it—and then pick me up right before my head goes under the water."

Talk about getting out of my comfort zone! And I thought that all I needed to do was to go for a long, hard walk and then teach for some hours.

ALMOST AS REGULAR AS THE BEEPING OF WATCHES, WAS THE NODDING OF HEADS

The reason I came, supposedly, was to teach. So I did this every morning for some hours. I had all my trauma theories spelled out neatly on A4 pages and brought props with me to help bring out my points. In the West life has a degree of predictability, especially when one teaches a class. The students sit in their chairs, taking notes. Depending on what the study is, you can figure out the demographics of the listeners and expect certain behavior according to this. Not so when teaching in a war-ridden nation.

First it was the setting: it was a bamboo structure without walls surrounded by jungle and mountains. This is the best way to air condition in the tropics—let the breeze move through the room, along with dust, bugs, and other debris—but there was always some activity going on outside. Since there were no walls or doors, anybody could come and go as they pleased. Most days while I was teaching a mule walked into the classroom. Who knows? Mules may be in need of some psychology too. It just stood there looking at me, and it was impossible for me to tell what it thought about my theories.

The classroom was equipped with benches, planks that had been leveled and made into fine sitting places. A few inches higher up were the desks, planks also, just like the benches. On the desks anyone fluent in Burmese could read short exclamations carved into the wood, probably with the knives the students carried in their pockets. The floor was just dirt, hardened and leveled. There was a blackboard.

While I taught I mostly thought of the students as cute! Cute in a tough way, I guess you could say. They were looking at me eagerly, wanting to learn, wanting to please. They all had cheap notebooks that were folded and stained, full of notes from other classes. While I spoke, I had a suspicion that many of them considered it an English lesson more than a psychology class. The students ranged in age from around nineteen to twenty-five. Most were men, but there were some brave women among them as well.

They were all given a survival kit when they arrived at the training session. The kit consisted of a green FBR T-shirt, a uniform, a sleeping bag, and other essentials for the mission they'd be going on after the training. It appeared to me that most of them thought the coolest item in the kit was a watch. It was the kind that beeped every hour, or, if you let it, it could beep every half hour too. I even think it could beep every fifteen minutes. So during the class thirty or so watches all beeped at regular intervals, reminding me that lunch was not far off.

The nodding of heads was almost as regular as the beeping of watches. Not nodding in agreement with my teaching, but nodding as in sleeping. Karen people have a gift of sleeping through any lesson. And they do so unashamedly. I too have been tempted to let myself take a snooze while listening to a particularly boring speech, but I know it's bad etiquette, so I force myself to stay awake either by eating gum or by thinking about my next vacation. The Karen just let it go. They will even snore. Once I taught at a Bible school for a whole week and the best compliment I got was, "Did you notice that nobody fell asleep during your class?"

But, besides the fact that some of them slept through my classes, I would still claim that they were bright kids. When I asked, "Why are the children important?" every time I started teaching, they answered enthusiastically, "Because they are the future!" "What is the most important quality you need to serve the children?" "We must love them." Then we spent time talking about how to practically demonstrate this love to the most vulnerable of all.

I felt humbled while I talked to them. It was easy for me to stand on the mud floor with my notes and ideas. The only sacrifice I was making was three weeks away from my kids and my husband, my hot showers, and the annoyance of hundreds of mosquito bites. The people I was training were going into a war zone. There were no promises of safety or comfort. They would probably never be rewarded for their efforts by getting a raise, a medal, or a day named after them. Instead hunger, fatigue, sickness, and even death might be in store for them. Yet they chose to embrace their calling with enthusiasm and joy. I could forgive an occasional catnap.

One of the students I taught during this time made a bigger impression on me than the rest. His head was shaven; around his neck was a string with a tooth on it. It looked like it could have been from a bear, but I wasn't sure. I had watched him and the others on his team do their physical exercise in the mornings and the afternoons. His physical strength was the level of a world-class athlete and caring for children was not a task I would have chosen for a man like him. A bodyguard, yes, but an early childhood counselor? Not really his style. His name was Kaw Blu Sei. "This is what I want to do. I really want to help the children of my land. In fact, I have already started helping them," he said proudly, the tooth necklace dangling as he nodded his head for emphasis. "A while ago I found four children aged four to ten wandering aimlessly around a village. They didn't have any parents. I helped them get to a refugee camp where they were taken in at an orphanage. They are all doing really well now."

I struggled some while trying to explain the concepts I had in mind, like the word *trauma*. I just got blank stares from most of the students, and I was starting to despair, or at least wondering if my teaching would have any value at all. That was when Kaw Blu Sei spoke up: "Yes, I know what that feels like. The Burma Army captured my mother and me when I was five years old. For a whole day they dragged us through the jungle without any food and water. Then they let us go. After that happened, I was always afraid. It didn't go away until I turned twelve."

I felt happy to get some help from Kaw Blu Sei, but it also made me realize something else: all these students had wounds, pain, and traumas too big for words in their hearts. How could they be expected to go out and minister to others when they themselves had so much baggage to carry around? I realized that the teaching I was doing was for them just as much as it was for the kids they would be reaching out to. Understanding this made me feel amazingly overwhelmed, sad, and hopeless. How to deal with a classroom full of so many unspoken hurts? I knew I couldn't do it, at least not all the way to the depths of their hearts where a movie was playing on repeat—a movie full of past events.

I did what I could do which was to speak what I knew to be true, to love them and to give them their props to practice with. Have you ever given hand puppets to refugees in their early twenties? It is an experience worth living for. When I pulled out a cute, fuzzy animal puppet for each one of them I got the feeling that at that instant, they all decided that all their suffering through push-ups and hard work had been worth it just to get that puppet. They forgot all about the teaching we were working on and spent the rest of the afternoon antagonizing each other with their puppets.

At the end of the week they had all learned the STOP model—kind of. It was a model I had learned from Phyllis Kilborn's book, *Healing the Children of War.* The STOP model is an easy way to remember what children need the most to get through trauma: S is for Structure, T for Talk and Time, O is Organized play, and P stands for Parental support, S-T-O-P. There is more to it, of course, but this is the essence.

At the end of the week we had a mini graduation where the students were certified Good Life Club counselors. We gave them each a warm jacket with a patch that said GLC. Kaw Blu Sei was grateful for the Good Life Club Patch that I gave him to put on his jacket. "This means you are a qualified GLC counselor," I told him. "We want this patch to be a symbol that children will start to recognize. When they see the GLC smiley face, they should know that here is a safe person who cares about the children." Saw Kiaw held the patch close to his jacket the way he might have done if it was a piece of his own heart. He wanted me to tell him where I thought he should put it, to the left of the zipper or to the right, or perhaps down by the pocket. It wasn't much, but it was a small symbol that let him know that we trusted him and he had been given a job that we considered supremely important. I thought that one day Jesus Himself would give him a patch too. He had chosen to follow Jesus' calling to serve the little children, and I believe there will be a real special prize for people like him—perhaps a patch that says, "Well done, good and faithful servant" (Matthew 25:21 NKJV).

TAKING THE COMMITMENT TO DO THE
RIGHT THING TO A WHOLE DIFFERENT LEVEL

Dave's wife, Karen, looks like she is related to Claudia Schiffer. She is petite and pretty, and has a smile that lights up the room. She says she loves coffee shops and shopping, and, I've heard, she's a very good biker. She likes to read and listens to classical music if she has a chance. I can envision her as a trendy *granola chick* in the Washington kind of way. Perhaps the kind of person REI markets for, or Real Simple, for all I know. Not sure if she prefers organic food.

But she is nuts. Together with Dave she has climbed some of the most complicated mountains in the world, and I think this says it all: they spent their honeymoon with former headhunters. (So they *said* that they've stopped the headhunting-thing, but how safe would you have felt at night? Wouldn't it be like putting a former alcoholic alone in a room full of liquor?) We thought she would mellow out a bit when she had kids, but no. Now she brings her kids to live in the jungle six months of the year. She did the walk I have been bragging about (the three day/night hike through the jungle) carrying a three-week-old baby.

We are good friends, although I suffer from incredible inferiority complexes when I'm with her. But inferiority complexes can be constructive. At least they are for me. They challenge me to become better—to strive for something higher and reach for goals I thought I couldn't achieve.

While at Tha U Wah Camp we would sit around at their bamboo house drinking instant coffee and chat in the afternoons some days. She had spent the morning homeschooling her kids and now they were flying around on horses as if they were practicing for a scene in a John Wayne movie.

"I want to teach my kids about generosity, hospitality, simplicity, and compassion," she says. "All these values I see in the Karen more than in our own culture. I want to teach them to love people, to help and care. What better way to do that, than here?" She will go on and on about how wonderful it is for her kids to grow up in this environment. She throws her arms out in a wide circle around her. "Look at this!" The jungle is their playground; the Karen students are their friends and guardians, there is no need for computer games in a world that has horses in abundance and a river as a close neighbor.

When the training is over, Karen brings her kids and an army of Karen people on a tour, The Good Life tour. For about a month they visit villages, and simply put: they bring love and laughter to the villagers, as well as supplies. Part of the program, besides playing duck-duck-goose for hours, is to do some basic hygiene teaching and other community development training. They also share the Gospel in a simple way. I have seen Karen's many photos from her tours, and, to be honest, I think that it's not so much the sharing of the Gospel in words that matters the most. It's that she, the children and all the Karen that are with them share the Gospel by living it out right there in the middle of Burma—to a people who were starting to wonder where all the love was.

Karen willingly admits that she finds her lifestyle hard at times. "You know, I don't like the jungle much, and personally I'd rather be other places. But every time I consider it, I see that this is the best place for my kids to grow up." She also prays more than most of us do (of course she does). She will tell me about difficult decisions she has had to make, like being away from her husband on Christmas, because he was out saving lives. Instead of doing what I would do, which is bawling and kicking and asking my husband if he really loves me since he wants to be away for Christmas, Karen takes it to God and gives Him her feelings and lets Him tell her what He thinks about the situation. Then she comes out from her prayer chamber all ready to take on new challenges. She makes it look easy. Most times I think only God knows how hard she really thinks it is.

At times I have thought to myself, *Shoot, why didn't I think of raising my kids in the jungle?* Here we were thinking that reading The Rainbow Fish, and, later, biographies about Gladys Aylward and Martin Luther King Jr. would turn our kids into compassionate and justice-loving citizens. We thought that going on weekend trips to refugee camps and villages, and letting them grow up in a cross-cultural environment might open their eyes to diplomacy and peace. Honestly, the thought of bringing my kids up in the jungle never occurred to me. And now I see that it's not such a bad idea.

In my mind, she has taken the commitment to do the right thing to a whole different level. During times when I feel the need to pamper myself, I'll compare my own commitment to that of people around the world who don't seem to commit too much, and I come out the commitment winner. This is a great game to play when I'm feeling down because, compared to many, I am ahead of the game. Once somebody told Steve and me, "You guys could just retire from doing good deeds right now and still feel good about yourself. You have done more good for the world already than most of us will do in a lifetime." Boy, did *that* ever feel good to hear!

Around Karen though, I fall short, and I'm reminded of an important principle: she doesn't compare her commitments and actions to what others do, but she measures her actions with God's standards. She will pray about most decisions she and her husband have to make, and more times than not, she'll end up voting for the option that is the least safe and comfortable. Of all the people I know, I don't think I know anyone who has given up her own ambitions, dreams, and interests to such a degree in order to see others succeed and in order to see others get to experience freedom.

Karen, I think, is a person worthy of our utmost respect. And I can see her waving her hands vigorously as I write this. "Paw leauw," she says to me in Thai—*Enough already*. But it's true. She could have probably made headlines in some fitness magazines or made a world-class nun (that's actually one of the things she contemplated), but instead she's living in primitive conditions in the jungle, seldom putting her own needs and desires first, seldom getting the kind of attention and admiration her husband gets, seldom getting to have a manicure.

I think of Karen as a person who has taken what she had—which happens to be a lot—and used it faithfully to serve and to give. The result can be seen all over Burma, in my opinion. It seems like God knew what He was doing when He made her. She glorifies Him with her life, and brings life to thousands of others.

So while I often compare myself to her and wish I had more of her verve and gifts, I mostly admire her and find that she is a great inspiration in my life. But I also have to admit that when I watch her kids whack each other on the head, when they refuse to do what they are told, or when they neglect to say *thank you* and *please*, it makes me really happy. She is human, after all, and her kids are too.

DOH SAY: KEEPING YOUR WORD
IN MY HEART, AND ON MY HEART

The days were all a blur to him. How long had he been here? He had lost track of time. His memory of his former life had blended together into a murky picture, much like the water in the river that ran through the camp. He was lying on the floor, pinned down with an invisible force called *excruciating pain*. He was like an invalid who needed help with every-thing—even going to the bathroom. He closed his eyes and with a heart full of unanswered questions he whispered, "Why did You let this happen, God? Why did You let me get shot when I had hidden Your Word in my pocket, not just in one pocket, but in two?"

Doh Say wondered if he was done now. Was his suffering and humili-ation finished, or was there more to come?

.   •   •

Doh Say found his favorite rock in the middle of the river. It faithfully waited for him, and every day he tried to get there before anybody noticed. When he felt secure on the rock he started making the swimming moves with his arms that he'd seen the other boys make. He desperately hoped that none of his friends would notice that he wasn't actually swimming. The water wrapped around him like a blanket did in the cold months of the year. Soon he felt so comfortable he put his head under, disappearing into a different world.

He held his breath for as long as he was able, looking around with blurred vision. Slowly he let go of his safe rock and moved towards the direction he thought the shore was in. As long as his head was under the water he hopped forward, pretending to be a frog. But when he lifted his head to get his directions he was painfully aware that he still didn't know how to swim. With a lot of splashing and moves that didn't really qualify as swimming moves he was able to make it to shore somehow. When he felt the ground under his feet, he coughed, spit, and tried to catch his breath again. His friends were watching him, laughing. "Doh Say, did you forget how to swim today?" He didn't tell them that actually, he had never learned how. He was more determined than ever and decided that tomorrow he would learn. Enough of being a fake swimmer standing on a rock, moving his arms like the puppets on strings he had seen at the fairs in town.

At the day's end he walked back to the village with his friends. They all went back to their parents and siblings. This reminded Doh Say that he was the only one in the village whose parents weren't there. He was going home to his aunt and uncle. The thought, like a small pain in his heart, had grown duller with time.

Doh Say was six years old and couldn't figure out why his parents had sent him away a year ago. *I must have been very bad, but I don't know what I did*, he thought. *I tried to be good, but sometimes I was mean to my sisters and brothers. Sometimes I was lazy. I was a bad boy. That's why they sent me to live with my aunt and uncle.* Then he was overcome with a sudden fear: *What if I am a bad boy for my aunt and uncle too? What if they send me away? Who would they send me to? Somebody very mean, for sure.*

It was hard to be a six-year-old trying to live to please the adults in his life. *I want to be a good boy so they don't send me away again*, he told himself as he dutifully did his chores. The scary thing, however, was that the adults were so hard to understand. Some times they would give him a smack for doing something he thought was a good thing. How was he supposed to know what adults liked? He wasn't an adult. It was very confusing and scary and every night he relived the day in his head. Had he been a good boy or a bad boy? If he got to stay another day that must mean he had been good enough.

•　　•　　•

Years later he was still living with his aunt and uncle. He had gotten used to his new family and rarely worried about them sending him away any more. His days were busy with school and chores. His aunt kept him busy most afternoons. "Doh Say, get the wood. Doh Say, go and get some water." In order to get some time to play with his friends he lingered on his way back from school. They threw rocks in the river, played with a ball that one of them had, and ran around chasing chickens. Most things were more fun to do than going home to hours of hard work. When he finally arrived home, his aunt was ready for him. *Smack! Smack!* "This is what you get for being such a lazy rascal! Don't you think I saw you playing with your friends? Who do you think is going to do your chores for you? Do you have a servant that you pay to do your duties, eh? No? Okay, then get working before I slap you again."

I don't care, I don't care, he told himself as he picked up the bamboo container, put the rope around the front of his head and walked down to the river to fetch water. He belonged to no one, therefore he could put up with their painful remarks, the occasional slap in the face, the constant nagging from his friends: "Hey, Doh Say! Who are your parents, eh? Where are they?" He has said the answer to those two questions more times than he could remember: "I don't have any parents. I just dropped down from heaven."

Then there were the happy days. They were as full of fun as the rice barns were full of rice—giggles at nighttime, games by the river before sunset. His uncle was prospering and they had more than enough to eat every day. He got new clothes more often than his friends, and more than once his friends had brought up his uncle's wealth. "Your uncle grows money on banana trees," they would laugh. "Our parents just grow bananas and other fruit, but your uncle, he grows money." Doh Say knew that his uncle was rich. He saw it with his own eyes every couple weeks when his uncle put wads of money into a big sack and walked to town to deposit his riches in a bank account that must have been fat like a pregnant lady.

Doh Say knew that the wealth didn't come from growing money on trees, but from owning several mines and more cattle than he could count. He knew that his uncle was considered one of the wealthiest men in all of Karenni State. It filled him with pride and comfort. *I'll probably never be poor,* he thought. After all these years he was more like a son in the family than a mere relative.

Karenni State. Doh Say loved his country. It wasn't an actual country any more although it once had been. Far away, in Rangoon, generals now ruled the nation, passing laws that got harder to live by the closer one got to the capital—or so he had heard. But here in Karenni State they did as they pleased. They saw little of the men in power, other than pictures of them on billboards, on the front of papers, and on TV that Doh Say had been able to watch on occasion. It was like they were still their own country, Doh Say concluded.

The state had an abundance of all the things one needed to live a happy and prosperous life—rivers that glided slowly or rushed down waterfalls, green forests, endless amounts of teak trees and evergreens, mountains, fertile plains, roaming wild elephants, and other animals. *What person alive could want anything that we can't provide here in Karenni State?* Doh Say wondered. It was as if God had taken this very small spot on the planet and made it like heaven.

·   ·   ·

Doh Say was a teenager now and had a job. A job that paid him a salary, however small, made him feel like an adult ready to take on the world. He was working at the local market, selling produce to poor villagers and rich merchant's wives. All day long he weighed up salt, rice, and other items that the customers wanted. "Here you go, mister: 200 grams of salt for you." "Here is two kilos of rice, auntie. Have a nice day." The few *kyats* he earned every day felt good in his pocket. He wasn't going to spend them until he had a lot. Thinking about what he could get with his money filled him with warm anticipation.

Then he had an idea. What if he could earn just a little more every day? Just a little, not enough that anybody would notice, but still enough to increase his savings over time. If he cheated the customers out of a few grams on all their purchases, he could keep the extra money for himself. Nobody would notice. A customer got 450 grams of salt when he thought he was getting 500. Would anyone ever find out? He doubted that any of the customers had a scale at home.

Doh Say's plan worked fine for days. He didn't cheat his customers out of a lot, just a few grams here and there. But as the days passed he got a nagging feeling in his heart: he was stealing. He was watching the poor villagers count up the few coins they owned—and for many of them salt and rice were the only two things they could ever afford to buy. The realization that these are the people he was stealing from, although he himself had everything he needed, was more than he could bear. In church he had heard of Zacchaeus who stole from the poor as well as the rich. Like Zacchaeus he decided to repent and never again steal from people.

·   ·   ·

It started with the season of worry and loss, of desperate pleading, and angry sobs. "But they belong to us!" his aunt shouted at his uncle. "This is stealing! The mines have belonged to this family for generations! How can they just take them from us? This is plain robbery!" His uncle just stood there in the middle of the floor looking resigned.

All around his town Doh Say saw men and women with the same worried looks on their faces as his aunt and uncle had. At nights the men would gather at the tea shops or the noodle stalls and talk in hushed voices. Some nights some of them had too much to drink and that was when men expressed their true feelings: "I'm ruined! Everything I have ever worked for is gone! What will become of me and my sons?"

He'd thought that Karenni State was isolated from the evil of the regime. He'd thought that they'd somehow avoid the painful lashes of the authorities. Instead they were lashed and salt was poured into the stripes. Overnight the government had decided that all industry was to be nationalized. The next day he was told what that meant: it meant that his uncle no longer owned his mines. The state did. No compensation would be given for his losses. The government was not in the business of mercy. Doh Say thought that they were not in the business of justice either.

Then they took their land too, and said that all the fertile land where the cattle grazed also belonged to the regime. Doh Say couldn't understand it. Why did they need all that land? How many men had decided this and how much land did they really need? They didn't just steal his uncle's riches. They took everything from everybody. Doh Say's family and their neighbors barely managed to keep their houses from the greedy hands of the rulers. Then they woke up yet another morning to find that the general had declared that all denominations of money that couldn't be divided by nine were of no value, the people's anger was like one of the big explosions in the mines—very loud and hard to contain.

They paid more attention to the news than before and understood that the discontent was not limited to their village. It was spreading all over the country like the fire on dry rice fields after the harvest. In his hometown some brave students arranged demonstrations as well. The next day they were gone. It was 8.8.88.

Doh Say's family was poor and in the months and years to come they lost more. The verdant forests that had covered the land for generations started disappearing at a rapid speed. The teak trees were valuable, but unlike the Karenni who had cut them down as the need arose, the regime cut them down as fast as machines could work. As they watched hundreds of logging trucks transport parts of their heritage, their country's soul, to the insatiable Chinese market every single day, they felt deeply betrayed.

Slowly the green forests full of wildlife and rare plants turned into logged brush, useful for very little. With the trees gone the wild elephants, the tigers, and the other wild animals disappeared too. The ones who stayed became easy targets for hunters, many of whom were villagers desperate for food and cash. The hunters who had hungry children and no prospects of other work to provide for them weren't greatly concerned that they were shooting and killing animals that might never be seen in their land again.

Doh Say watched his uncle and aunt, his cousins, and community struggle to make a living. Their glory days were gone. They looked defeated. The proud stature he had admired in his uncle was replaced by sunken shoulders and sad eyes. They took jobs at the mines they had once owned, earning a meager living that way. Doh Say was aware of the regime's oppression every passing hour and waited for the day when he could fight them.

When he turned twenty his desire to fight was almost uncontrollable. When he went to sleep he fantasized about carrying a gun and shooting the enemy, and when he woke up he could almost feel a gun in his hand. As soon as an opportunity arose, he took it. He joined the Karenni resistance movement to fight the regime. He was done with peaceful negotiations; they only ended up with slaughter anyway. To fight with an AK-47 was the only way.

It felt good. Doing the morning routines and the drills made him feel more alive than he had felt for years. He excelled as a soldier and gladly accepted new challenges. He secretly hoped that an encounter with the enemy would be imminent.

It happened sooner than he had expected. Within weeks he was fighting the biggest battle the Karenni had ever fought with the Burma Army.

The sound of bullets flying in the air became a constant noise that only stopped during the dark hours of the night. Doh Say spent his days in the trenches, keeping his gun steady and aimed in the direction of the myriads of enemy soldiers. They were outnumbered four to one and if he let himself think about it, he knew that he was fighting a battle neither he nor his fellow Karenni could win. His optimism, however, was as bright as the burning sunlight that penetrated the canopy of trees above him. He was sure that God must be on their side, since they were fighting an enemy as evil as the Evil One himself, and his Karenni brothers were fighting for all that was pure and right. Surely God would be on their side, strengthening them, and guiding them like He had the Israelites when they fought in the Old Testament.

When men started dying around him, fear entered Doh Say's heart, and with the fear came the doubt. Was it possible that they'd all die? He watched mortars hitting the trees, and the trees falling over like they were thin bamboo sticks. Terror percolated through his whole being as he thought about one of them hitting him.

I must do something to protect myself, he thought. *But what?* Suddenly he remembered the story he'd heard of a man who had written Psalm 23 on a piece of paper, folded it, and put it in his pocket. The story was that God's Word, neatly written out, had saved the man from being killed by a bullet. Doh Say thought it was worth a try. With bullets raining all around him he meticulously wrote out the whole psalm and put it in the left breast pocket of his uniform. Then, for good measure, he wrote it once more and put it in his right pocket. He smiled. Surely God would protect him now. He had His Word in his pockets.

He walked into the battle with a new spiritual confidence. It was not long after that he was shot.

Later his friends told him that they had been close to just leaving him in the ditch. His face was ashen and he was hardly breathing. Blood gushed out from the bullet wound and they knew it would only be a short while before he was gone. But he was breathing weakly and they had heard of miracles happening before. He was transported together with the rest of the wounded to the hospital in a town on the Thai side of the border. That was where he finally woke up.

He looked around and saw dead people. They were all dead. For a second he thought he might be dead too. Dizzy and confused he called out. His voice surprised him. It was groggy and weak, the way his whole being felt right then. The nurse who came in looked more surprised to see him alive than she would have been if she'd found him dead. "We didn't think you'd make it," she explained. "That is why we put you in this ward. This is where we put the dying … the ones who are beyond any hope. But I guess your time hasn't come yet."

As the days passed in the hospital Doh Say wondered if it was a mistake that he didn't die. What kind of life would he live now? The doctor had told him that he'd never again be able to do physical activities. He'd be a burden on his family and his community for the rest of his life. Better to be dead.

Some time later he was in a refugee camp and his mood was as dark as the clouds gathering for rain.[12]

---

12   This story is based on several talks with Doh Say, at our house, in the jungle, and other places.

AN ANIMAL THAT IS SMART, KIND AND STRONG

There's one person who is seldom missing on the soccer field every afternoon. He is one of our family's good friends and plays soccer as if he's trying to qualify for the Champions' League. He is Doh Say from Karenni State.

The first thing I noticed about Doh Say was his legs. This may not be smart to admit since it reveals how carnal I am. But the truth is that I did notice those very strong legs with the well-defined, tight muscles—dark brown and not very hairy. This was a while ago and we were on a trip to a camp right on the border of Burma at that time. Doh Say told us that this was the camp he had lived in for two years while recovering from a gunshot wound.

We had hiked through the night to get this camp. It was my first time to go on such an adventure and I was ecstatic. There were several of us on this trip. Mark was one of them, and he's the kind of guy I absolutely love being with. He's hilariously funny. This is what I like the most about him. The second thing I like is that he's so smart that I get smarter just by associating with him.

Anyway, Doh Say's legs. We had many good laughs together comparing his legs to Mark's. The conclusion was that Doh Say definitely had the legs, and Mark had the brain. This didn't mean that Doh Say wasn't smart, but it did mean that Mark's legs weren't very sexy. When I got to know Doh Say better I didn't focus so much on his legs, but on his heart.

His laugh is refreshing, like children's giggles. It comes easily because he has the ability to see the humor in small things. Then his eyes become narrow lines in his kind face. Once we were in Shan State with Doh Say and we didn't have a lot to do for a few days. We sat by a rustic building overlooking the Himalayan foothills while thinking of party games we had played when we were kids. We laughed so hard we got stomach cramps, and the one having the most fun was Doh Say.

He loves intensely, is more disciplined than I will ever be, and Jesus is his best friend. He receives guidance and comfort from Him. While he reads his Bible daily, Doh Say admits that some of its teachings provide him with challenges. "You know, I mostly just read the verses that I like and understand, and most of all the ones that make me feel good," he says with a shy smile. So from time to time, my friends and I refer to the "Doh Say Version" of the Bible. That's a version we all like.

He is the only person I know who doesn't actually live anywhere. All his belongings can be found in his backpack. He will say, "I really don't need much—just two poles so I can hang my hammock." When we give him some extra money at times, he smiles and says, "Thank you. This is great, because now I can help more IDPs."

Not many run as fast and as hard as Doh Say does on the soccer field. Sometimes he takes off his shirt and tucked between big muscles are nasty scars on his back and on his chest. The battle wound will always be there, but that's about the only thing that reminds us that he was once almost dead.

One time my daughter Elise was ten, she was sitting on a wooden bench looking out at tall mountains in Shan State. "What is an animal that is kind, smart, and strong?" she asked. "Why are you thinking about that?" I asked. "I want to compare Doh Say to an animal, and these are all the things he is," was her answer. During the past few days she had gotten to know a man who had become more than an uncle. He was almost everything she thought a good person could be.

Doh Say serves his people by being a full-time relief team leader now. Parts of the year are spent training new relief teams in the art of saving people who have been attacked by the enemy. Then he spends months in the jungle walking from village to village, and from hiding site to hiding site visiting the teachers that Partners supports, and giving them their salary for the next few months. There are no ATMs in the jungle and bank transfers are out of the question. The only way to get money to the teachers is to physically hand it to them. The teachers are doing heroic acts by teaching the children in a war-torn country. Doh Say is the hero who makes it possible for the teachers to teach. "When I go and hand them the money for their salary, their eyes light up because somebody cares about them. That makes my heart very full of joy."

But before he gets to experience the joy of seeing the smiles of the teachers, he has to wander through the valley of the shadow of death—literally. He told me once, "The soldiers were so close I could hear them talk. If they had looked in my direction, they would have seen me. All I could say was, 'Jesus, make me invisible.' I kept talking to Jesus while walking, reminding myself that He was there." Later he said, "It's not that I mind so much being killed by them. It's what they would do to me before they killed me that scares me." He admitted, "The hairs on my back stood up while I snuck by the soldiers. I was so afraid."

I guess one of the things that have impressed me the most about Doh Say is his humanity. He's not a superhero who has no fear and worries about tomorrow. He feels great fear at times, but chooses to do the right thing in spite of his fear. He isn't afraid to talk about his weaknesses and shortcomings. "I wish I was a better person," he said once. After one of his trips when he hadn't wanted to help a family that was in need, he lamented, "I was selfish and thought about myself first." It inspires me to meet a person who, like me, has struggles, but who consistently chooses to disregard his fears, his weaknesses, and his limitations. Instead, he chooses to follow his Leader into territories that aren't safe, nor comfortable, but are where he's supposed to be.

I wonder how he does it, and the only answer I can think of is this: he has his eyes fixed on heaven. He knows that life here isn't the end. And I believe that when Doh Say meets Jesus face to face one day, he will know that all his sacrifices were worth it.

When Doh Say is done playing soccer he goes for a swim in the river. He's one of the best swimmers at the camp, and he teaches the students to swim and rescues many from drowning.

September 14

Dear friends,

After returning from the Kyaw Kho Maw IDP hideout and meeting with the people I had met including many children from the boarding house and some teachers, I have become sadden, knowing that I will have to leave them soon, A few days ago I had mixture of happiness and sadness: the reason I was happy was that there were only a few days left to return to Thailand; the reason I was sad was that I had to leave the children, the teachers and the IDPs I have met.

For me all the children should have the right to be happy and the right to have what they should have. This afternoon, I believed that they had a happy childhood for some hours. I just wish they always had a chance to be happy like that. We were just like a big family: (we were like parents) playing together with the children.

In the same time, I was very sad, knowing that I have to leave them in a couple of days. I had to hide my sadness.

This afternoon I found out more about their needs. It was painful to know that they do not have soaps, washing power, enough clothing. For instance, girls or boys have only one or two under wears which are no good for the rainy reason. K'Chay and me arranged with a teacher to buy more clothing for them.

Many of them, I am sure that they are missing their parents. I tried hard not to happen to ask them "Do you miss your parents?" because I do not know what to say to them if they said yes. Like we mentioned in one of the emails about a young girl who is as young as 11 years old and is separating from her parents. Almost all of them are just like that young girl, being away from their parents for education. For me all the children around the world should have a chance to live with their parents till they grow old enough.

I still remember when I was a child; I was crying a lot as my father leaving me with one of my aunts in a big city for a better education. Although I had everything I wanted, I was stilling crying for my father.

I want to add a little bit more by saying that just like I told you several years ago, my main spiritual objective is to have a chance to go to Heaven when God wants me to come back and together with friends in Heaven.

I wanted to have this and that a lot, mainly about materialism until I was 30 years old. I have been slowly able to realize what I really need and just try to become a good person and be useful for the needy ones.

It is now become clear and clear to me that my second objective is to see everyone, poor or rich, educated or uneducated, to have the right to live peacefully and without fear. So I would like to request you to pray that: 1. everyone in Burma stops killing each other solve all the problems with peaceful mean that we are facing and peace and harmony for everyone prevail in Burma, 2. everyone in the world stops killing each other and peace and harmony prevail in this world, 3. everyone gets enough food to eat and, 4. everyone has a reasonable things that he or she needs to live on.

Thank you very much for your understanding the time you spent on this letter.

God bless you all and the world.[13]

Doh Say

---

13   This letter was written by Doh Say to some of our staff. We have left it in its original version, even though there are some grammar errors. To read the letter in the form Doh Say wrote it, is like hearing him speak.

WHEN I HAD TO LEARN KUNG FU FROM DOH SAY

After three weeks in the jungle together with some of the world's finest people, I was heading home. And guess what I was thinking about? Food. I was so excited about all the things I was going to eat when I got home that my mouth watered at the thought of yoghurt, fruit, bread, veggies, beer, cheese, and chocolate. I would say it was in that order.

Obviously there were other things on my mind as well. Hugging the girls and cuddling with Steve. Hearing what mischief they had gotten themselves into. Sleeping in a bed. Taking a hot shower. Shaving my legs. But first, creamy yoghurt.

It would have been nice if the thing on the forefront of my mind had been, *How can I better serve?* I have to be honest and say that was way back in the line, even after Starbucks. I am so ashamed to even admit this.

The hike back was as long and strenuous as the walk there. No mountains had been removed, nor had any of the rivers. We still had to cross them. The difference was in me. I was three weeks wiser, stronger, and more experienced. Dave walked with us for part of the way. He chitchatted about this and that, such as skipping on stones in a river while bullets rained around—all of them meant to kill him—or about getting fungus in Honduras. We had to cross one river on a bamboo raft because it was deep and wide (like God's love). We placed ourselves on top of it while Dave swam behind, pushing it. When we had crossed over, he swam back, and on the other shore he bowed deep with his hat off and waved. It was like we were going off to a different world—which, in a sense, was true.

Doh Say was our companion and with him and the other Karen we were in the best of hands. The night we walked was a gift from God. A cool breeze played in the trees, there was a full moon in the sky (making our headlamps almost unnecessary) and the jungle was playing a song that lasted all night. We trotted on, determined to make it to the river by dawn.

On this trip I had the privilege of another girl to keep me company. Kiryn had become a good friend during the weeks in the jungle, and now she was walking back with us. She was an amazing person, talented and strong, and with a character that resembled Jesus (she also shared her chocolate). I decided that when I grew up and turned twenty, I wanted to be like her. She had some problems with her shoes on the trip though. The reason was easy to see. Her shoes were an old pair of sneakers that somebody had donated. They had lost their bottoms, but Kiryn easily fixed this with duct tape. But, no matter the quality of duct tape, it can't withstand jungle moisture. So every hour or so, we had to stop and let Kiryn re-bind her shoes with more tape. And did I mention that her shoes were a couple of sizes too big as well?

Some of the guys tried to make small talk with us while we were climbing the steep mountains. After a while, Kiryn said what I had been thinking, "You know, I'd love to tell you all about that, but right now I can only think about how to take one step after the other. So can we please talk later?" We came up with a smart trick though, and that was to make Doug do all the talking. He was a talking machine and every forty minutes one of us would think of a clever question to ask Doug. He would be as happy as a puppy and would gladly spend the next half an hour giving a detailed answer to our question. This was a great way to learn about new subjects while walking, and it was also a way for us to avoid spending any energy on talking ourselves.

That night I learned about Catholic priests, Chopin, California, communion, the Church, non-Christians, home schooling, piano lessons, hiking in Poland, stretches, youth problems, Satan, national parks, stories of people, stories about Dave, how to get a job, and a lot of theology that was a little too advanced for my liking, but interesting nonetheless—all from Doug.

Suddenly we heard the sound of the Salween River, hours before we had anticipated it. Our team had set a new speed record and Doh Say was so amazed he didn't know what to say. So he said, "It was just like you were cannon balls that got shot out of the cannon, over the mountain, and down to the river. That is how fast you were."

A small problem was this: we had walked too fast and there were no boats by the river yet. To call for one would have raised some suspicions from the wrong guys, and we could get ourselves in trouble. There was nothing else to do but wait. The jungle at this particular place had no strong trees upon which to hang our hammocks. We were exhausted and it was 2:00 a.m.

Doh Say had a mischievous look in his face while we, dripping with sweat, wondered how we could sleep. "I will teach you Kung Fu," he said. "We're going to sleep on the banana leaves." He laughed at this funny joke himself, but we must have looked so bewildered that he felt he needed to explain: "You know, Kung Fu that will make you sleep in the air, on banana leaves." We still didn't get the joke, but laughed a little like: "Yeah, I got it now. Kung Fu in the banana leaves. But, honestly Doh Say, what are you trying to say?" What he was trying to say was that we would cut down some big banana leaves and spread them on the ground. Then we could sleep there. It would be a lot easier than to actually sleep in the trees, on the banana leaves—like Kung Fu, he explained.

So we cut down some banana leaves, made ourselves a nest and went to sleep. I had no idea what surrounded us, or what we were sleeping on (other than banana leaves, that is), but at that point I didn't care. I slept like a baby until the first rays of the sun woke me up in the morning and we could head towards home, food, and family.

Steve and some others had come to pick us up at the meeting point. It was in the middle of the night. (A new night. We had to walk two nights, you see.) All Steve could do when he saw me was laugh. He couldn't believe what a jungle rat I looked like. My clothes were caked with dirt and mud. I was wet. My shoes were soaked. My hair was plastered to my head like a rust-colored cap. I had mud streaks on my face. I smelled like … I'm not sure what. As soon as we stopped walking I started shivering with cold. He plugged his nose and let me into the truck and we headed to a hotel in a border town where the girls were sleeping, waiting for mom.

For the next few days I was happy enjoying all the luxuries I was given. Brie cheese had never tasted so good. Nor had olives. And the sensation of hot water streaming down my body like a gentle waterfall! To live in a world of hot showers is truly a privilege to be thankful for.

Orchid

SMALL TRIPS CAN BE BIG, AND ALL PEOPLE HAVE
SOMETHING GREAT IN THEM. ROACHES ARE BAD AND
ONE SHOULD NEVER, EVER GIVE UP.

PICKING FLOWERS ON DUSTY ROADS

A few times I have observed a pig being slaughtered, skinned, gutted and cut into dinner-sized chunks—which we later ate. The pork went with us in people's backpacks for a few days until it was all gone, and by that I mean, not one piece of the animal went to waste. I got to watch the guys doing their laundry in the river, making fires to cook the meals (that I got to eat with them), and watch them carry heavy loads in wicker baskets tied to their backs with long pieces of cloth.

To go on a trip with the Karen from Burma is a rare privilege that has more surprising elements to it than you can ever imagine.

On many trips I've been the only female. That may sound like a lot of farting, burping, and grunting, which it is—but not so much around me.

Once on such a trip the sunshine sieved through the gaps between the bamboo leaves and the tropical birds sang their symphonies. As often happens, I almost forgot that we were walking in the territory of one of the worst dictatorships in the world. It seemed too perfect for that. On the top of a hill we met a woman whom I thought confirmed that this was a place of fairy tales, not of murder and atrocities. She emerged out of the jungle like a fifty-year-old fairy—I can almost picture her wings. Actually, I think she was sitting on a log taking a break after a long hike from her village. She lit up when she noticed us. We were a rare sight.

My backpack must have looked like something from another planet. Not to mention my big shoes. She wore cheap flip-flops on her feet, and they had seen better days. Still they looked elegant on her dark, flat feet. The sarong she had tied around her waist was the color of sunshine and Washington apples. Her smile made me think of my mother. But it was the flowers in her hair that I will never forget. She had picked them on her walk on the dusty roads. The headband she had tied around her hair held a wreath of orange flowers whose bright color seemed otherworldly. They had become her tiara and she was the queen of the jungle.

"I'm on my way to the village down the hill to sell my chili peppers," she informed us. "Then I will use the money I make to buy dried fish from the villagers there. After I have done that I will walk home again. My village is four hours away." It would take her all day, and she would maybe earn sixty cents and a bag of dried fish. A day well spent. We smiled back at her and I tried to shake the feeling of being in a different world. Then we walked on.

My feeling of contentedness and peace ought to have been right in a place like that. One should be able to walk through the jungle to sell one's chili peppers and pick pretty flowers while humming a song. The meeting with the jungle queen was a picture of the utopia Burma ought to be.

In the village we entered, people looked at us both suspiciously and curiously. The bamboo houses were spread in a small valley surrounded by mountains that looked like they were covered with lots of broccoli. It was as primitive as it had been hundreds of years before. It appeared that there was nothing in the village that hadn't been found in the jungle or made by the villagers. I had brought a teddy bear hand puppet that I used to teach the children hygiene. The puppet had a stomachache because he hadn't washed his hands properly. He also had a toothache and other ailments due to lack of hygiene skills. But with some soap, a toothbrush and toothpaste, life got better for the puppet. The women laughed heartily, showing their stained teeth, but never loosing the pipes they were vigorously smoking. The children were more afraid than amused. The men tried to look unaffected, but I could tell they were entertained.

I noticed some whispering and friendly tugging in the crowd, especially among the women. It was as if they were saying, "You ask her!" "No, you!" "No, you do it!" At long last the bravest of the women stepped forward. She asked if she could ask us a question, which we of course told her was okay. She asked, "Is the puppet alive, and does it really know how to talk?"

Then we gave all the children bags with toothbrushes, toothpaste, and soap. They lined up without saying a word. When they received their bag of stuff, they shook our hands with great seriousness. It was a solemn event to get one's first toothbrush.

Our little performance had a bitter taste, though. The Burma Army had its outpost not far from where we were. They visited the village regularly, making sure that the villagers behaved according to their rules, and more importantly, to collect taxes in the form of money, rice, meat and other produce. When times got tough they would demand forced labor as well. To say no to that demand would mean severe punishment, such as torture and death. The villagers talked about the Burma Army in hushed voices without a sign of panic. In their minds the soldiers were just an annoying presence that they couldn't get rid of, like a pesky fly. They seemed to have accepted that the enemy would be in the proximity forever and the best way to cope was to keep on living as normally as possible.

We had hoped to find a free floor to sleep on in the village, but to do that would have put both the villagers and us in grave danger if the soldiers found out. Picking up our walking sticks and heading for a village further away was a much better option. It was sad walking out of this small valley of pipe-smoking women, rice-farming men, and curiously dirty children. Again I had the feeling of peace and innocence. I kind of wished I hadn't heard the real story about soldiers hiding somewhere under the broccoli.

That village is gone now. It wasn't long after we visited that the enemy attacked, doing more than just asking for some rice. They leveled the village and took what they wanted before they burned the rest. The people have scattered, the houses are probably all gone and, like thousands of other villages, it's just a memory of days lived in simple innocence.

We left that day not exactly sure where to go. But we were in the land of the most hospitable people in the world, so we trotted on, convinced that there would be a floor for us somewhere. We ended up at a place hidden between two mountains. The village was glued to one side of a mountain overlooking another like an Asian Switzerland. The houses were scattered down the hill like ornaments, making the scene more perfect. We put our backpacks down and went looking for a place to stay. Some of the guys just hung their hammocks between trees down by the river. I wished I had been a Karen man right then, because then I could have joined them. Instead I was escorted to the biggest house in the village where they decided that Russ (He is our good friend, and, at that time, one of the leaders in Partners. He is a very tough guy who can do loads of pull-ups.) and I would sleep with some of the wimpier Karen. (Wimpy for the Karen means the ones who prefer an occasional night on a floor and who own a sleeping bag.)

I rolled out my mat in one corner and Russ made sure to find the place in the house that was the farthest removed from me. His biggest concern the whole week was *not* about getting killed by a snake or a soldier, but that somebody would think I was his wife. I thought it was obvious that I was not.

Then we went outside to join the villagers in the fun. When living in a place as removed from anybody as this place was, a visit from people like us was first-class entertainment. The medics on the team made a clinic on a mat on the ground and everybody who was sick in some way lined up to get treated. That turned out to be most of the villagers. I think that some of them may have thought that it was impossible to know when a doctor would be there next, so even if they weren't sick, they would see the doctor in advance. Surely, sooner or later, it would be of some benefit. Nobody confirmed this suspicion, but I thought that had I been a villager in an area where doctors were as rare as pink pigs (pigs in Burma are brown), I would've come to the Partners clinic too—for prevention, or just in case.

When the evening came to an end at around 8:30 I headed back to our house. As I approached my mat I noticed something crawling—a couple of cockroaches. I brushed them off and turned around to get my stuff. Then when I looked at my mat there they were again, as if they had just swung right back. Distressed, I noticed that now their aunts and uncles were joining them too. They came marching down the beam heading for my sleeping place. I took a deep breath. This was a test. I was not going to become some screaming woman the guys had to deal with. I would rather sleep with roaches. So I went to find Russ.

"Russ," I said, "it appears that my sleeping place is next to a cockroach nest. Would you mind if I move my mat a little closer to where you're sleeping?" Russ, being the gentleman he always has been, said bravely, "That's no problem, but rather than that, how about if you just take my place and I take yours? I'm not scared of roaches." So we agreed that would be a good solution. Then we went outside to join the rest.

Later that night, on the way back to the house, we met Chris and Matt who shook their heads and looked at us as if we were going to our own funeral. "Sorry, you guys," they said with concern. "Wish there was something we could do." We thought they might be recovering from a heat stroke, because that kind of compassion is rare from those two.

As we climbed up the ladder leading to the house we noticed a basket that seemed to be moving. Although I have never been on an acid trip, I thought it might feel like this—moving baskets in the dark. A closer look revealed the cause of the movement: hundreds of roaches having a party. I detected the slightest consternation in Russ' voice as he said, "Sure hope they are all on that basket and not anywhere else." That was wishful thinking. As we entered our sleeping area it was like an animated horror movie. We were the giants that had entered the kingdom of roaches, and the roaches were going to war. They had mobilized the troops from all the surrounding kingdoms. There were waves of them coming, and their marching bands were blowing their horns.

Russ screamed as soon as he saw his backpack sitting on the floor. It seemed to have become the headquarters for the battling roaches, and just like the basket we had spotted, the backpack too seemed to be moving. We couldn't even tell what color it was any more. Russ took the bag and threw it in the air, sending roaches flying in all directions. "That's it!" he said while wiping the roaches off his pants. "I can't sleep anywhere close to this floor." The Karen with us chuckled. "Thraa (teacher), they don't bite," was all they could say between their giggles. Russ and I didn't really see the humor at that time. All we were concerned about was hanging our hammocks high up away from the battle scene. We must have looked funny though, jumping around on the floor trying to get the roaches off our clothes. Russ finally strung his hammock and mine on the only available beams in the house. We wrapped our mosquito nets around us like we were trying to dress up like mummies. Then we turned out our headlights and went to sleep. No roaches bit us that night.

The next morning we woke up with the sun and thought the previous night's experiences may have been a nightmare. But we noticed handfuls of roaches going back to their sleeping places (which were inside the bamboo logs) after a long night of intense activity. After a strong cup of coffee we were brave enough to approach the hollow bamboo logs and, sure enough, their insides were crawling with thousands of roaches. They were preparing for the next night's attack, of that we were sure.

NOW YOU ARE KOH-LA-WAH IDPS

A day later we faced other foes than roaches. There were soldiers from a Burma Army proxy force in the area and they were headed our direction.

We were all squatting close to the ground in the jungle somewhere. Jonathan, our Karen guide and bodyguard, chuckled. "Now you are Koh-la-wah IDPs," he said and then he had to laugh again. The thought was so comical that it kept him smiling for a whole five minutes. Our other Karen friends found the joke hysterically funny too. The thought of us Koh-la-wah (foreigners) living in the jungle on our own for any length of time was so absurd that they could only laugh.

Personally, I could think of other circumstances that were a lot funnier—having to listen to the New York stock exchange, for example. The lush jungle around us seemed schizophrenic, acting like a friendly shelter and hiding place one second, then the next moment, a foe hiding unknown enemies under its protective arms.

My imagination became like that of a four-year-old who was afraid of the dark, even though it was still light outside. I thought I could hear gunshots and branches breaking, and imagined I could see the shadows of uniformed men behind every cluster of bamboo. If a Burmese soldier had come swinging down on one of the thick vines above us, shouting Tarzan words in Burmese, I wouldn't have been very surprised.

As we were sitting there I had the kind of thoughts that I have every time I rock climb with Steve. I do that from time to time as an act of love for my husband who has dreams of us two climbing around the world—harnesses, shoes and a good supply of Shiraz and Brie cheese (the essentials) in our backpacks. I go rock climbing with him to keep his dream alive, and to find out if I have overcome my very irrational fear of heights. The peaks I climb are not very high, but they are vertical and that's all I need to know in order to feel fear. While climbing, looking desperately for hand- and foot-holds at the same time as I try to avoid looking down, I ask myself the same question every time, "What in the world am I doing, and why did I get talked into doing this?"

That was exactly what I was asking myself while squatting with my friends in the jungle. While my fear was completely out of proportion, our situation *was* a bit sticky. The Burmese soldiers were headed our direction, they had guns, and judging from their reputation, they didn't follow any ethical standards. In their book we were intruders, and showing them the teddy bear puppet that we had used to teach hygiene in the villages, or the medicine kits we had used to treat the sick, would be as useful as what? Nothing. We had to hide, and remain that way.

My instincts told me to run. Sitting on a log not fifteen minutes from the village the soldiers were approaching seemed a bit passive. I guess it epitomized me and my outlook on life: Why wait when you can run? Why sit still when you can do something? Why trust when you can worry?

Karen soldiers were with us and their job was to protect us. I should have trusted that they knew what they were doing since they'd been in battles before. In an odd way they reminded me of God, and my clattering teeth reminded me of all of mankind. I was totally dependent on the Karen here, and my worry did nothing to make the situation any better. In a similar way I'm dependent on God, and me worrying about stuff doesn't help Him, or me, one bit.

I could've taken a clue from one of the soldiers who were there to protect us. He strung his hammock between two crooked trees, lay down on it and fell fast asleep. The carefree sound of his breathing should've told me that an attack wasn't imminent. And when and if there was a battle, he would be rested—unlike me, who by now had spent quite a lot of energy thinking of worst-case scenarios.

The seconds passed slowly that afternoon. We started passing M&Ms around. I looked at Chris. He was enjoying himself. Chris is one of my best friends, but I think of him more as my little brother. He belongs to a breed of people that think that the more uncomfortable, the more dangerous, the more challenging, the more strenuous a situation is, the better. He thrives on crisis and enormous challenges. I love to go on trips with him because in him I have both a bodyguard and a friend who has read more books than me. I hoped he wouldn't let me down now, in my time of need.

Then the sound of branches breaking was not just in my head, but it was as real as the sounds of the sleeping soldier. I looked at the rest of the Karen for an indication of what was happening. They seemed unaffected—like God when He doesn't seem to understand my incredible troubles. I wondered if running up the mountain would be my best bet of survival.

I don't remember the face of the man who emerged from the bushes, only his infectious smile—a warm, genuine smile on a tough, dark, and worn face. Using palm leaves for potholders the man with the smile had carried a pot of noodles up the mountain to our hiding place. He had plates and spoons for the picnic in a cloth bag slung over his shoulders. Still smiling and chatting with the others, he started serving us the noodles. "You just couldn't run through the jungle with the enemy on your heels without eating a good meal first," he reasoned with us. They found the thought of running anywhere without lunch as hilarious as the thought of the white faces being Koh-la-wah IDPs. It was impossible.

As I took the plate of noodles that they gave me I thought of God's grace: it's a plate of noodles in the jungle. It's strength to run the next few miles even if there are enemies right behind you.

Then we walked into the jungle with all its dangers. I didn't feel brave, but I felt ready to walk. I knew that with the Karen who walked with us I was in the very best company I could be. I thought about how nobody really knows how life will turn out. There are unknown enemies hiding in the jungles of our lives too. We may never know what will happen, but we still need to keep walking in the direction that seems right. Along the way we'll encounter people such as the brave and beautiful Karen who will guide us through the brush, over the hills, and right home. That is what they did for me the day I was a Koh-la-wah IDP.

PAW HTOO: SHE HAS CHOSEN A
WAY OF FORGIVENESS AND LOVE

A halo of frizzy, dark hair topped a chubby face streaked with dirt and dust. People noticed her eyes first. They burned in the presence of injustice, but sparkled the way fireflies do when she experienced something humorous. The village was her playground and she belonged there the same way the small bamboo houses and the roosters did. The village was familiar, safe, and with abundant hiding places. It was a childhood haven.

She picked up one of the village puppies. It was dirty and malnourished, and bugs were feasting on its skin. The dogs in the village were mostly left to fend for themselves; their main responsibility was to fend off intruders and to kill unwanted vermin. While they were puppies, however, they were favorite playthings for the children.

She wanted this puppy to be hers. She carried it gently in her arms while she petted it and whispered little secrets in its ear. "I will take care of you forever," she promised and got some of the leftover rice from breakfast. Sometimes her mother or grandma would take the leftover rice and fry it dry over the fire, making it crispy and a little black on the outside. It tasted almost as nice as the deep-fried bugs they sometimes ate. So she was careful to only take very little; she knew that her parents wouldn't approve of her feeding the dogs the food that they needed to survive on. The puppy eagerly ate the rice from her hand. Paw Htoo giggled as it kept licking her hand long after the rice was gone.

Only when she heard her mother calling did she remember that she had been asked to fetch water. She picked up two of the hollowed-out bamboo trunks that they used for fetching and storing water and tied the thick twig attached to the trunks around her head. On the way to the river she stopped and invited her friend to join her. Together they skipped down the well-worn trail on bare feet. She hardly noticed the rocks and the branches on the trail—the soles on her feet were hard as water buffalo leather.

Down by the river they met other children who had also come down to get water. They were in no hurry to go back, so before filling up their buckets, they took a bath. Paw Htoo laid her head all the way back into the river and let her hair swim. A butterfly was playing chase above her head. Its large wings were canvases painted by God, velvet black in the background, intricate red patterns twirling on top. Paw Htoo thought it looked like it was dancing in the air. She closed her eyes and hoped the butterfly would land on her hair. If it did, she would turn into a princess. But the butterfly didn't care about Paw Htoo's dreams and fluttered on towards the jungle. She got out of the river and let the sun dry her wet body before she filled up the water containers and climbed up the trail with her friends.

Her mom, grandma, and sisters were waiting for her back at her house. Her dad also came and sat on the floor with a sarong tied around his slender waist. He had been taking a bath in the river too. The day had started early, but he wasn't too tired to pat Paw Htoo on the head and ask her what she learned at school today. She showed him the crumpled notebook she used for her lessons. Her name was written on the front page in round Karen letters. "This is what we did in Burmese and on the other page is Karen," she said proudly. Toward the back of the book was her math lessons, numbers lined up as orderly as a newly-planted paddy.

While talking about the day's events they ate their dinner consisting of rice and fish paste, a grey-looking salty soup made from fermented fish, salt, and chilies. They used their fingers to eat. Their four fingers and thumb held together were as good as any spoon. Between mouthfuls they talked about the approaching harvest season.

Paw Htoo always looked forward to this time of the year. They would be moving up to the simple shack they had built by the mountain rice fields. She loved the days in the fields, harvesting the rice and playing with her sisters and their neighbors. Her mom and dad would walk, bent over, cutting the rice and tying the straws into bundles. Paw Htoo and her sisters would then help by shaking the bundles on a mat on the ground, making the rice fall off. The whole village would take part in the harvesting and they all had well-defined tasks. For example, only the men were allowed to throw the rice into the air, making it fly like bugs. They put the rice on large woven bamboo trays and tossed it up. The breeze would blow away the dust, dirt, and other unwanted debris, leaving the rice that fell back down almost clean and ready to eat.

I wonder why only the men can do this? Paw Htoo would think from time to time. But it was just how things were done, and she accepted it the way she accepted that the rainy season followed the hot season. She didn't know why it was so. It just was.

While the men winnowed the rice, the women cooked special meals—dishes reserved only for this special time of the year—cucumber soup and pumpkin stew. Paw Htoo could almost taste these delicacies as she thought about them. And when the rice was harvested they would put some of it inside hollowed-out, tender bamboo and cook it on the fire. When it was done, they would peel the bamboo off the way they peeled a banana. The rice inside would have become a loaf that could be broken off into bite-size pieces. Paw Htoo couldn't think of a better treat.

Months ago they had cleared the field where the paddy now grew. Every year they cleared new fields. It was hard work that her parents did from dawn to dusk. Paw Htoo and her sisters helped too if they weren't at school or doing other chores. When the land was clear, they burned it. Then, as soon as all the vegetation was burned to the ground and the rains had begun, they would plant. Her dad had explained to her that the black ashes gave food to the paddy, making it grow and become food for their family.

Paw Htoo remembered the days bent to the ground planting the rice. They had used a sharp stick and poked holes in the ashes where they dropped a few seeds of rice. Her parents always worried about the paddy not producing enough food for them, so it was very important that they did the planting right. She knew that the rice they produced would be all the rice they'd have to eat for the coming year, so she understood her parents' concern. Some of the people in the village conducted special ceremonies to different spirits and gods asking them to protect the paddy and make it produce enough food. Paw Htoo had never seen the spirits and wondered what they did. Sometimes rats and other wild animals came to eat and destroy the paddy, and they had to chase them away. She thought that they might have been sent by some spirits who had become angry.

Paw Htoo fell asleep that night thinking of angry spirits. During the night she dreamed of the spirits burning the paddy fields and her family trying to stop the flames from devouring all the food they were going to live off. She woke up at dawn to the sound of voices. She didn't recognize the voices, and although she understood the words spoken, they were in a different language. It took her a few seconds to realize what was happening, and as soon as she did, her heart sunk. The soldiers had come to harass them. *What will they do today?* she wondered as she looked around the room. She usually liked it better if her parents were still in the house when she woke up, but today she was happy they had walked off to the fields well before sunrise.

Quietly she got up from her place on the floor and peeked through the cracks of the walls. A few of the villagers were talking with the soldiers. They all looked worried and disturbed. The men in the green uniforms reminded Paw Htoo of snakes. She had learned that when she saw a snake she must be very careful not to scare it or make it angry, because that was when the snake would strike and kill her. She thought that the soldiers would do the same. They had never killed anybody in the village, but she still had a bad feeling about them and she would never, ever trust them.

The oldest one was talking to the village chief. "A lot of work has to be done for the development of our beloved country," he said. He then told the chief the reason why they were there, but all the villagers had already guessed it. They needed a few of them to porter and work for the army. It wasn't the first time they had come and asked for help. The timing couldn't be worse. The harvest season had started and nobody felt like they could go away to help the army. The work they would be forced to do was usually hard and dangerous, and they wouldn't get any pay for it. Paw Htoo had heard that they didn't get much to eat.

After a few minutes of talking, two of the men from her village stepped forward. Even if Paw Htoo hadn't heard what they had talked about, she knew what the villagers had agreed to do. They would take turns volunteering when the soldiers came to ask for help. The rest of the village would then help the families who had volunteered by assisting them with their harvest. They all knew that one of the next times it would be their turn.

Some days later Paw Htoo's father came walking down the trail and there was a sparkle in his eyes that she didn't recognize. It was as if he were carrying a secret and the secret made him happy. She ran towards him and asked why he was smiling. From inside his shirt he pulled out her dream: two furry puppies. "I got them in the neighboring village. They look strong and healthy," he said. He smiled as Paw Htoo cuddled the love-starved pups. "I want them to become my hunting dogs, but you need to help me," her father explained. "It will be your job to feed them every morning and night, and to make sure they're healthy." Paw Htoo couldn't have been given a better responsibility. This was not a chore. This was happiness on four feet—times two.

She fed the dogs dutifully for years, making sure they were the healthiest dogs in the village. "I can feed the pig too," she offered to her mom and grandma as they sliced banana trunks, making a fibrous mixture for the family pig. But the pig was too important for the family, and they never trusted anybody but themselves to care for the precious hunk of meat. Paw Htoo thought it didn't make sense because look at the dogs: they brought her dad into the jungle and helped him kill wild boars, snakes, and deer that he brought back for the family to eat. She wondered if they would have all that meat if it hadn't been for the dogs. Paw Htoo felt incredibly important. She was practically responsible for feeding her family.

·　·　·

Darkness. There were no colors in the dark. When a person entered the cell they left the world of colors and stepped into a place of black and grey. In this world there was no music and birds singing, there was no laughter and children playing. This was a place of silent sobs, loud screams, and lonely thoughts of, *What if?* This was a place barren of justice and beauty—a laboratory to experiment with humans and their tolerance for pain. This was a place where dreams turned into nightmares and it always felt like night.

She put her hands on her growing womb and thought sadly, *This isn't the kind of world I had wanted for you.*

·　·　·

It had started with her unquenched thirst for learning. Paw Htoo had finished the years of schooling the village could offer, but she wanted more. Her parents were poor, however, and no matter how many times they thought about their small savings, they weren't enough to pay for further schooling. This was why she had joined the resistance. They promised her an education if she would serve with them. She could study to become a nurse and then help treat the soldiers and the civilians hurt during battles. Paw Htoo, who had just been treating scabbed dogs, thought this sounded like a life of her dreams.

I didn't join to fight the enemy, she thought sadly while she leaned against the concrete wall of the prison cell. *I just wanted to find a way to learn.* Naively she had believed that the worst thing the government did was to send soldiers to the villages demanding that the villagers work for free. That was bad enough, and she'd never considered that they'd commit worse crimes than that. What she had learned shocked her and made her wish she had stayed in her village, ignorant and happy. Although she now knew that even staying in her village would sooner or later have exposed her to the military's brutal behavior.

She had soaked up the things she learned. Dressing wounds, giving injections, delivering babies, and checking for malaria. Every bit of her education was new and exciting. She couldn't wait to practice.

Paw Htoo remembered one of the first trips she had been on with the resistance, the KNU, the Karen National Union. Her ignorance now amazed her. They'd had to move during the night to not be seen by the enemy. She'd thought until then that the jungle was her friend, and her feet were companions that would take her anywhere she wanted to go without ever failing her. This was before she was forced to walk after dark in a jungle so black that only by blinking did she know that her eyes were open. They were strictly forbidden to use any lights—that would have alerted the enemy. So she hobbled along like a blind person until one of the soldiers had mercy on her and let her hold on to his hips. Then he guided her through the dark jungle. "Rock coming up!" he would whisper. "Watch out for the root in front of you."

Then there was the fiasco of stringing the hammock. How could *that* be so hard? Her dad did it all the time with no difficulty at all. She hadn't wanted the others to know that she'd never strung a hammock between two trees before and tried to get it tied in a way that would allow her to lay in it and not fall to the ground. It was useless. After some minutes they all knew that they were with a hammock novice and helped her get it strung just right—not too tight, not too loose, but securely so it didn't fall down during the night.

They helped her and made it look so easy. They could walk in the dark and string a hammock, but none of them could put up with the way the monsoon rains started drizzling as soon as they lay down. They managed to rest only two hours, and then it was time to start walking again.

The next day they reached the river. The river was swollen with water, having been constantly filled for the last months of the rainy season. To wade across it was not an option. Neither was swimming, since none of them had learned how to swim. They looked helplessly across to the other side, wondering how they were going to get there. Their rescue came in the form of some villagers and an elephant. The sure-footed elephant carried them across the river, and they only got their feet wet.

Paw Htoo hadn't thought about marriage much before she met *him* —a soldier in the resistance. Then everything changed. She fell in love and for a while it seemed that nothing mattered much except the moments she had with him. Soon they ware married and she had some dreams that she now thought incredibly childish and uninformed. They were dreams of a quiet life with her husband in a village by a river. They could have children and she could open a clinic while he perhaps could become a teacher. Was that *such* an impossible dream? It appeared now that it was.

He was strong and agile, like a panther on two feet. He could maneuver through the jungle, always prepared to be ambushed by the enemy. He was not violent by nature. He, like her, just had a strong and deep desire for their people to be free, and at the moment it seemed like the only way to do that was by fighting the regime, and, more importantly, by protecting the civilians that were always the target.

Their honeymoon had been walks through the jungle on missions to new areas where villagers had been displaced. Privacy was as rare as a decent meal. But somehow they managed to find some moments to be alone, and those were the moments she would savor.

Then the fighting escalated and one day there was a battle that destroyed her. The sun may have been shining that day. She didn't know. The birds may have been singing. She didn't hear. There may have been laughter in the morning. It didn't matter now. All that mattered was the sight of him falling when they shot him, his injured body tied to a rope and dragged across the jungle floor as if he were a log that needed to be moved. Before he died they took his clothes from him, removing his last scrap of dignity. Then they stabbed the body she loved more than her own flesh with knives many times. As a final act of morbid cruelty they took their guns out and one of them shot him in the mouth. After that they came for her. She cried, kicked, and screamed, but they were stronger than her, and determined to not let her go. They had a place reserved for her in the prison.

Paw Htoo was sentenced to two years. Two years for what crime? She didn't know and there was no use asking for an explanation. She had tried that and it didn't end well. *I'm just the enemy,* she concluded, *and the enemy must be crushed even though it was an enemy who just treated sick people.* She knew she should be thankful the sentence wasn't longer. Still, two years seemed longer than her whole life.

The baby was due to arrive any day now, but it didn't fill her with the joy and anticipation the way a firstborn usually would do. Sorrow and worry, dread, and fear filled her whole being as she thought about delivering a baby in prison, and about what the baby's future would be. She'd been in the prison for months already and the days had become a kind of routine. They swept floors, made baskets for sale then swept some more floors. Like living dead they walked around—seldom laughing, just trying to make it through one more day. At the end of each day they were one day closer to freedom.

When she'd started feeling the first contractions she wanted them to go away. She wasn't ready for what was to come. But she knew there was no stopping them. She had never missed her husband more than she did those hours as she moaned on the floor, the other prisoners sitting around her, encouraging her to not give up, but none of them sure what else to do. Some moments she was glad for their presence and encouragement, other times she told them to leave her alone—and she did so in explicit terms. She had never anticipated a pain so intense and merciless. Death seemed like a good option. She thought that if she just let go, she could perhaps die, and in an instant be with him, her husband and father of the baby she was about to give birth to.

Finally the baby arrived, wet and scrunched up, and with a loud voice that sounded through the hallways of the prison. Now, when she was beyond danger, they were allowed to call on a doctor. He came, checked her and said she was fine. *How little you know. How little you understand,* she thought bitterly, almost sneering back at the doctor.

Paw Htoo's son gave her more pleasure and comfort than she had dared hope for. Nursing him and feeling his body close to hers brought out emotions that she thought she had buried the day she buried her husband. "I love you so much. That is why you can't stay with me," she whispered to him. Not that it was her choice to send him away. The prison policy was clear: babies weren't allowed. So six weeks after he was born they came and took him away. It was her loneliest day.

He'll be staying with my husband's family, she told herself. *They'll love him and give him a good life. I can't take care of him here in prison. I can't even care for myself. This is the best for him.* Still, the ache was unbearable. It felt like a part of her body had been ripped away from her without giving her anesthesia.

Slowly the days became routine again. *If I just obey they won't beat me,* she resolved. There was just one thing she was unable to do: wait until 7:00 a.m. until she went to the bathroom. They were awakened at 4:00 every morning and had to do their chores for three hours before they were allowed a bathroom break. Paw Htoo just couldn't wait that long, and daily endured the punishment in order to make it to the bathroom in time. The rest of the day she did what she was told, asked no questions, complained about nothing. They never went outside. Two years, and she never saw the sun. She never saw flowers and butterflies, water trickling down a lazy creek, or black storm clouds gathering on the sky. The only way she knew if it was day or night was by looking through the small peepholes up by the ceiling. It was their only source of light.

The day of her release finally came. She had planned for this day every hour since she'd been imprisoned. She was let go, and her husband's family was waiting for her, holding her baby whom she wouldn't have recognized had she not known it was him. He was a toddler now. He had teeth and could walk and say a few words. He didn't know who she was and didn't want her to hold him when she tried. It wasn't easy to keep her tears back then. She had missed him so much, and now she wanted to make it all up to him. But first he'd have to let her hold him. She hadn't anticipated that.

Paw Htoo's first days of freedom were consumed by her son and by regaining her strength. She tried to think about her future and what she was to do now. She was a lot more hopeful than she'd been in prison. Still, there were all the unanswered questions.

She didn't have to wonder long. She was surprised when one of her fellow prisoners showed up at her door one day. This was a woman she'd confided in while in her cell. She had felt a connection with this lady and enjoyed their times of talking. Now she entered their house and seemed anything but friendly. Paw Htoo was surprised and shocked when the woman confessed that she'd been a spy, hired by the enemy to get all of Paw Htoo's secrets about the resistance. "As your friend I am here to warn you," said the lady. "You need to get away from here quickly or my leaders will come for you. At any rate, your son and your family won't be safe if you remain here."

She said goodbye to her baby again and walked away without looking back. In a way, she thought, it was good that he didn't know she was his mom. It made the parting less painful. She walked into the jungle. It would be fifteen years before she saw her son again.

•   •   •

"I'm tired all the time now," Paw Htoo said as we sat and talked in a house in a refugee camp across the border from Burma. "I don't have the energy to walk in the jungle." She was forty-one and one of the most beautiful women I knew. It had taken me days of walking in the jungle with her to get as much of her story as I had. Maybe her pace wasn't the same as it once was, but it was my observation that she walked just fine in the jungle. Paw Htoo didn't like to talk much about herself, and she especially didn't like to talk about the hard stuff. "It'll just make me cry," she said. Her voice was soft and unassuming. She wouldn't tell me anything unless I asked, and even then I had to ask very detailed questions.

We were talking about the place she and her second husband Baw Boe had been given as a gift. "I just like to have a nice garden and trees to shade my house," she said. "We call it Paradise. I want it to be a paradise. But do you know what kinds of trees I should get that will give us lots of shade?" We talked about trees and other stuff.

Her life hadn't been easy. To say that it has been full of life's poison ivy might be a better way to describe it. And yet, here she was, kind and generous, beautiful and calm, talking about her love for peanut butter on toast and black coffee, not the sweet stuff the Karen prefer.

She stayed with the resistance after she left her son and her in-laws. She walked across the country helping the sick, delivering babies, caring for the needy. She had become a Christian over time. She worshipped in the churches of the internally displaced and prayed with the ones who had lost their loved ones. She could relate and she knew what they felt.

"Then my sister died when she gave birth to twin boys," she told me. "She was still living in my village, but they were so poor now and she was very malnourished. She just didn't have the strength to deliver those babies. Her husband was too upset about his wife and he couldn't take care of the babies, so I went back to my village and took the twins with me and raised them. That was eleven years ago." Her parents were dead and one more sister was living in a refugee camp. Paw Htoo and Baw Boe raised the twins. Some years ago her son also came and joined them. All the years apart made it hard for mother and son to reconnect and they went through some difficulties. Now he was going to a high school some days walk from Paw Htoo's home and seemed to be doing well.

Paw Htoo's new husband had a story to tell as well. "My name is Baw Boe," he said, smiling. "Do you know what it means? It means walking stick. That's because I was badly injured during one of the battles with the Burma Army. I carried some heavy ammunition, fell, and almost broke my back. For months I had to walk with a walking stick. That's why I have this name."

"We are all in this battle," he continued. "I joined when I was fourteen. But do you know what the resistance leaders did when I told them I wanted to fight? They said, 'You're too young to fight. Go back and finish school. We don't want you.' They were so strict with me. My mom had died from cancer, and my dad drank himself to death. Ha ha. Very funny story."

With a big smile he continued, "Steve asked me, 'Where did you learn English?' and I said, 'The jungle.'"

Now Baw Boe had another passion. He wanted to train and empower the people in the villages. "You know, so many leaders just tell the people what to do. And they don't trust them. They act like they think the villagers are stupid. But I don't think so. We need to train the villagers to care for themselves. We need to help them, Thraa Muu

(Teacher). We need to do, what do you call it, community development. And slowly, slowly we will strengthen the local people. You know, we Karen have this saying: 'Don't throw oil on elephants.' What we mean by that is that if you throw oil on elephants it will just come off anyway. It is no use. It's no use to have leaders who do everything and make every decision either. We need to give responsibility to all our people."

"Thraa Muu, so many sad stories about my people. Thank you for helping us."

I smiled and looked at Baw Boe and Paw Htoo and thought, *Me helping you? No, I'm just a small vessel and you're the huge porcelain water container—the kind that sometimes is outside of Karen houses to collect rainwater. You can use me to scoop out some of the water that you contain and give it to all the people around you, the ones that you have been destined to help.*

I wondered sometimes if pain strengthens us or if we have been given the strength in advance and that is how we manage pain. I asked myself how I would've tackled all of Paw Htoo's challenges, or the challenges of many of the other Karen I have befriended. I usually claim that I don't think I could've handled it and most likely would've ended up at some institution. The thing though is that Paw Htoo probably wouldn't have seen herself as a candidate for survival either, had she known thirty years ago what she knew now. It seems like grace is doled out to us in appropriate portions when we need it. Just like the manna in the desert. We can, of course, choose to receive it or we can resist. Paw Htoo has chosen to take what she can get from God, and she has chosen the way of forgiveness and love. This, I believe, is why she was now able to laugh. I thought it was important to remember that she cried too. One does not carry losses like hers lightly.[14]

---

14   The story of Paw Htoo is true. She has told me bits and pieces of if whenever we have been together. There is a lot more, but that you will just have to find out yourself when and if you meet her.

BORN TO KILL

I went on a trip inside Burma with Saw Doh and Paw Htoo. For days we visited villages and met people who shared about their lives. Becky from the U.S. was with me too. She took photos like nobody I have ever seen. She crouched down on the trail and took pictures of the leaves, of the ants, and of the trail itself. *She really wants to remember everything from this trip,* I thought. Later I was so happy for all those pictures. They were like a journal of all the small and big events.

We walked with a handful of other Karen as well. One of them was a pro-democracy resistance soldier named Saw Mue. I loved this guy. His upper body looked like a tattoo artist's sketch-paper, with the words *Born to kill* being the most prominent statement among many others. Observing him with his people on the trail, I started thinking of him more like my cute little brother than a fierce soldier. But, he would tell me, he'd been in more battles than he could remember. And he'd killed more Burma Army soldiers than he could remember too.

"When you are in a battle you shoot, or they will shoot you first," he explained. Once he was shot in the leg, but that didn't stop him; he had kept running, holding his leg. The bullet wound made an impressive scar on his leg. He also talked about rescuing twenty women who had been forced to porter for the Burma Army. Women never just porter. Portering is what they did before being forced to be sex-slaves for the men who humiliated, abused, and killed them. The Burma Army did what they wanted to the women then disposed of them the way one disposes of used equipment that no longer excites. They were sent away towards their homes, like second-hand humans.

What the women didn't know was that the soldiers had lined the trail they were walking on with landmines. So when Saw Mue and his team met the women they were—in Saw Mue's words—a bloody mess. His team did the only right thing, which was to treat them and bring them home. In that way they saved their lives. I thought he should get a tattoo that said *Born to save* instead. It would match his personality better.

The previous night I had given Saw Mue a blue knitted hat and a vest. It was a fake down vest that could be worn inside-out—a piece of clothing never before seen in the hills of Karen State, of that I was sure. He was the luckiest man in the house and got quite a few envious stares from the other men. But, generous guy that Saw Mue was, he let them all have a go at wearing the vest for part of the night. All night long different men wore it, inside-out or inside-in. They would give compliments and make each other stand up so that they could get a better look. I learned that night that men, even hard-core soldiers, were as vain as women. And *one* vest as handsome as this one didn't fill the obvious need for vests among Karen men. That too became evident. Next time I would bring a few.

On this day we were going to a village to meet some people who had walked for many hours to share their stories. Paw Htoo had been restless and unhappy-looking in the morning. "I know we will hear a story that will break my heart," she explained. "I will start to cry and it will hurt." Her fear of crying was not a fear of crying in public or of feeling pain as much as it was fear that the stories she was going to hear would rip up old wounds—wounds that had taken a long time to heal.

The village we came to was so pretty I wished I could move in. Tall orange and red flowers twisted their slender stems around antique bamboo fences, creating lace-like hedges, porous and delicate. The houses were clean and well-kept. It looked like they had put their finest on just for us. For the first time in days we had come to a village with a toilet. You can only appreciate this after you have fought off pigs and curious villagers every time you have to go pee-pee. The toilet was a simple squatty potty inside a basic bamboo structure. But let me tell you, it felt like the bathrooms of the Shangri La.

After the initial welcome and greetings we were invited inside the village chief's house for a rest, and to see the people who had come to meet us.

ENTERING THEIR SOUL

Walking into a Karen house is like entering their soul.

First, we take our shoes off. We always take them off at the bottom of the ladder that leads up to the house, which is anywhere from an arm's-length to a couple of meters in the air. All our shoes will sit there waiting for us—like deserted toys in a dusty sandbox. It's a wonderful custom that illustrates how when you enter a home, you enter a sanctuary. A sanctuary that seldom has a lock.

The homes are beautiful in their simplicity. They are built on bamboo poles that have been secured in the ground, supporting the weight of walls and floors that are organic in its purest form. I like to sit in a Karen home at dusk, watching the light change, turning everything grey, hiding details, and bringing the day to a slow end. Then the orange light of a fire reveals kind faces, daily activities that haven't changed for centuries, and perhaps the house kitten that looks anemic and clinically depressed. This animal's purpose obviously is not to lounge on a couch, but to keep vermin away. I often wonder if it has the guts.

The floors sway and bend when you move. The bamboo has been split, flattened out, and secured by rope that was also made by that very utilitarian plant. The floors are always teeming with holes and cracks, making it easy to sweep the floor and dispose of rubbish and water—not to mention spit. A sealed floor is inconvenient indeed. Sleeping on a bamboo floor must have been the way God intended sleep. With only a thin mat between me and the floor, I'm able to enter deep and relaxing sleep, waking up only a couple of times a night to weird sounds. At such times I ask myself whether my eyes are open or not. The darkness is so thick that only by blinking my eyes do I know that I must have them open. Cozier still is hanging my hammock between two poles and going to sleep looking like a cocoon with strings.

I have lain in my hammock many nights and thought, *I am totally content and need nothing*. When with the Karen, the essence of what we really need to survive and be happy narrows down to just a few basic items. Sometimes I've decided that nothing matters more to me than my headlamp; other times it's been my backpack or my good shoes. I have at times worshipped the security a mosquito net has provided, or my all-purpose titanium cup. That I ever considered a shaver an essential is beyond me during those times.

The walls of Karen houses are art. Again it's the bamboo; it has been flattened to sheet-like paneling, which is then woven between horizontal poles and tied with bamboo string. Jungle tapestry of the most exquisite kind. Air and light get free access through apertures of the room dividers, making the inside feel a lot cooler than the outside. And although there are no lamps, there is plenty of light.

You kind of learn to live without artificial light. Getting up with the sun and going to bed with the chickens establishes a healthy routine, and it's the one that most villagers follow. During the hours with little or no daylight, however, small candles may be used. We drip a little wax on the floor and make the candle stick this way. Then when it's burned down it gets blown out unless it dies by itself.

The abundance of small peepholes in the walls makes it possible to spy on the neighbors and the occasional visitor without being noticed. As you walk through a village you see eyes behind almost every thin wall. They are dark and curious, and probably consider the sight of a white person in all her strangeness more entertaining than a show on Disney Channel.

The downside to the airy architecture of Karen houses is, of course, that it gives bugs and sound free access. You quickly learn that the disadvantage to having lights in the house after dark outweighs the benefits because the light attracts all the bugs in the jungle—and there are many! One also learns to speak in whispers unless it doesn't matter that all the people passing by the house hear your words. Some mornings I have woken up and it sounds like all the toddlers in the village (or in the camp) have started crying at the very same moment—a choir of unhappy voices chiming in at the same time to show the world their discontent. I can put up with the crying of babies and find it strangely comforting, as long as one of the voices isn't my child.

The real annoyance is when Western civilization enters the world of tranquility. Sometimes, to the distress of some of us Westerners who like things the way they were, and who have observed our own world taken captive by media, the villagers will carry a TV to their communal meeting place. Once Steve and I spent Christmas in a remote village that was, in our minds, the picture of perfection. We looked forward to sleeping in the airy environment and waking up to the song of the roosters. But four strong men, a television set and some bamboo poles crushed the dream. The way to carry anything heavy through the jungle is to use two stiff beams of bamboo. The item is secured between the two poles, and the two people lift them on their shoulders, one on the front end and the other on the back. When the weight is evenly distributed, things can be carried a long way. This is how the TV was brought into the jungle and the village. Behind the TV porters came two more men carrying a generator.

The village was rife with excitement all afternoon. It was going to be a party and it was only fitting that world-class entertainment was provided. As soon as the moon replaced the sun, the TV came on. All night we were entertained by the noise of Chinese war movies, and the sound effects left nothing to one's imagination. The last movie was over at around 6:30 the following morning and by that time Steve and I had cursed Philo Farnsworth many times for inventing the boob tube. We also sent longing thoughts to thick walls with layers of insulation, and could affirm that ear plugs do *not* work, not when Chinese gun fights fill the air.

Back to more pleasant memories of idyllic Karen houses…

The fireplace inside the house is the coziest place. Usually a box-like enclosure of smaller bamboo poles has been built on the floor and is filled with sand and ashes. Perfectly-shaped rocks are placed in the box and serve as the stand for pots as rice is being cooked. You can usually see how old the house is and how much food has been cooked by taking a look at the ceiling above the fireplace. The ceiling of an old house will be stained as black as night with pieces of grease hanging from the bamboo beams like Halloween ornaments. The ceiling gives the history of many meals and hours in patient preparation. There are cooking utensils all around the fireplace, simple items that all have a clear purpose. A cutting board has been made from a thick slab of teak and on this one board meat is minced, bones sliced, delicate herbs ground, and vegetables chopped up. The baskets are an exhibition of artistry and skill. There are always many baskets—some for sifting rice, some for carrying food, some for catching fish, and some for putting the machete in. Then there is a wok and a pot for cooking the food. The pots are always covered with clay that has hardened and burned dark. This is to keep the pot inside alive longer. A clay mortar is also one of the kitchen essentials.

Bouquets of dried herbs hang on poles and natural hooks, waiting for their next use, and some vegetables are usually laid out for drying as well. I have sat with men and women while they have cooked. It's as if time doesn't pass. They sit on the floor and pound the herbs, mince the meat, and sometimes gut the chicken. My assistance is usually limited to a smile and a nod, and if I ever try to help, I do it wrong. Chilies can be cut in many different ways, and for sure I'll choose the wrong one.

I often think of these homes when I'm not there. I realize that stuff is overrated and wonder how I'll be held accountable for stashing so much for myself. As I whip together dinner before heading off for soccer practice, I think about the beauty of the biotic way they cook and long for it. In the villages the food travels short distances: from the field to the cooking spot, from the forest to the mortar and pestle, from the pigpen or the chicken coop to the pot. Some times the villagers trade with each other and walk to neighboring villages with their goods, but I wouldn't say that the wear they put on their flip-flops by doing this puts a big strain on the planet.

I blush inside when I think about the food we eat or prepare that has zigzagged the world before ending up on our table, just so we can eat the best and the most exotic ingredients, satisfying our increasingly picky pallets. I wonder how many village hospitals could have been erected with the funds saved by all of us eating locally-grown food instead. How many schools could have been funded by the cost of furniture advertising? Sometimes I think about the stuff I have and wonder whether it's more than all the stuff in a Karen village combined.

While I believe that these are thoughts are more than just romantic musings from a naïve person with too simple solutions to everything, it's the losses that really bother me. When the army boots enter the villages the homes no longer are sanctuaries, but battlefields where dark, brain-washed creatures, like Orcs out of Mordor, fill the air with fear and terror. When they attack with morbid glee, the bamboo and the baskets turn into kindling. The forgiving floors become the stage for gang rapes and humiliation, and the thin walls do nothing to muffle the screams. The rice that was painstakingly cultivated on steep hills or flat paddies burns along with the herbs, the vegetables, and the roots that were meant to provide life. Mixed with the smell of burning crops is the stench of burning animals whose flesh would never feed hungry bellies.

I have never been in a village that was attacked, but I have sat in refugee camps speaking to many who have. I have heard stories that I don't even want to repeat, except to say that if you imagine the most grotesque and heinous things that one can do to humans, then that is what they do—and worse. When the villagers are scattered or killed, the homes left in ashes, the soldiers will finish off the job by jagging their machetes through the cooking pots like a final business card from the military junta. Then they bury landmines around the village to kill and maim those who dare return. What was once a picture of serenity is a pile of ashes with only the most stubborn teak logs left as a testimony to the community that once resided there. It's now a scene fit for a horror movie where ghosts of fear and desperation linger.

NOW WE ARE ALWAYS AFRAID

Western women fall in love with Karen men left and right. As a woman I have to say I understand why. Even the plainest-looking Karen man is more handsome than George Clooney. They have high cheekbones, muscles that look like Michelangelo's *David*, and smiles that melt hearts. They are quick, agile, strong, and brave like tigers. While they could kill flame-throwing dragons, they will also take delight in cuddling babies, cooking a meal, or playing a ballad on the guitar. What is there not to like about men like these?

Meh Hah was one of these perfect specimens that make women's knees weak. He made the room come alive. He had a smile that lit up his face and revealed kind lines around his eyes. He never sat completely still and his eyes were forever searching the space around him, noticing every little detail while he enthusiastically told stories, laughed, and used his hands to add flavor to what he was saying.

I felt like I was in the presence of a man I'd like to follow. *His village is lucky to have a leader like him,* I kept thinking while I wondered if my hair was cute. I asked him to tell me a little about his life. "I am just so tired," he said. His eyes became narrower as he smiled again—a sorrowful smile this time. "I am tired of always fighting. I am tired of having to deal with the Burma Army. I am tired. I just want to quit."

His village has been under the control of the Burma Army for many years. When the Army takes control they do pretty much as they like. Meh Hah said that the enemy soldiers would come to his village on a regular basis and demand food and services. They would make the villagers their slaves, forcing them to do hard manual labor and portering. I asked if they got paid for the labor and Meh Hah laughed. "Never!" The villagers struggled to get enough food to eat. Meh Hah explained that the soldiers made it even harder for them by demanding parts of their crops, and by restricting their movement. Sometimes they would tell them that they weren't allowed to leave the village to tend to their fields. When the villagers still did so, it could have tragic consequences. Last December a young man was captured and killed when leaving the village without permission. "Right now there is a villager missing too," Meh Hah recalled. "He went to his fields and that is the last any of us saw of him."

"We would be fine if it wasn't for the SPDC," he explained, referring to the official name for the regime in Burma, the State Peace and Development Council. "But now we are always afraid. The worst is when we have to be minesweepers. " (You probably don't know what minesweepers are. It's grotesque. When the Burma Army knows that there may be landmines in the area and they don't want to step on them and get killed or get their legs blown off, they force villagers to walk in front of them so that if a mine is detonated, the villagers will get hurt or killed, not the soldiers.) "My mother stepped on a landmine and died just four years ago," Meh Hah told me. "I also had two cousins who did the same thing. One of them died, and one lost both legs. My aunt also died from stepping on a mine. Just this last year four people from our village had to walk as minesweepers. One of them stepped on a landmine and died."

Meh Hah told me all of this while he was chewing some betel nut and smiling with sparkling eyes. I was amazed that he could tell me such tragic stories with so much calm and gentleness. Every event was laced with pain and sorrow, but he shared the way I would have shared about my summer holiday.

It is the only way to survive, I realized. When living in the shadow of the oppressor one has to decide if one wants to live or die. This was a man who had chosen to live although he had no guarantee that he'd be alive the next day. He felt fear, yes, but he had chosen to not be controlled by fear and obsessed with bitterness. He had chosen to embrace each day as a challenge that he could overcome. He had learned to laugh easily and to enjoy the small moments of pleasure that life provided.

I wanted to give him something. Freedom for him and his people would have been nice. But this was not in my power. I told him about our work and how much we too longed to see Burma free. "Tell the world," he encouraged me. "Tell them what you hear. The Army hates it when the world finds out what they're doing."

I smiled and promised to keep telling the stories of the Karen until they are free. Then I took a headlamp out of my bag and gave it to him. This was the highlight of my day. The village headman who had carried so many burdens for his people over many years smiled like a boy who just received a new toy for Christmas. He held the lamp in his hand and studied it. He outlined it with his fingers, tried all the different settings and wished it could get dark soon so he could get to try it. Becky and I were in a giving mood, so we gave him a knitted hat from Norway too. He put it on and lit a cheroot. Then we gave him and his friends T-shirts for all their family members. We were desperate to do something for these people, and since we couldn't give them what they needed most we gave them all kinds of other stuff.

Little Emily Paw was playing on the floor. I gave her a pretty dress that had belonged to Kristin. She acted just like my three girls had at that age. She twirled around like a princess at the ball, showing everybody how pretty she was. She was almost three and although she was living in a primitive village in the jungles of Burma, she was still a little girl so much like my own children.

It was time for her mother, Naw Moo Wee, who had come with Meh Hah, to tell her story.

"We have to leave our village in order to work on our fields," she explained. "We can obey the rules of the soldiers and starve, or we can disregard their rules and hope they don't notice that we're gone." One of the rules the soldiers enforced was that no villager was allowed to leave the village after dark.

Naw Moo Wee's husband disobeyed the rule and went hunting for food for his twenty-three-year-old wife and daughter one evening. They were poor and finding enough food was often a challenge, so twenty-five-year-old Paw Koh went hunting animals in the jungle.

The soldiers guarding the village found out that he was missing, hunted him down, and made sure that the villagers understood the severity of breaking their laws. They met Paw Koh on the road and shot him to injure him, tortured him, and then finally shot him twice, killing him. He was left on the road for the other villagers to pick up the next morning.

Naw Moo Wee told the story without shedding a tear. She was looking down as she spoke. I got the feeling that maybe there weren't any tears left. While she was talking Emily Paw was busy unwrapping some candies I had brought. She seemed unaffected by what had happened. The most important thing for her at the moment was to get the candy in the mouth so she could get up and run around again. But when she heard her dad's name mentioned, she stopped, looked up at her mom and said, "Where is my Daddy? I miss him."

We gave Naw Moo Wee some money so that she could buy food for a while. We also gave her and Emily Paw some more clothes. But what we gave them seemed so insignificant. What they needed was their husband and dad back. What they needed was freedom. What they needed was to be able to grow their rice in peace and to go to bed at night without the threat of soldiers lingering over them.

I felt a little hopeless that day, but it made me determined to fight harder and longer to bring justice and peace to Burma.

Meh Hah, Emily Paw, and Naw Moo Wee had to walk back to their village before dark. Nobody could know that they had been talking to us. We said goodbye and went in opposite directions. On my way back I carried sadness with me, but also a new sense of faith. I knew that in the end the Karen people would conquer the enemy. I knew this because there are people like Meh Hah who will never let their hope die and who will continue to smile in the face of his advisories, and because there are little children like Emily Paw who will learn that love can conquer evil, forgiveness conquer hate, and righteousness prevail even though evil may have a stronghold.

We got back to our village and I took a quick bath in the river before joining the villagers in their evening activities.

WHEN DID I LAST HEAR MY NEIGHBOR SING?

It's no secret that we in the West are masters at spending our lives running for the wrong reasons. We've entangled ourselves in a net of expectations and commitments that's harder for us to get out of than it is for a fly to get out of the spider's web. We all know we need to stop before the spider eats us alive—sucking all the juices out of us until we're dead.

A political party in Norway asked in one of their election campaigns, "Why aren't our lives any better when we have so much more?" We live in constant climate control where we never need to get too cold, hungry, or tired. We have a life with hardly any wants and where the definition of a 'need' is constantly redefined. A computer didn't use to be a need. Neither were phones that had encyclopedias and music stored on them. We certainly didn't know that we needed an iPad, and some of us are still trying to figure out why we do. The net is getting tighter and tighter.

After meeting Meh Hah, I was sitting in a Karen village watching life unfold. I was an outsider and was able to observe without really taking part. The challenges of survival were more complex and involved than I probably understood. Only a few kilometers away the Burma Army loomed, carrying with them the threat of death. Minutes earlier I had talked to villagers who had shared the burden of not having enough to eat and not knowing how they'd survive the year on so little rice. The children were poorly dressed, and many had runny noses and coughs. And yet I saw joy and heard laughter. I felt a sense of peace that maybe was divine.

I always heard singing and it came from everywhere. Not exactly Elf-like, but honest and unpretentious songs that I imagined were about love and bravery. Men who were working the fields or walking through the jungle, women who were doing the laundry by the river or carrying their babies up the hills, and children who were just running about, being kids, sang. I have never heard as much singing as I have in the presence of the Karen. I wondered, *When did I last hear my neighbor sing, or my colleagues as they came to work on Monday morning?* We have a reason to belt it out. We live in a free country, we have pantries full of food, microwaves, and walk-in closets, but the sounds coming from us often lack tunes.

On this evening I had heard the singing coming from simple huts on the hills while I stood outside watching the myriads of stars dancing on the dark sky. There were no other sounds than the sounds of the jungle and the little piggy-snores coming from three piglets that were huddling together in a ditch in front of one of the houses.

I walked inside and sat on the floor with the others. There is something calming about Karen people talking. They speak with softness in their voices, like they're lined with tranquility. There was no rush and I felt that life was happening there and now. There were no worries about tomorrow or regrets about yesterday. There was tobacco to smoke, betel nuts to chew, and the ingredients for a meal about to be prepared. The vegetables were washed in a bucket of water that had just been carried inside. Meat, herbs, and vegetables were chopped on a slab of wood or ground in a mortar then prepared over the fire on the floor. The fireplace clothed the room in orange, casting shadows around the room and making the serene scene feel almost magical. Many hands joined to make the meal, and those who didn't have a job were content to sit and watch. Some smoked their pipes; others just enjoyed the conversation. Children were sitting with the adults. Their presence wasn't a nuisance, nor did they get any special attention. They just seemed to belong and acted as if their place in the community was as well established as the village chief's. Laughter came easily, and the jokes often referred to the singles in the room and who would be a good match for whom.

While sitting in the presence of villagers who seemed to have understood the value of community and a lifestyle that hadn't ever been compared to a rat race, I was tempted to think that they got the better deal. Something in me longed for days when my main concern was survival, not hundreds of unanswered emails, piles of laundry, meetings, deadlines, soccer practices, and math homework. As I sat on a bamboo floor with only candles to give light, listening to soft voices conversing with the sounds of the jungle as background, it felt like a moment of perfection. I thought that if we just nixed the Burma Army, this would be an ideal life.

In my world the cars and airplanes move faster every year, the computers are breaking new records for speed, and fast food is a necessity. Since we have become such masters at doing everything speedy, we can pack more into a day than previously possible. Although stress-related diseases have become more common than the cold, we still think that our efficiency is great. Fast is a virtue. Busy is a condition we're proud of. But in our quest for speed, we've lost some of the most valuable things in life. The Karen sitting with me on this night had not.

I have to watch my attitude so that I don't become like the eccentric anthropologist who thinks that the more primitive and distant a culture is, the better it must be, and that change of any kind is always bad. As I looked around the room and saw skin infections and heard deep coughs coming from children with runny noses, heard of malaria and labor deaths, I obviously wanted to improve healthcare. When the village chief asked me to please send somebody to help get rid of the bugs that were eating their rice, causing them to have much too little to eat, I thought about Partners staff members who specialized in these kinds of things. In my mind, even a simple toilet in the village would have been a welcome addition.

It wasn't that I was opposed to hot showers, Omega 3 pills, and all of our sophistication. I was excited about drinking a bottle of wine, putting on my slippers and listening to Miles Davis. Sleeping on a hard bamboo floor was a refreshing change for a couple nights, but after many nights of the same, my own soft bed actually sounded nice. Still I felt that our Western lifestyle keeps us so busy improving our lives that we don't take the time to enjoy what we have, and nurture the most important things in our lives. Annie Dillard says, in her book *Pilgrim at Tinker Creek:* "It is dire poverty indeed when a man is so malnourished and fatigued that he won't stoop to pick up a penny. But if you cultivate a healthy poverty and simplicity, so that finding a penny literally will make your day, then, since the world is in fact planted in pennies, you have with your poverty bought a lifetime of days. It is that simple. What you see is what you get."[15]

The people I was sitting with didn't have the unlimited credit cards and the fancy wallets to store them in. But they had learned to stoop down and pick up the pennies (or the *kyats*, the Burmese currency), so to speak. While we chase happiness as if it was something we need to run after, waving our dollar bills at it, the Karen seemed to care more about relationships, hospitality, and generosity. A meal is a sacrament, not something we chow down by the kitchen counter or on the way out the door. A guest is

---

15   Annie Dillard, *Pilgrim at Tinker Creek*, (Harper Perennial. Modern Classics 1974)

a visitor from God, not an interruption. He or she will be honored as such and given the gifts of time, food, and possessions. Children are God's provision for the future and are treated with love and tenderness, not as inconveniences that mess up our lives.

I lay down to sleep when the candles had burned down and all the neighbors had gone back to their houses. The wind moved through the house and I zipped up my sleeping bag. Then I made sure the mosquito net was tucked under me, making it impossible for tiny, six-legged intruders to get inside. Our hosts were still whispering while they too got ready for bed. They had asked me questions about my country and I know that the things I told them had sounded like a fairytale. I hoped I hadn't painted a picture that made them think less of their own world. I wanted them to understand that skyscrapers and elevators aren't equal to happiness, nor are wide roads or garbage disposals. And if there ever will be a day that there are microwave ovens in Karen State, I hoped that they would still choose to sit together and talk about this and that while they push the buttons and watch the plate move round and round.

Bamboo

HOW HAVING KIDS HAS TAUGHT ME ABOUT DICTATORSHIP
AND POLITICS, HOW TRAVELING GETS EASIER WITH A
SUITCASE, AND BELONGING TO A TRIBE IS ESSENTIAL.

DICTATORSHIP HAS A CERTAIN APPEAL IN THE HOME

My life is divided into many befores and after: Before Jesus and after. Before Steve and after. Before the refugees and after. Before my period and after. Before kids and after. While Jesus, Steve and the refugees changed my life radically—and so did my period to a certain extent—nothing has changed me and shaped me as much as my kids have. I'm not at all the same person now as I was before kids. To become a mother is the world's most amazing, frightening, life-changing, plan-revising, laughter-bringing, tear-jerking, routine-altering, expensive, messy, exhausting, rewarding, energizing, painful, joyful, and eventful happening. I'm not being irreverent. Being introduced to Jesus and deciding to follow Him has an everlasting impact on my life and I wouldn't change it for anything. But you have to admit, it's easy to fake it with faith. At least we think it is. With children there is no faking it, and I am 100% sure that this is what Jesus intended.

Something changed in me when I delivered a child. I became a mother and my responsibilities soared. Like a freshly-opened plastic can of play dough, my child could be formed into anything I wanted. At least that's what I thought and I determined to make her the most perfect person the world had met. I followed the advice of the pros. They delineated plans and strategies for the upbringing of perfect humans. It all looked so easy. This was until they wouldn't sleep on schedule nor eat their mashed carrots that I'd bought at the organic store. It looked easy until they hit their friend and refused to share. Surprisingly, they didn't find it particularly exciting to go hiking with mom and dad on a Sunday morning when the alternative was to watch a cheesy show on TV with their friends who had slept over. My acquired theories on childrearing didn't prepare me for all that.

I quickly understood that giving birth to children is one thing, but bringing them up to be the kind of people you want them to be is a totally different ballgame. The basic skills are easy: changing the diapers, living with little sleep, cooking Mac & Cheese. But try to make children do the right thing instinctively! I imagine that making a cow dance Swing would be easier. Since I don't always do the right thing myself, that complicates things. Children don't just shine the light on their own imperfections by their behavior; they've brought my own shortcomings to the light too. They're clear as day and dark as the night. I am impatient like a wasp, selfish, and I hoard my chocolate. I lack wisdom and say mean things. The standards I set for my own kids I need to live by myself too, I assume. This is a problem. Dictatorship has a certain appeal in the home.

While speaking of dictators,[16] one would think that fighting some of the worst ones—the ones in Burma—would be the world's biggest challenge for a person like me. The task is overwhelming, and there are days when I want to laugh when I realize that here I am, trying to combat an enemy that is bigger than the Grand Canyon. It probably ought not to be so, but it's actually easier to turn the switch off to *that* challenge than it is to turn it off to the bickering of my own children who bump into each other in the car. Human nature is both complex and infantile.

Sometimes though, I wonder if the principles applied to my kids could be applied to most humans in order to make them behave. If those principles aren't applied then we end up with spoiled rascals that are not very pleasant to be with. This I have learned about children: there must be consequences for bad behavior and rewards for good. See, kids don't generally just behave well and do the right thing just because that is the right thing to do and because they really, really want to be good, for goodness' sake. (I have some acquaintances whose kids do but they are hopelessly nerdy, like the kids in Barney—way too perfect and nothing like real-life twits.) Nope. They masterfully disregard the voice in their hearts (the voice that often sounds like mom) and do whatever they feel like doing, unless there is the promise of a reward. Then you can get them to do almost anything, just like puppies that want a treat. They're also less likely to commit the same crime twice if they've been grounded at a particularly unfortunate time.

There must be punishments that sting and rewards that you can buy stuff with. (Hugs are terrible rewards according to my kids.) How many

---

16   You may know that there was an election in Burma in 2010. This supposedly brought the military dictatorship to an end. There have been some changes, and more may still come. We are allowed to be optimistic. But not until the Army has less power, the ethnic people are treated with respect and dignity, and new leaders are in place, will Burma experience what we think of as democracy. Read more about the political situation in Burma in the Afterword in the back of the book.

politicians, lawmakers, rulers, and leaders do you know who aren't motivated by the exact same thing?

Some of my politician friends think that they can change the ways of dictators by visiting them, having tea at their offices and talking about how they must stop doing bad things and start doing right things. I can tell you right now that this isn't going to work at all, and the reason I know this is because I am a mother and I know it wouldn't work with my own kids. Dictators, politicians, kids … they all respond to similar stuff.

This is something else I have learned:

There is a certain glory involved in helping the poor. One gets hero status, at least among some. Saving people's lives, bringing help and hope to the destitute, speaking about fancy concepts such as *sustainable development*, the *marginalized* and *crisis management* sound educated and cutting edge. It's interesting and makes people look at you in a different way—*admiringly*. Not so when you talk about where diapers are on sale or about spending the afternoon watching your five-year-old practicing for her ballet performance. They will look at you, some with pity on their faces, and most of them will think, *Boring.*

I had kids and loved being a mom from day one. But I also was challenged more than a bullfighter. My children have pushed every button there is to push and made me give up more of myself than I thought possible. They have pushed me into the bathroom where I have sat on the toilet with my head in my hands crying and telling myself that I am unfit to be a mother … in fact, I am unfit to be called a human being. Then, sometimes on the same day as the toilet episodes, my heart has erupted in an enormous love volcano and I know that the love I feel for my kids and my commitment to them cannot be matched with any other love. I feel like the most privileged person in the world and I can only stare at my girls in dumbfounded wonder. This is what it is like to be a mother: our feelings yo-yo up and down and around, feeling every extreme emotion that exists in the dictionary, and all of these extremes are focused on one or several human beings who probably have no idea of the turmoil they're putting their mom through.

I was wondering whether or not to write about my kids in this book. It seemed so far removed from Partners, Burma, and refugee lives. Who wants to read about raising kids in a book that boasts of being about

Burma? Wouldn't it be the same kind of people—the children's grand-parents—who enjoy hearing you talk about potty training, spelling bees, and endless soccer games where the players don't even know which team they're on? But I've concluded that as in nature, everything is connected in my life too. I can't separate my faith, my work, my kids, my relationship with Steve, my relationships with friends and the people at the grocery store. It's all connected into one big play dough sculpture called My Life.

It may not be this way for you, but the way I see it, I've been given a calling to love and respect all people. I've been called to love my neighbor like myself, and that includes my children as well as the people living in the jungles of Burma. I can't break it into neat little compartments, like I've been doing with jigsaw puzzles, crayons, and blocks. If I fail at giving my children the attention and love they deserve, I've failed in my work with the people of Burma as well. Faithfulness begins in small things—like not rushing off to important tasks when your little girl wants to serve breakfast, like I almost did a while back.

That day was moving on without me it seemed. There was a pile of unfinished tasks cluttering my mind, and Kristin was still sleeping in my bed. She needed to wake up and get ready for school. She was late, and I was late for all my assignments.

I walked up to the room to take a look at the sleeping beauty. Nobody I know enjoys sleep as much as she does, except perhaps cats. Kristin sleeps with her whole being. Every part of her body had found the spot in the bed that it seemed to enjoy the most. She reminded me of Pinocchio with her legs sprawled out in different directions, her arms pointing northeast and south. Her long blond hair was a big mess, like a bird's nest. Once in a while I could hear a small giggle, then a contented sigh. Life as a sleeping child can be so void of worries about tomorrow.

I worried a bit though. When would she decide to wake up? The clock had already moved passed 9:00. The rest of the world had been working for a while.

But I didn't want to wake her up. I believe that there are times in your life when you should be allowed to indulge in sleep. One of those times is before you turn six. Kristin was weeks away from turning five. She could sleep as long as she wanted even though she might miss circle time at pre-school.

At 9.30 she sat up in the bed, rubbed her eyes and stretched her miniature muscles. She was happy as a bird. Now the day could start. Not a minute too early, neither a minute too late.

For me it got a bit hectic now. The child was awake. She should get dressed, eat, and I'd take her to school. Then I'd have to speed myself up to meet the deadlines of all the projects that were supposed to be finished. Surely, surely, Kristin too would want to hurry to get to her best friends. Maybe they'd be learning a new letter today! I made the bed and walked downstairs to make her favorite oatmeal.

"Don't come into the kitchen! I'm making something. Don't look!" I could barely see her bird's nest hair over the kitchen counter. I felt a minor panic attack approaching, but came to my senses. "Okay, Kristin. I'll hide in the office, and then you call me when you're ready."

I walked into my office and saw my computer looking at me with longing in its eyes: "Come and use me. There are many files inside me that need help." I decided to ignore the pleading and enjoy the moment. Seconds later the little voice from the kitchen squeaked again, "Hey, you can help me too." "What are you doing, Kristin? Are you making toast?" "No, mom, I'm making breakfast for you and me." I took a peek through the door and saw the Kristin project: a basket with crackers and bread, cheese, jam, and mustard. She was carrying all the condiments for the gourmet meal to the dining table—her feet moving so fast, her eyes full of zealous determination.

At long last she was ready. "You can come and sit down now, mom." So I sat down to eat my second breakfast at 10:00 a.m. in the morning, when I should've been at the office for a couple of hours already, and Kristin should've been at her school reciting the names of shapes and the days of the week. We ate dried bread with cheese and jam, and drank lukewarm water from coffee cups while we talked about important matters such as which color is nicer and who is the "meano" at school. It was a collection of moments that was more valuable than any document I could have created on my computer, it was more valuable than missed deadlines and unanswered emails. It was valuable because I had remembered to stop and listen, stop, and watch, to stop the business and enjoy the moments that were given to me.

They were moments of life and moments of heaven—heaven seen in a little girl with messy hair who likes to sleep long in the mornings and who appreciates the finer things in life.

I have fully embraced Partners' vision, which is to give free, full lives to the children of Burma. This free, full life is a life where not only is there enough food to eat and warm clothes to wear during winter, it's also a life where a child can be allowed to laugh in her sleep, be with her mom when she wakes up and be able to talk about school and friends with words that don't include losses. Kristin showed me the value of such a life.

WHAT PIECE OF LEGO IS AN ION?

Recently I sat with Elise on the couch helping her get ready for a science test. That I am scientifically inept is no secret. I still find it hard to understand the whole thing about atoms and ions. Those atoms are the smallest things that things can be broken into, right? Just like the smallest pieces of Lego when you have built an amazing castle. But then they bring in the ions and now I'm lost. I can't think of what piece of Lego an ion can be.

Elise and I sat there and I tried to make it sound like I understood the material she was studying. Being a ninth grader, she was beyond the Lego stage, and she needed real answers. "So, what do you know about salt breaking?" I asked her. We tried to imagine the ions flying apart like surprised little trolls, bumping into each other and getting mingled with their own kinds, such as the positive kinds. I was pretending to be enthusiastic and interested in the particular subject—salt, but honestly, I found it about as interesting as Leviticus. (Before you judge me, let me assure you that I'm sure there's a lot of useful stuff in Leviticus, it's just that I can't relate to most of it. I'm still trying to understand and live the Sermon on the Mount.) I often find details tedious and a waste of my time. Wouldn't it be enough just to know that the salt broke into pieces when we smashed it with a hammer? I want to know: what's the bottom line?

But … I guess, for some reason it *is* important to know how things are broken down in order to know why it acts a certain way. We need to do that with people at times too. Most of our behavior can be explained if we only break ourselves down into personality atoms and ions, it seems. Personally, I have, at times, an unhealthy need for affirmation. So I end up doing all kinds of activities just to be noticed, affirmed, and appreciated. This must, no doubt, be extremely tiring for the people around me, and I suspect some of them roll their eyes behind my back and think that I am such a self-absorbed person to be with, that there are times they wish they could just hang out with a weather forecaster instead. But, if you break me down and get to my innermost core, you will see that this odd and unhealthy behavior stems from a longing I have had since I was a girl, and then, all of a sudden you'll understand, and perhaps start to like me more.

And hopefully I'll realize that all this activity just to get attention is unnecessary because I'm loved already.

A while ago our team at Partners had a staff team-building day. Don't ask me why, but we decided to talk about what we were afraid of. As we sat in a circle talking about fears of lizards, divorce, and flying, I thought about my fears. I realized that I was afraid of so many things that it would take very long to list them all. Besides that, I didn't think it would be very constructive for the rest of the team to hear about all the ridiculous phobias I have. What struck me, however, was that all my fears could be narrowed down to two categories: fear of failing and fear of losing control. After I thought about it for a while, I decided that is probably why most of us do (or don't do) the things we do. Perhaps this is a bit like the atoms and ions—they act a certain way and it affects the whole structure, turning it into either a chair or a spaceship. People do all kinds of crazy things that actually hurt others or that hurt themselves; it stops them from living their dreams and from loving another person; it puts people on their butts instead of on a mission to rescue the princess, the prince, the dog, or whatever. All because of two silly fears: fear of losing control and fear of failing. In the end the fear-atoms turn into huge towers that make a loud crash when they fall.

Volumes have been written about Burma and other places where tyranny rules. There have been many attempts at explaining why a nation can fall into such misery, and why its leaders not only allow it to happen, but actively take part in the destruction. I think it can be explained with one word: fear. My guess is that if we were to peel off the hard exterior we would find a scared and insecure boy inside every dictator's outfit. I realized this as I was trying to understand basic chemistry. Everything has to start with something. And at our core, we're not that different—dictators and I. We have just mingled with different kinds of atoms and the outcome of our fears has been different.

One fact still remains though, and it is this one: I still don't really understand the difference between ions and atoms.

Prayers at the end of many days:

"Jesus, I pray that the refugee children will not only get blankets and food. I want them to have toys too." Elise

"God, I am kind of tired of always praying for the refugees. Now I want to pray for me. Thank you God for making me." Naomi

"Dear God. I pray that the Burma Army will get constipated and afficuated I pray that they will fly away on a kite, fall into the ocean, and get eaten by a shark." Kristin (She doesn't know what either word means, but they both sound horrible in her mind. How would you like to get afficuated?)

"We pray for Doh Say tonight." Elise, Naomi, Kristin
"We pray for Doh Say tonight." Elise, Naomi, Kristin
"We pray for Doh Say tonight." Elise, Naomi, Kristin

GOING FOR A BEAR HUNT

We have taken our kids to many refugee camps over the years, but this trip was different. It was remote and hard to get to. In order to get there, we had to walk after dark. For part of the walk we weren't allowed to use flashlights and we could only whisper basic instructions back and forth. Gummy bears came in handy when the going got rough. After we had gone up the mountain, down the mountain, and over the river, the camp was finally within reach. It was on the top of a hill and we climbed it as fast as we could. Only when the houses of the refugees surrounded us, making us almost disappear among the dark shadows of bamboo houses, did we feel relatively safe. Nobody had seen us get in. It felt like a scene from a movie.

In the camp it was the same heart-wrenching stories: "There was no food for us to eat in our village," Saw Noh Noh told us. "The soldiers don't allow us to go to our rice fields, so we're starving." "I couldn't feed my children," said another man who had been living under the Army's control for years. "We are slave laborers working for free for the Army. If we don't do what they tell us, they will beat us up. We were only allowed to work to provide for our families a few days a month."

While we were talking to the refugees, the girls busied themselves with showers. It was a challenge of great dimensions. First they had to undress in the same room that we were sitting in without revealing any private parts. This they cunningly did behind their colorful sarongs. Then they had to tie their sarongs around themselves like the Karen girls do and make them stay. If they had fallen off it would have been disastrous. Then, with the sarong tightly tied around their bodies they had to climb down a bamboo ladder wearing their flip-flops. Perhaps you could compare this exercise to rock climbing with your body wrapped in saran wrap. The comparison breaks down, I know, but, you have to admit, it is a funny image.

In this particular building we had the luxury of a bathroom. Often this isn't the case, and then you shower publicly, which is more challenging. But this place had a room downstairs with a door. It had a dirt floor, bamboo walls, and a roof made with teak leaves. Spiders lived there too. Who would want a tiled bathroom with plumbing and a tub when you could experience this? Not us! Once inside, the girls could pour cold water over themselves and the sarong. The water was in a large basin that had been filled by hospitable Karen. This is important to remember: although you're inside a room with a door, you should never take your clothes off inside a Karen bathroom. The reason is that there are too many peep holes in the walls.

When the girls had washed their bodies to the best of their abilities, they would wrap a dry sarong around themselves, pick up the wet one and do the whole exercise in reverse. Then, because it was so hot, as soon as they got dressed they'd want to take another shower because they were already sweaty again.

We filled the day with other activities too. For example, did we bring beads and pipe cleaners! Those are items that will provide hours of unforgettable fun in a refugee camp. There is a word we use in the West that I despise: *bored*. To hear my own children say they are bored and ask, "What can we do?" sounds much like Styrofoam rubbed on glass. I automatically go into a mild rage and say things like, "Figure it out yourself. You have more stuff than 90% of the world's children, so don't ask me what to do." I will go on and on for a while, preaching like some kind of end-time prophet, and then realize that the kids left already. They're playing a computer game.

I'm not the first person in the world who is concerned with the damage we're causing our children by bringing them up in a world that moves so fast and that's so full of activities that they've lost their ability to imagine, wait, be still, and create. The fast food world we live in has taken a lot away from our kids. Here we were thinking we were doing them a favor by inventing dolls that poo, books that read aloud, Gameboys, interactive computer games and websites, Facebook, iPods, mobile phones, remote-controlled cars, electronic wands, and karaoke. While it is wondrous stuff it may be wise to ask ourselves if it wouldn't be an idea to send our kids outside to play some days.

A few times a year our family makes a point of going somewhere (not necessarily a refugee camp, although that's a perfect place for this exercise) where there is no electronic- or cyber-based entertainment. We also prefer that it's a place where none of us can interact with other friends. Quite simply, we're stuck with ourselves and our imagination for some days. Without exception, those times have been our favorite times together. For days the girls won't utter the word *bored* once. They will keep themselves busy and happy playing games that none of us knew existed, and *sibling rivalry* is a term that doesn't apply. Suddenly seashells become people and flowers are as interesting to study as a fashion magazine. It's harmony like the families in cereal commercials experience. We ride our bicycles, hike the mountains and laugh while our hair blows in the wind.

Young children in the refugee camps don't make a conscious effort to remove themselves from Western entertainment gadgets. They don't even know they exist. And I don't think it's a bad thing. In a refugee camp you'll never see a bored child. They play all day long. Their imaginations are their biggest resource, as well as all their friends.

So here we were with beads and pipe cleaners. The word got out, and before we had arrived at the school where we were going to do the craft we saw a parade of children marching up the hill to where we were. They looked like a string of colorful beads themselves, weaving up the narrow trail. Some of the older kids carried their younger siblings on their backs, mothers that were only teenagers also joined. When they were all inside the building we pulled out the goods and had the best craft party ever.

I was a proud mom as I watched my girls sitting with groups of refugee munchkins stringing beads and making silly glasses from pipe cleaners. It could have been any Sunday school class in the West. Except that it was a thousand degrees and we were in a bamboo structure with very dirty and very cute refugees. It was a fun day. The children beamed with pride as they put their necklaces around their necks. Precious stones wouldn't have been prettier.

Then we did a drama about David and Goliath. Kristin was brave Dave, and our friend Sid was Goliath—a role that he really got into, in fact: he roared like a giant and slapped himself on the chest. The rest of us were Philistines and Israelites. I'm not sure that the kids understood anything about the story, but there's no doubt they thought we were entertaining. They were so fascinated watching us that they probably didn't pay attention to the person translating the story.

When we left a few days later it started to rain. The expression *raining cats and dogs* took on a whole new meaning that afternoon. It was like somebody held a showerhead with water gushing out over our heads for the whole walk. We had to take a detour in order to not be seen, and when it rains in the jungle it gets slippery. There was some slipping and sliding, but no complaining. This is when the book, *We Are Going for a Bear Hunt* came in handy. Through the jungle we kept chanting, "Can't go over it! Can't go under it! Got to go through it!"

We crossed the river under a tarp so that nobody would see us and then kept walking on the other side. The trail we had walked on going there was now a rushing river. The girls trotted on, half amused, half irked. I was impressed by their attitude and spirit through the afternoon and into the early evening. The one who got cheesed off was me. It happened when Steve revealed that he had accidently packed the headlights in a pack that was being shipped down the river, to meet up with us the next day. "You did what?" I bellowed, forgetting all manners and the commitment to good attitude. "So you mean we're going to walk this perilous trail with three kids and no light, do you?" What could he say? We were in the middle of the jungle with no flashlights. It wasn't like we could stop by Target.

So we stumbled along. Steve last, me fuming in the front. Baw Boe, who was our guide and best travel buddy, probably lost a lot of respect for me. Elise finally set me straight: "Mom, he just forgot the flashlights, okay? Now we just have to make the best of it." You never feel smaller than when your child puts you straight, and you know she's right.

We made it fine to the meeting point where a truck waited for us and took us back to a world of alarm clocks, traffic jams, and scheduled meetings.

Once we were safely back we shared feelings and thoughts about our experience. Naomi said, "Mommy, I was scared that night, but it made me think of what the people fleeing must feel like. For us it was only a couple of hours and then we knew we'd be safe. Imagine if we never felt safe."

I thought that if we'd done the whole trip only for my girls to learn that one lesson, it was worth it. The second most important lesson was that it was possible to walk in the jungle after dark without flashlights.

MOM, I'M DOING THIS BECAUSE IT'S THE RIGHT THING TO DO.

Elise was only a year old when our friends' daughter, who was the ripe age of two, pushed her so that she fell on the floor, just so she herself could grab the toy Elise had been playing with. Steve and I were appalled by our friends' absolute lack of control over their child. We'd never let our little angel get away with such mean behavior—not that we thought she would actually ever become such a brat. I'm embarrassed to share that we even mentioned this to our friends. It only took a few months and we were eating humble pie. Our little Elise could take on the character of a mafia chief who'd had too many double-shot espressos just to get what she wanted from her friends, or in order to avoid sharing what she had with others.

We've been teaching our kids to share ever since. When we have a lot and somebody else doesn't, we share. That's the mantra. This is a hard life-lesson to learn, and I often admit to myself that as the mentor, I need to work more on my own performance. The roles change sometimes and my girls turn out to be the ones teaching me. Elise does this all the time. She has moved away from the push-to-get-what-you-want stage to a much more beautiful stage.

She may actually be an angel in disguise. With her dark eyes and earthy beauty she radiates kindness. She just wants to make the world happy and feels that she needs to play an active role in the process. My aunt wonders if perhaps she was born without the original sin that the rest of us are stuck with. Obviously, my aunt didn't see Elise when she was two, or when her sisters get on her nerves, but she has a point though. My vote is that she's just a very, very nice person who has some bad days too.

Elise's conscience and commitment to do the right thing sometimes gets in her way. When she was eleven she was at a gathering with some particularly annoying kids that nobody wanted to play with. Halfway through the day Elise approached us in a very bad mood. "I just can't stand these kids," she informed us. "I know that they're acting the way they do because they're insecure and they may have had some problems in their family and they may have been hurt. But, you know, it doesn't make them any nicer to be with. Can I please be excused from them?"

After the trip to the remote refugee camp we heard a story that troubled us. A new family had just arrived at the camp in distress. Hser Gay Paw, one of our Karen staff members, told us, "The dad just died, so the mom walked for days with her four children and arrived to the camp just days ago. As soon as they got there, her only son died also. Now she's alone with her three daughters aged seven and under. She's falling apart emotionally and they have nothing. No clothes, no mosquito nets, no blankets, no food. Do you think you could help them?" Hser Gay Paw is short and round like a Karen version of the Russian stacking dolls. Her face is almost always a big smile, her eyes smiling as much as her lips. But this day she only looked very concerned.

That night we talked about the tragedy this woman and her daughters were experiencing. We remembered the days in the camp and the children we'd met and who'd moved into our hearts. All the three girls were upset by the story. "Imagine if that was us, Mom. Imagine if Daddy and one of us girls both died in one week. Then we lost our home and had to walk to a camp where we had nothing. How would we feel?"

Before going to bed that night Elise handed me an envelope. In it was all the money she owned. It was one thousand baht (thirty dollars).

Besides being a very kind person, Elise is also the most forgetful and absentminded person north of the Equator. She has gone to school and realized when she arrived that she forgot to put on her shoes. She has on several occasions forgotten to bring her backpack to school, and it is the exception from the rule if she remembers her lunch. For her birthday we had given her her first mobile phone, a pink wonder that had several annoying ring tones. You probably know the rest of the story. Within two months she had lost it.

Elise's devastation was so acute that we almost went and got her a new phone that very second. But that would have been the wrong thing to do, of course. Her absentmindedness may be genetic (I blame Steve), but we still have to help teach her some basic routines and rules so that as an adult she won't forget her kids, for example. We told her we were sorry that she lost her phone, but that she was 100% responsible for the loss. So we wouldn't get her a new phone. She'd have to save money to buy a new one herself. She agreed and started doing the dishes with new determination.

The money she gave me was the money she had saved for her new phone. She was a third of the way toward reaching her goal. "This is for that family," Elise said. "But, honey, this is all the money you own. Are you sure you want to give it all away?" "Yes, I am. It's a little hard to do, but I still want to do it." "But why?" I asked, out of touch with the inner voice Elise no doubt had listened to. "Mom, I'm doing this because it's the right thing to do."

Elise's money was enough to buy mosquito nets for the whole family and blankets for all of them.

Quite frankly, her act of generosity and obedience was a challenge for me. What she did was right and true. She didn't have much, but she gave everything she could. I asked myself if I would do the same. How far am I willing to go in order to be the answer to the many prayers coming from the thousands living in constant fear, in constant need, in constant hunger in the right now?

Bono said something very challenging recently. "To love your neighbor as yourself is not a piece of advice. It is a command," he said. The pointed words, only slightly softened by his gentle Irish accent, pierced my heart. We don't give to the poor out of pity or from charity. We do it because, like Elise said when she gave all her money away, it's the right thing to do. She had come a long way from being a two year old, maybe further along than me.

SHE MAY BE GOING THROUGH SOME
KIND OF AN EMOTIONAL TRAUMA

She was dressed in overalls and carried her pink Bodyshop backpack. It never left her side. Inside were her most prized possessions: a potato-person made by Elise (it was quite wrinkly by now), an empty film container, a passport photo of Daddy and a cut-out picture of Mr. Bean. Naomi was two-and-a-half we had just spent some time at the bookstore. As we walked down the cobblestone street holding hands, she stuck her free hand deep into her overalls pockets and pulled out a small note-book. "Ta-*da*!" she exclaimed, leaving me too stunned to speak. Where had I gone wrong in my childrearing theories? What would become of a child who knew how to steal at the age of two?

A couple of years later, Naomi had, mysteriously, managed to acquire a number of items that we didn't know the owners of. We would find stuff she had hidden under her pillow, inside drawers, under her bed and in all her purses. When she, as a four-year-old, managed to steal almost all the art supplies at a Vacation Bible School program without anybody noticing, we were alarmed. We envisioned first-page news of bank robberies where we'd recognize Naomi as the main hooded dude. Luckily, our faithful psychologist friend, Glen, was back in town, and since we often fed him dinner, we thought he owed us free counseling.

"You know, Naomi may be going through some kind of an emotional trauma," he suggested. We had just had a new baby, and she went from being the youngest in the family to the child who might now suffer from the "middle-child syndrome." Glen thought there could be other issues as well. He then suggested that we had her draw with us, and that we should start by having her draw her family.

He explained that the way she would draw her family would let us know a little more about how she felt about herself. For example, if the baby was disproportionately large, we should assume that she thought the baby got too much of our time, and that she'd begun stealing because she thought that was a way to get our attention. (She was right about that!) As soon as Glen said this, I started feeling like a mother who had blown it with my little No'mi. I felt so bad that she probably felt all unloved, unvalued, and un-special.

Steve and I couldn't wait to give her the paper and markers the next morning. Steve, who doesn't like old and scruffy stuff, had gone to buy a new drawing pad and new markers just for this occasion. We asked her to draw us a pretty picture of our family and waited to see what she produced.

Glen had told us to be calm and not shrink-like while doing this exercise with her. We should act just like we always do so that she would draw as natural as possible. So Steve sat down to draw a picture himself and I read.

"I am *all* ready," said Naomi after some minutes. Her hair was in pig-tails and her one dimple on her right cheek was like a deep wishing well. We fought to get a first glance at the masterpiece that would help us find the missing pieces. Our suspicions were quickly confirmed. The picture had five people on it; one of them was large. This one was looming over the rest as if she were trying to take over the whole world of the Gumaers. We thought that it was so sad that she felt like the baby had taken her world away from her. "Now, tell us who they are, honey," we said, sounding like amateur counselors. "This is mommy, daddy, Elise, Kristin," she said as quickly as only Naomi can, pointing to the smallest people on the picture. "And this one, this one is ME! Me, *me!*" The person bigger than all of us combined, and with a smile that went from one end of the face to the other, was none other than Naomi herself.

From this exercise we found out that Naomi had no problems with her self-esteem whatsoever. But we still didn't understand why she stole people's stuff.

After some more thought and a few more incidents we concluded that what mattered to Naomi was to get what she wanted, at whatever the cost. That it was morally or ethically wrong was only a minor problem as long as she ended up with all the teacher's stickers or any other attractive item. So we decided that she had to lose something more important as a punishment. At four and a half that would be her makeup.

I still remember Steve taking all her lipsticks and other beautifying items away from her for a whole month because she had stolen her friend's toy. It was devastating. She felt like her life was over. She was not going to give up without a fight. Once she threw her hands in the air and said, "I have no mascara! How can I go outside?"

She didn't grow up with a mother who looks like a model for Mary Kay, this Naomi. It's quite a mystery to us why she was so fond of makeup. We thought it might be because she was artistic. At least it seemed that she was trying to express herself rather than make herself pretty when she came downstairs for breakfast with lipstick outlining her lips all the way up to the nose and purple rouge that made her look like a victim of domestic violence. Whatever the reason was, taking her makeup away from her seemed to do the trick.

One day I went to Naomi's class to talk about ethics, faith, and serious stuff. It was a most entertaining lesson. With twenty seventh graders you need to know your stuff and you need to be animated. Memorizing the Buddhist creed won't satisfy. We got into a hefty discussion about whether all people are of equal value, and there was some disagreeing when it came to Hitler and Idi Amin. Then we moved on to talking about the gnarly generals of Burma. They were all angry at their behavior. Rightly so. Everybody I ever talk to gets angry when they hear about their actions. We have a sense of right and wrong, after all. But when I said that I think they too (the seventh graders in front of me) have to carry some of the responsibility for all the suffering in Burma and elsewhere in the world, they looked at me like I was short a few screws. "We're not responsible for what they're doing in Burma," they said, indignantly.

The truth is that we all are. If we passively let unrighteousness happen and keep eating our steaks as if nothing's wrong with the world, I would say that we are not only stealing, we are lying too—and worst of all, we are responsible for people dying.

It's a little bit like Naomi when she was four. We know what we want and we're going to get it at all costs. Even if it means leaving others hungry, sick, destitute, and oppressed. We have this idea, in this part of the world, that we deserve it. Aren't we all acting a little bit like toddlers when we say things like that? Naomi changed when she realized she would lose something more important to her if she kept her behavior up. I wonder what we need to lose in order to realize that stealing is wrong?

After a while Naomi got a new nickname. It wasn't my idea, nor was it Steve's. Her friends named her *The Giver*. As fast as she would nick people's stuff before, she now would give her own stuff away to people who needed it, wanted it, or merely glanced at it. This quality has stuck with her the way her dimple has. And my hope is that as my little Giver grows up to be big, this quality will be her trademark.

The BFG
and his observations on human beans

Some of my favorite things are children's books. I was so happy when I had kids and had a reason to buy them. I love the many illustrations and the simplicity of the messages that sometimes are just plain silly, but other times have serious messages hidden between the lines. I haven't found the hidden meaning of *The Very Hungry Caterpillar* yet, but *If You Give a Mouse a Cookie*, however, is a brilliant devotion.

Of the many people who write great books for kids, I think Roald Dahl is one of the best. His imagination beats almost everything I have ever read and I wish I could just have a small piece of his quirky humor. We recently read a very exciting book by him called *The BFG* (short for the Big Friendly Giant). This book made me look forward to the evenings when we could cuddle up together and find out what on earth the Big Friendly Giant was up to next. We learned the worst English grammar ever, and the giants totally lacked manners. "It's filthing! It's disgusterous! It's sickable! It's rotsome! It's maggotwise! Try it yourself, this foulsome snozzcumber!"[17] the BFG exclaimed while talking about the only vegetable he could eat in giant country where the other giants' diets consisted of people—children in particular. Later, when explaining another issue, he clarified: "What I mean and what I say is two different things." I can definitely relate to that.

I would recommend The BFG to most people before many Christian devotionals. Some of those books are okay, but I have to admit that with many of them I think: *Yawn! I got the message already.* Not so with Roald Dahl, and not so with the BFG. You'll be on the edge of your seat to the very end.

---

17   Roald Dahl, *The BFG*, (Puffin Books, 1982)

While the BFG himself is a devoted vegetarian, the other giants in the country are a foul, reeking bunch of man-eating monsters. With names such as *Meatdripping, Fleshlumpeater and Gizzardgulping* you can't really expect anything else. There's no excuse for their ghastly behavior. Sophie, the main character, who is eight, is very distressed about the terrible giants. She has to hide from them inside the pocket of the BFG to avoid becoming dinner. The best word she has to describe what she is observing is that it is "awful." A fitting word. But, and here's my point, the BFG points out something rather interesting:

"'Human beans is killing each other much quicker than the giants is doing it.' 'But they don't eat each other,' Sophie said. 'Giants isn't eating each other either,' the BFG said. 'Giants is not very lovely, but they is not killing each other. Human beans are the only animals that are killing their own kind.'"[18]

He ends his speech by saying that he also condemns the behavior of the giants, because, "One right is not making two lefts."

One day it dawned on me that what the giants did was less hideous than what I allow to happen to children around the world, and I wonder if that was not the point Roald Dahl wanted to make. For example, no less than 25,000 children die from lack of food every day, and we tolerate it. We don't exactly tolerate it by saying we think it's okay, but by being passive and allowing it to happen. The BFG pointed out that human beans (His English is not so good since he never went to school, so he frequently gets his words mixed up) are the only animals that are killing their own kind. It's a barbarous idea, but it turns out that it's true.

18   Ibid

SOMETIMES THE TEACHINGS OF JESUS ARE ANNOYINGLY CHALLENGING

A few churches I know wouldn't allow Jesus into their congregation. Some people would find His talking and behavior so offensive that they'd warn their congregation against Him. I'm fairly confident of this.

He wouldn't conform to the dress code that had been implemented by the elders; He'd invite street people to join the service; He could possibly have a beer with some of the newcomers after the service—in the parking lot. Imagine the hullaballoo it'd cause if Jesus showed up with single moms and their kids, recovered drug addicts and even prostitutes to celebrate church! I can see them putting a blanket on the floor and having a nice little brunch while laughing and singing. A few churchgoers would have a very difficult Sunday. Many would worry immensely about stains on the carpet and the smell the new guests might leave on the newly-purchased chairs.

Sometimes I find the teachings of Jesus annoyingly challenging myself, so to a certain degree I understand the focus on the interior and the sound system. Not that Jesus spent much time talking about it, but such diversions keep us comfortable. I understand the attraction to the cotton candy version of the Bible, where the focus is all on us and what we can get from Jesus. It's like the seagulls in *Finding Nemo:* "Me, me, me!" We memorize verses that say that He will give us the desires of our hearts. We feel safe and comfortable with our own kind of people, not with the ones who smell funny. It's awkward when Jesus comes and messes everything up.

Some time ago I read a book by Shane Claiborne that made me a bit uneasy. It was called *The Irresistible Revolution.* In it he writes about how he perceived Christianity at first. He thought that as long as he stuck to certain behaviors and followed a set of rules, then he'd be safe and make it to heaven—which, of course, is the goal. But when he started reading the Bible more thoroughly, and especially the teachings of Jesus, he found a different kind of religion. It turned out that a lot of the rules in the church were not rules made by Jesus, and a lot of the rules that Jesus *did* make were simply not talked about, or, if they were talked about, they weren't lived. He started looking for people who actually followed Jesus' example and lived the way He said we should, and for the longest time his list stayed embarrassingly empty.

Shane wanted to meet a real Christian, but all those he found, such as Francis of Assisi, were dead already. After he'd almost given up hope of finding a true follower of Jesus, he finally ended up with Mother Teresa. He went to live with her for a while and spent time caring for lepers.

While reading this book I was able to think about all the Christians I knew who don't live up to what Shane Claiborne said the standard should be. I felt smug. I was working with the poorest of the poor, bringing hope and love to children who were victims of war. For years my husband and I lived on so little that we could only afford to order the appetizers on the menu if, once every blue moon, we went out for dinner. We had dedicated our lives to the destitute. Could it be that Jesus had me in mind when he preached the Sermon on the Mount?

During this time I often drove our car through a traffic intersection where two young girls, the age of my kids, were selling jasmine flowers on the street. One in particular stood out. She was very pretty and had a smile that penetrated me. After a while she started to recognize my car whenever I was paused for a red light. She came running up to me, smiling. I would give her twenty baht, which is fifty cents, and she'd give me a flower. Sometimes we'd have some seconds to chat. Her Thai was poor, but I found out a few things about her and her family over the weeks. Every time she stood by my car, she looked inside. It had air conditioning and music. Sometimes my girls were with me and we were off to some function, ballet or soccer. I would tell her this, smile at her and be off when the light turned green.

I always drove away with a bad feeling in my stomach. A voice told me that fifty cents a few times a week was not enough. It could've been the voice of Shane Claiborne, but more likely it was Jesus whispering, *What do you think I would have done for her?*

I came up with so many excuses not to get involved with her. They ranked from my acute lack of time, to: She could be ADHD, to: Would she even know how to pick up after herself? For all I knew she might have been HIV positive. Then think of the mess! My excuses were so many they'd always take me all the way back home where I'd forget about her until next time I was stopped at the same light.

The bottom line was that I just didn't want to get involved. Helping this girl would mess up my life, and I didn't want it messier than it already was. Kind of like the church people with the carpet.

I knew the danger she was in. Any young and pretty girl on the streets in Thailand is a target. The fact that she came from a hill tribe and was almost illiterate made her even more vulnerable. Human trafficking is a daily occurrence in the cities, and I, the very sanctified follower of Christ, knew this. But I chose to let the days go by and kept working on my excuses. One of my best ones was that I had heard others in the community—Christians like myself—talk about this girl. Why didn't they do anything for her? If *they* didn't, why should I?

Then one day I came to the intersection and she wasn't there. I never found out what happened to her and I'll probably never see her again.

This is one of the stories in my life that I'm not proud of. It hurts to think about how far I am from living like Jesus did. I'm faced with my own selfishness and see that my heart is full of the same gunk that the people I've been judging left and right have in their hearts.

One of my biggies is Christians who buy airplanes for themselves. This is where I draw the line: at the airplane store. When people I've respected in the past go and buy themselves a flying machine, I question their salvation. You may think this is very silly and intolerant, and maybe it is. But I know Christians who do the same thing about other issues. Some think that all Christians have to be Republicans, for example. I don't. I think Christians shouldn't own airplanes. They can fly commercially, they can drive, and best of all, they can use public transport. This is better for the environment, it'll save money that they can give to the poor, and it will ultimately bring them closer to God.

Some days I obsess about this airplane-thing as well as other issues I have with Christian brothers and sisters. I've seen so much injustice that could easily have been fixed if only we were a little more willing to be a little more generous with our time and resources—and by resources I mostly mean money. Some days we sit at our office in Thailand and look at our numbers. There are times we have to agree that one more clinic in this or that area (where there are none), is more than we can afford. Those are the times when there's an impulse in me that wants to go out and whack people on the head—especially when I also get to see children from the same area, sick and dying without any medical facilities. Then, after the meeting, I go and buy myself a latte.

I deserve my latte, I explain to myself, and enjoy the bitter-mellow taste, using a spoon to eat off the delicious foam on the top, humming to Feist. It's been a long and hard day. But if we're going to think black-and-white here, I don't deserve my latte any more than my friends deserve an airplane. Why do I think I deserve anything at all? And where exactly in the Bible does it say, "Thou shall not buy airplanes"? The really hard thing to realize is that I don't deserve anything, not even instant coffee. Everything I have has been given to me for free. And most of what I own is more than the people in the jungle own. If I'm going to follow my own logic, then I should also only own one shirt and no shoes.

I justify myself by saying that the money used to buy an airplane could feed a lot more people than money spent on a latte, which, actually, is true. But who sets the standards? Who decides at what point we must stop spending money on ourselves? If an airplane is wrong, then is a car okay? And are two cars allowed? How about an RV? As I think about it, I have to admit that this really is none of my business. My main responsibility is my own heart and my own actions. I want to stand before the Jesus I want to resemble on earth, and hear Him say that I was a good steward and that He's proud of me.

My second responsibility though, is to speak the truth, which I think is to point to Jesus' teachings and His life, but also to speak about the people in the world we're called to share with. I won't stop doing that, but I will try to have a less arrogant edge to my words, because as it turns out, I have a few issues myself.

MY HEART OFTEN SMELLS OF DIESEL

Kristin was depressed. Her face was brown from playing in the sun; a few freckles decorated the chubby face along with some dirt and traces of chocolate—proofs of a day spent in childhood heaven.

"Mom," she said, her voice full of concern, "what am *I* good at? There's nothing I can do that Elise and Naomi can't do better. They can read better and bike better and do everything better than me. What is it that *I* can do that I'm better at?"

How well I knew the feeling: trying so hard to be decent at something, feeling that I'm getting there, and then realizing that I'm *so* average or below.

"Kristin," I said, "there's a lot that you're good at. There is, for example, nobody in the world who gives better hugs than you." "Yeah, but that's *nothing*. I want to be good at something *important*." We talked for a while and I tried to come up with things that I thought she could do well, but she wasn't impressed. She just thought of her humiliating status in the family. No matter which area we talked about, she was the baby. And she feared it would always be that way.

"When I lose a tooth, Naomi and Elise have lost all theirs already. I swim across the swimming pool, but Naomi and Elise can swim a thousand meters already. I try to read *Sam I Am*. Naomi and Elise read huge books, for example, *Harry Potter*. They can do everything better than me." I could read intense frustration in her upset face, and a look that said, "Don't try to fool me. I know what I know, and that is that you just *say* I'm the best at something, but actually Elise and Naomi are always going to be better."

I hugged my favorite six year old and told her that she was great and I loved her. Although I know she believed that, I'm not sure she was pleased with the outcome of the talk.

Gunhild, her three-month-younger cousin, is one of Kristin's favorites. She's one of those kids who could read and write at such a young age that people, especially grandparents, think they're geniuses. Of course, this had been noticed by Kristin too, who was still trying to remember the days of the week, and how to spell *Gunhild*. They are best friends nevertheless.

Most of their time together is spent in a world where only the two of them are present. I'm sure that if a parade of naked men and elephants came walking by, they'd continue whispering their secrets and acting in their role-plays, noticing nothing.

But one day Gunhild's role as best friend was seriously threatened. She showed up at our house—hold on tight—with a missing tooth *and* a brand-new, sparkling, shining, expensive-looking, un-scratched, un-dented, no-training-wheel bicycle. She was as proud as a peacock as she sashayed across the driveway and into our house. Imagine the betrayal! The look on Kristin's face was almost as if she'd been a wife whose husband had just told that he'd taken on a mistress. Her jaw dropped, she tried to say something to the face-minus-a-tooth, but no words came out. It took days before she wanted to see her cousin again, and it wasn't until daddy had bought his girl a new bicycle too. Just as shiny. We couldn't do anything about the teeth that wouldn't come loose, but we could give her some dignity by providing a bike that was a respectable size. Since she's a Christmas baby, she got a halfway-through-the-year birthday gift.

Later she went on to become the family's best hoola-hooper. Her big sisters didn't stand a chance. Neither did Gunhild. She was unbeatable and even made it into the newspaper. With six hoola hoops around her waist, all swishing around at an amazing speed, it was no wonder that she caught the attention of the media.

It's a cute story because the main character was only six. The truth is that we all struggle with our need for importance, and I suspect that you, like me, compare yourself to all the perfect people in the world, and either dislike them or yourself in the process.

Once I was at a meeting where there were other groups of people that did aid-work in Burma. These were wonderful people with clean clothes and spotless smiles. Their presentations oozed with integrity and passion and I'm sure they would've gladly given up their own dinner in order to feed the hungry. And I sat in the meeting room wishing that they would just stop it. *Go back to the place of your birth and become photo models or dermatologists,* I thought. I wouldn't go as far as to say that I was jealous. The feeling in my heart was hard to label. It was more like a fear that they'd surpass me, that they'd do a better job than us, that they'd be noticed and I wouldn't, that—heaven forbid—they'd end up helping more people than us and get a better website too.

This ugly feeling slowly stained my soul like a bottle of black ink that had just tipped over, and I hoped nobody noticed my sulky face. I asked myself what my real motives were as I had given my life to help the people in Burma. Had I been fooling myself and the world by saying it was because I wanted to help? Was it more that I wanted to be noticed, admired, looked up to, and loved? If I disliked it when I heard of others doing similar things in order to help the people that we wanted to give freedom and life to, then something didn't match up. Like Sherlock Holmes I took up my magnifying glass and tried to find some clues.

The clues I found, in the form of dirty fingerprints on my soul, led me to conclude—again—that I'm no better than anybody else, and not much different either. The job I do doesn't purify my heart any more than putting on a new dress makes my dirty underwear clean—if you know what I mean. I also had to admit that while the work I did was both important and noble, my motives were sometimes not purer than the honey some of my refugee friends had once given us. They had found pure jungle honey in beehives in the old trees in the rainforest then had cleverly put this honey in an old diesel container. We found it a bit hard to enjoy the honey on our toast with its unmistakable smell and taste of diesel.

My intentions may be good, and the work I do pure as honey, but my heart often smells of diesel. Here's a little truth about me and how I feel when somebody is better than me: I struggle with the balance between watching other people who are amazing and learning from them, and watching other people who are amazing and feeling like crap because they're so much smarter and better and prettier than me. Whether it's raising kids, running a marathon, or making a spreadsheet in Excel, there are always those A+ people who make me look ordinary or worse. Comparing myself to others in order to see my own shortcomings is a great way to keep me from spending my energy on useful activities. It takes my *oomph* away and leaves me sitting in a pool of self-pity unable to even do the dishes. It's a condition that creates insecurity, animosity, and strife. It causes me to be inefficient, unhappy, and unpleasant. It's not good for me, the people I live and work with, or for the children of Burma.

Our kids are genetically unfortunate. Both their parents are math-challenged. While in math multiplying two negatives makes one positive, this seems to not be the case in real life. Two parents with low math IQs don't equal three children with high math IQs. When the kids were small, we heard that babies that listened to Mozart would become better at math. Our girls listened to so much Mozart that they could whistle parts of the Magic Flute when they were three and hum along to the Marriage of Figaro before they could read. They would come home from school and turn off the pop I listened to and put in their favorite Mozart concertos. I think it was the Flute and Harp Concerto in D Minor by St. Martins Academy. But did they become math geniuses? No.

One day Elise, who happens to be a perfectionist, cried over her bad math grades. "I hate grades, and what's the point of them anyway?" she sobbed. "The point is to let you know how good you are at something," I said sounding like I was quoting a textbook. "Well, I actually know how bad I am, and the ones who get the A's know how good they are without these stupid grades to tell us," she continued. "All grades are for is to make the good people feel good about themselves and the bad people feel bad about themselves."

I have to say I agree. We grade people from the day they're born until they die. We compare each other's babies and wonder if my baby will have problems in life because he got his first tooth a month later than super-star baby Jack down the street. Or what if he can't walk before his first birthday? Then he may never get to play on the soccer team. Instead of marveling at the wonder it is that teeth actually grow through our gums, we compare the speed at which they grow. Instead of marveling that a kid actually can figure out how to multiply fractions, we compare them to the ones who can do algebra.

Our values system is all screwed up. Mine is. Instead of comparing myself and my accomplishments to what God is expecting from me, I compare myself and my accomplishments to the rest of the world. Who decides what is more important? Does the Bible spell out a list? Does it say there that in order to receive God's favor one must be five foot seven inches tall and wear a C cup? Does it say that good math grades are better than good grades in art? Does it say that the more money we have, the closer we are to heaven's gates?

It doesn't say exactly that, but it speaks a lot about God's unconditional love, about doing His will and about resting in His peace. To Kristin I say that when I look at her I don't care so much about what everybody else can do. All I want for her is to find her special gifts and get good at them. All I want for her is to feel happy and know that I'm proud of her no matter what, as long as she does her best, and doesn't give up. I wish I could remember that's exactly what God is trying to say to me too. He loves me—even though my stomach isn't flat, my writing is more spontaneous than organized, and I suck at the Karen language. He wants me to use my talents, however few, to glorify Him, serve others, and make the world a little happier.

That somebody will find a better way to help the people of Burma is as certain as it is that somebody will run faster than me, keep a cleaner desk, and make tastier canapés. And when they do, I can rejoice. *Good for them!* I can think. *These people have good talents, and so do I. I am, for example, very good at looking at people while they talk to me, and I've been told that I have a nice smile.*

WHY DID YOU JOIN THIS TRIBE OF PARTNERS?

"It must be so hard to work with refugees," people will say and look at me with jealous concern in their faces. "How do you handle all the suffering?" I tell them a little about how I handle it, and sometimes *not* handle it. But I rarely tell them that the thing harder than working with refugees is working with other people (all the ones who aren't refugees). They can be a real pain. They're also a lot of fun.

Some days I feel like I'm married to Partners. Not Partners as a legal entity, with the personnel manuals and the budgets, but to Partners, the flesh, blood, and bad breath—the staff, in other words. Most of them are the best kind of human beings you can find on the market nowadays. That they have chosen to work with us is a sign of God's mercy in my opinion.

Occasionally though, we run into some differences in the ways we want to do things. We get annoyed by each other's constant chatter or we can't figure out where to put each other on the flow charts. I personally find it hardest when my friends (staff, that is) don't want to be with me all the time—like, live with me. They're my family and I want to be with them as much a possible. But Steve is not into the idea of having them all move in with us, so I just have them over for dinner a lot. An okay compromise.

Working with Partners is more than just a job, I say, because this is definitely true for my family and me. It's a lifestyle. If you're looking for an 8:00–5:00 job and a thorough job description then you should apply to work somewhere else. But if you're looking for passion, love, no routines, little money, a cause to live for, and a lot of fun, then, yeah, come and join us!

Some years ago, Steve and I were waiting in line to cross the Thai-Burma border the legal way. What we were going to do was to just walk over the line that turned Thailand into Burma then turn around and walk back into Thailand again. When we got back to Thailand, a border official would stamp our passports and we'd be able to stay in Thailand for another three months. This was one way to stay and work in Thailand, but not a very good one. After a while we got an actual visa and had to deal with immigration officials only a few times a year (which, if you know immigration officials, is more than enough).

We were waiting in line together with mostly back-packers who also wanted to stay longer in the country where you can sleep in a guesthouse for only a few bucks a night and where pot is as cheap as candy. It was going to take a long time to reach the end of the line, and we were bored. In front of us was an interesting Rasta-dude. Steve has many gifts, and one of them is to befriend people wherever he is. So he tapped Rasta-man on the back and said, "Hi." It turned out that Rasta-man was friendly, though a little surprised to be approached by such clean-cut people as us.

He smiled under the red, green, and yellow Bob Marley hat that held the braids somewhat together. He wore a hand-woven shirt with stripes and loose-fitting pants, the kind that the farmers in Thailand wear. They are like a sarong with legs, extremely comfortable and good for the environment. That he was wearing sandals (Birkenstocks knockoffs) was no bombshell. What else would he possibly be wearing? Nikes? A tribal shoulder bag hung over one of his shoulders. In it, I imagine, was a copy of *The Bohemian Manifesto* and perhaps *How to Tie-dye a T-shirt*. Absolutely all back-packers carry a copy of some version of a *Lonely Planet* guide-book as well.

"Hi, I'm Steve. What's your name?" Steve said in his endearing way. "I am Rafael," said Rafael with a very French accent. "Nice to meet you, Rafael," we said. "What brings you to Thailand?" "Ouh, I am a chief," he said in a way that made us think that he felt like we should have assumed that already. "I am a tribal chief." "Really?" "Yes (dumb-heads), my tribe lives in Pai." "Well, Rafael, it's an honor to meet you. I've actually never met a tribal chief before," said Steve, acting as if it were a respectable job he had, leading a tribe of pot-smokers in the mountains of Pai. We talked a little longer about this and that, but we must have seemed very trivial to Rafael. When it was his turn to get his passport stamped he didn't even say goodbye and he never asked for our address.

As we walked away with a three-month visa freshly stamped in our passports, I nudged Steve. "You wish you could be a tribal chief too, eh?" Steve looked at me and smiled. "Yes, of course. I'd like to sit on a throne and have lots of women dance around me while I drink my tribal brew." "Get a life, Steve."

Then it dawned on me: "But you *are* a tribal chief already! You lead the tribe of Partners!" Steve's face lit up. We laughed at the idea and almost ran back to see if we could track Rafael down. "Hey, Rafael, I just remembered: I'm a tribal chief too. And this is the queen here. She dances really well when she's had some tribal brew."

The idea of a tribe kind of stuck. I read a leadership book where the author actually talked about tribal culture, and how we all end up belonging to some kind of tribe that we identify with. So when we planned the Partners retreat the next year, the theme had to be *The Tribe of Partners*.

For me, our staff retreats are the highlight of the year. They're like the dessert. We go to a nice place with a pool and air-conditioned rooms; we eat yummy food and have lots of coffee breaks with more pastries than we're able to finish. It's true luxury. Some people—like myself, I have to admit—have questioned the wisdom of doing this extravagant event every year. It does cost money too, you know. But then I get a lecture from Steve, the tribal chief: "Our staff works harder than many people I know. Most of them don't even get paid for the work they're doing (they're volunteers who raise their own support, you see, which means that to some of them splurging on a meal at a restaurant or spending a night in air-conditioned bliss is out of their budget), we don't give them any benefits (other than a job that's mostly exciting and helps save lives), no retirement plans—shoot, not even a good job description in many cases. I think that the very least we can do for them is to give them this gift once a year."

This is true, and when I come to my senses, I see that a staff retreat is a small price to pay in order to keep our tribe happy.

The other thing about the retreats is that for years they have been my creative outlet, a place where I've felt like I could put my wackiness to good use. We do all kinds of crazy events (that usually involve getting dressed up in some outrageous costumes), games, dances, songs, and other stuff that make us laugh so hard we think we may fall over. I have fallen off my chair laughing on at least one occasion. It's true.

I made Steve and me costumes from fake leopard skin. We put on some facial paint and looked very tribal, especially Steve in his primitive skirt and hairy legs. Our kids and some of the other kids joined us in a dance to officially start the retreat. Then we gave everybody a carton of juice that we mixed together to make a tribal brew and we danced around the totem pole that was decorated with portraits of each one of the Partners tribe members. Later we spent time making head ornaments, chants, and even some other costumes. Stu got into his role more than the average staff member. He got himself a small sub-tribe with Craig as his closest follower. Their tribe's main objective was to have fun. Some of us liked our head garments so much that we wore them to the teaching sessions.

The teaching was about how to be a victorious tribe. Our good friend, Glen (whom Steve frequently refers to as Obi-Wan Kenobi), had so many revolutionary ideas about how we could stay unified, reach our goals and overcome obstacles that it made our jaws drop open and we wanted to drink some more tribal brew in celebration. I won't list all the points Glen made, but I'm sure he'll be happy to send you his notes if you want to learn how your tribe can overcome the enemy.

There was, however, one question that Glen asked, that has stayed with me since, and it was: *Why did you join this tribe of Partners?*

I still remember that day, sitting in the cozy meeting room at the Chiang Mai Sports Club. (That was the name of the hotel since it had a cement tennis court, a moldy squash court, a few sets of weights and an Olympic-size pool.) I was listening to the cicadas outside and the humming noise of the air-conditioner inside. *Why did we join this group of wild people (or so it seemed after the last days of tribal ecstasy)? Stu was grunting and Craig was making sure his feathers were straight.* It was certainly not the money. I'll be as frank as to say that it wasn't because of our good looks either. It could've been the nice staff retreats, but that was unlikely.

The answers were revealing. We did a brainstorming-thing where we just shouted out all the words that came to our minds instead of going into long elaborate devotionals about why we were here today. I liked it that way. It got to the core of things, broke it down to atoms. When we were done, the core looked something like this:

On the edge, Adventure, Family, Community, Passionate, Love, Excitement, Not normal, Faith, Fast, True, Moving, Risk, Risk-takers, Giving, Fun, Fearless, Different, Unorthodox, Bent, People-focused, Righteous, Justice.

The list went on for a while, but the words were similar. I wrote them down in my journal and marveled at what I read. There was not a single word on the list saying anything about refugees, about Burma, about sustainable development, relief, strategy plans or advocacy. Not one word. The critic may say that our staff just assumed that we all knew that we were there because of Than Shwe[19] and the mess he and his team have made out of Burma, which is probably true.

But I think there was another message there too: people joined our tribe because they wanted to be a part of a movement of people who put community and love before results and strategic thinking. Our people liked to be different than the masses, to take chances and risks in the name of righteousness. They liked to live for something bigger than themselves and while doing this, having fun with the adventure. It appeared that flow-charts didn't make it on the list.

I looked around the room—which I do frequently during all our staff retreats— and, as usual, I got tears in my eyes. (This sounds so cliché that I hardly dare to write it, but it's true. I've always had a hard time holding my tears back and it's embarrassing at times.)

Here was a group of people that looked like very unlikely candidates to change the world. I didn't know how many of us could even change a tire. There were people from ten different nations, and several different ethnic groups sitting there. Some had good degrees, others didn't. Most spoke English, but many didn't. There were children crawling and giggling, some of them whispering secrets to their best friends. We weren't sure how we were going to pay for this retreat, much less how we were going to meet next year's budget. Some people were spending their own savings in order to stay with us and work with us. There were people who could've had a successful and lucrative career in the world, with money by the truckload. There were people who had risked a lot to get here from Burma. There were Thais who said they were Buddhists in their villages, but who worshipped Jesus when they were with us. There was my former drug-dealing husband and me.

What an unlikely crowd to make it! What an unlikely flock to succeed at anything really important, other than making cute head garments! What a good opportunity for God to do something!

We wanted to be a victorious tribe, so we'd take Glen's words to heart and do our best. But I think that most of us also felt that some setbacks and defeats would not be failures as long as we stuck together, loved, and forgave each other. Success would be to still believe in each

---

19   This Burmese military leader was chairman of the SPDC and head of state from 1992 -2011.

other when some of us tried to climb the mountain, graceless and slow, but determined to never give up. Success would be to help each other get back on track again when we fell all the way down to the ground. Success would be to cheer when one of us made it to the top while some of us were still fumbling around way down close to the ground.

It wasn't long after this retreat that many of us actually attempted to climb a mountain together. I need to share that story.

THE TRIBAL CHALLENGE

I'm not sure why Partners doesn't attract the super-star athletes of the world. Our friends and co-laborers, the ones we look up to with shameless admiration, the Free Burma Rangers, get all those. They have the staff with the high cheekbones and abs that look like washboards. They grit their teeth and go running for hours while the sun is blazing and the landscape only provides uphills. Their staff does push-ups before all their meetings and they don't consider sleep a daily necessity.

We want to be like the FBR too, and we have from time to time made moves to get there. The results have not been very convincing. During our staff retreat that focused on us as a tribe, I bravely arranged the first (and, as it turned out, only) Partners tribal challenge. I really wanted our staff to get in shape and to discover the vast joy of exercise. What feeling can compare to the feeling of a body spent after a strenuous workout, a shower, and then some ice-cold OJ for reward? I can only think of a few.

Optimistically, I challenged all my fellow tribe members to something that I figured we all could manage: over the next couple of days walk or run five kilometers and swim five hundred meters. None of it needed to be done all at one time; they could swim a lap a day and do a kilometer in the morning and one in the evening for the whole retreat. A mouse could manage more.

I got up with the sun the next morning and did some half-hearted stretches while waiting for all our staff that, no doubt, were just around the corner, ready to start the day—and their new life— with a leisurely jog through the sleepy neighborhood. After forty-five minutes of doing the only three stretches I know, I had to admit that I'd have to do the run by myself. While doing the short loop I wished that I had followed my gut and promised the winner of the race a flat-screen TV. Instead we had agreed that nobody needed to be special and the reward for completing the race would simply be the feeling of satisfaction. Any moron should have seen that would not motivate anyone.

At breakfast our tribe happily indulged in scrambled eggs or the Thai version of breakfast: a spicy rice soup with herbs and fried garlic. "Where were you, guys?" I asked, trying to look incredibly pleased with my fantastic morning run. They had mostly been enjoying the cozy beds, and some had been out praying. None seemed particularly unhappy about missing the run. In fact, they all seemed … content.

For the rest of the weekend I kept asking for volunteer runners, and every time they all had much more important things to do such as reading a book by the pool, going for coffee in the lobby or taking a nap. The end of the story was that four people completed the challenge, and Steve and I were two of them. Steve, of course, only did it because he felt sorry for me and was worried about the consequences if he didn't go for a sweaty run around the compound. I really wanted to reward Shaune and Chris with a flat-screen TV for their amazing feats, but they just got a compliment.

You may think that I'm writing this to point out that our staff is lazy. Not so. They just don't like to run much and that Olympic-sized pool was very long. They also have an above-average ability to enjoy life and to take joy in life's simple pleasures such as foot massages, magazines, and afternoon tea. In today's busy world where people fall over from burnout left and right, this is an important skill to have. Besides, Partners staff members are way better administrators than FBR, and we keep our office much cleaner than they do.

It was around the time of the above-mentioned staff retreat, however, that some of our staff members decided they wanted to go a tad more hardcore. We do some work in Shan State, a place in Burma that used to have their own independence, rulers, and traditions. The Shan are beautiful people, many living high in the foothills of the Himalayas. We were slowly falling in love with them, like we had done with the Karen. They are resilient and determined to survive, a thing you cannot take for granted if you're an ethnic group in Burma. The Army has been doing its utmost to erase the Shan from the territories they've owned for centuries. The methods are familiar: pillaging, torture, rape, the burning of entire villages, slave labor, forced relocation, arbitrary arrests, and denial of healthcare and education. It's a simple way to get rid of an entire people group and to keep the ones who survive in the dark.

There is a military outpost that belongs to the Shan right on the Thai-Burma border. The outpost has turned into a refugee camp as well since people feel protected from the attacks of the enemy there. While there, I sometimes have to remind myself of the terrors of the war, because the surroundings are spectacular. It looks so peaceful and the air tastes like freedom. The place reminds me of a medieval fortress on the top of the mountain, fenced in by hundreds of other peaks, stretching high and far.

While we were getting started with our work there, we were told that most of the time we'd have to walk to the camp. There is a road leading there, but it wasn't advisable to drive since, strictly speaking, we were doing something illegal by crossing the border into Burma. (I always struggled with this. Who talks about *illegal?* We wanted to cross the border to help people in need that were deprived of their basic human rights because of what? An illegal government, who, I believe, had not done a legal act during their whole time in power. They may have driven on the right side of the road, but that was about it.)

A group of our staff was going to do the walk there, up the mountain. They were going to help train medics and do other meaningful work together with FBR. There was no doubt that they'd be immensely useful once they got there. The challenge was, however, that they had to get there on foot. The tribe that had preferred the bed to a 5K run was looking at a substantial challenge. The hike would be strenuous, and there'd be no coffee shops along the way.

Six weeks before the trip we started training for the hike by doing walks up a local mountain. Walking up and down the mountain a few times would give the impression of being in the jungles and mountains of Shan State. Of course, it would be seven times longer and harder ... but still. The first hike we did will forever be etched into our memories as a milestone in Partners' history. There were Greg, Craig, Shaune, a few volunteers, plus Steve and me. Steve was the Commander in Chief. "We'll be walking at soldier pace today," he said. "That means we won't take many breaks and we need to keep a steady pace." "Yesss, sir!" We were all excited about the challenge and ready to venture into the wild unknown of Doi Suthep Mountain (There is also a three-lane paved road up to the top of the mountain where Thailand's most revered temple lays. Thousands of tourists flock there daily, so to call the mountain a *wilderness* may be a stretch. Although, where *we* walked, we were alone with the snakes, spiders, and vines that hang from the trees like Oriental Christmas ornaments). The goal was to make it up and down the mountain in less than two hours.

Greg carried so much water with him that he would've been better off paying for a pack mule to help him carry all the bottles. It was no surprise to those of us who knew Greg. He's a man who likes to plan for the unexpected and who rarely is unprepared in any situations. In fact, Greg is a man you want to have on your team on any mission, be it a war or a camping trip, because he thinks of everything, worst-case as well as best-case scenarios. And one thing is for certain: you won't go hungry if you follow Greg. It's great to have a person like him on our team because he helps us remember, in our enthusiasm, that (for example) we need money to accomplish some of our zealous goals. He analyzes and details, and recalls facts as if they were … facts. Then he gently reminds us to get down to earth.

The amazing thing with Greg is that he sticks around, year after year. He was our first staff member, and he's stayed with us through the very worst. And he'd tell you so himself, it hasn't always been easy. I think there are days he'd rather have worked at a bank. If loyalty could be described as a person, it would be called Greg.

So Greg grunted under the weight of his water bottles and trotted on. It's pretty in the jungle, especially after the cacophony of the monsoon season is gone and the trees and birds once more display their beauty in song and color. We chitchatted up the slow slope that was surprisingly easy.

A ways up the trail we passed a waterfall that was a refreshing sight for us who were used to the concrete jungle of Chiang Mai. The water rushing down the rocks while lush bushes and jungle flowers line the sides was therapeutic. We had to walk on a teak log to cross over a trickle of the waterfall, and the log marked the end of easy and the beginning of hard.

Our friends looked bewildered. This trail was going up at a grade that seemed unacceptable. We had to take a break. Some snacks were passed around and Greg emptied one of his bottles. We could do this. And here the fun began.

For the rest of the walk the trail inclined at an unmerciful angle. The uphill was very much up. At first we just endured by leaning forward and battling the hill like we imagined soldiers would. But when it never got easier, Craig started cussing.

I think this illustrates more than anything how hard it must have been because Craig doesn't cuss. He's one of those very straight Christian guys who thinks *stupid* is a bad word and who will have a Coke when we have a beer. I love Craig for all his conservative straightness and his uncluttered life. He has showed me that a person can have fun even though he goes to church every Sunday. I think he's twice as tall as me and perhaps three times as animated. This is why, when Craig has something on his heart, we all know about it. Like Tony Soprano (this is Steve's nickname for him) he waves and gestures and speaks loudly and makes even a very small story into a very entertaining one.

He takes you seriously, Craig does. Most of our staff put him on their list of 'My Best Friends in the World.' This is 100% true. He makes us all feel like we're so special and our problems are so interesting and he can't think of any better way to spend his workday than to sit on a chair and listen to us share about our very hard lives. It's also nice to have somebody so uncluttered around. I bet you could lick his desk and not even get a speck of dust on your tongue, and there won't even be an ice-cream wrapper on the floor of his car. When it comes to work, he helps us do one thing at the time and not fill our days with all kinds of *pjatt* (which is a Norwegian word for *nonsense*). My personal interest in Craig is that he makes me a better English-writer since he has edited most of my writing. He restructures sentences and points out grammatical errors. He straightens out the hodgepodge of my jumbled thoughts and then says that I'm a great writer. If *that's* not a good friend, I don't know what is.

But here we were and Craig was cussing. He blamed us all for taking him up there and when we encountered a cement pole on the trail he ran (well, *ran* may be an exaggeration) to it and hugged it as if he hadn't seen a sign of civilization for weeks. We named the pole *The Pole of Civilization* and the hill became *Craig's Cussing Hill*.

By now there wasn't a lot of talking. There was a lot of breathing. Someone could have easily followed our trail by the drops of sweat and tears that were left behind us. Shaune was crying. "It was all no use," she kept saying behind me. "What was no use?" "All the exercise I've been doing the last months and now look at me. If I can't even get up this mountain how can I ever make it to Shan State? I'm turning around and going back home now."

The single mom who had come to Thailand and joined Partners with almost no money and a teenage daughter whom she home-schooled was saying she wanted to quit! I don't think so. Shaune, I think, is the inspiration for the title of the book *Good to Great*. She keeps getting prettier and smarter and kinder, and if she keeps it up I think we need to tell her she's too good for us. She's a nurse whom I admire for her skills and her commitment to sick people. I can hardly see blood or smell disease before I get nauseous and feel like I've been riding a roller coaster. Shaune cares for refugee patients in all kinds of conditions and she doesn't even plug her nose. She does her work with tenderness and love and she genuinely cares about the sick. I've known her to spend her free days going to hospitals to visit and check up on patients that Partners is responsible for. Many times I know it's not strictly necessary, but St. Shaune goes anyway. She really wanted to do this trip because she wanted to help the Shan, but it was also a personal challenge for her. She needed to lose weight and get in shape. This trip would motivate her to do both. But now she wanted to quit.

"No way, Jose," I said, putting on my bossy attitude. "We're going to make it to the top today. Let's not think about the hike to Shan State now, but about making it to the top of this mountain." And then we kept going. The hill of this particular breakdown was later named *Shaune's Slope of Tears*.

The rest of the hike up was uneventful in that we had no more breakdowns, less cussing from Craig (he was too tired to say much any more), and no major accidents. Greg kept emptying water bottles like a water-holic. Not much was said. The last part of the hike was the steepest and unfriendliest. But then we were at the top. Like rugged wanderers who had fought our way through the Gobi Desert our team stumbled over the invisible finish line and fell down to the ground, heaving for more oxygen.

Then we had to go back down—which, it turned out, was very hard too. Now we had to figure out how to get our legs to go down the hill before the rest of our body. There was some tumbling and almost falling, but no broken bones. At some point I was having a conversation with Greg, but he was uncharacteristically silent. I turned around to find that he wasn't there. I knew he'd been right behind me only seconds ago. While I was wondering what had happened he crawled out of a hole he'd fallen into. He brushed grass and branches off himself and kept on walking. The hole may have been the home of unnamed critters. But now, half way down the trail, we had another landmark: *Greg's Hole*.

About four hours after we started, we were back down by the trailhead. It was not looking good for Shan State. While we were happy to have accomplished such a strenuous achievement, our team was a bit discouraged too. We had spent twice as long as the longest time we were supposed to spend. I was slightly pessimistic. At this rate, we wouldn't even be a challenge for soldiers or tigers.

It was time for some straight talk. Shaune said, "You can just tell me now. I know I can't go to Shan State." But the ever-optimistic Steve had a different idea. "I think today was a success," he said, and I wondered if he understood the meaning of *success*. "Really, it was. None of us gave up. We all made it up and then down again, didn't we? We didn't do it as fast as we need to, but that can be fixed. I say you do this trail a few times a week for the next few weeks and then we'll time you again before we need to make the final decision."

For the next weeks there was indeed a steady stream of us walking and running up and down the trail at all times of the day. Half way up the trail there's a Buddhist temple with orange-robed monks meditating their days away. It must have been a curious sight for them watching us pace back and forth. Thais generally don't walk if they have the option to drive. And they especially don't like to walk in the jungle. The one and only reason they would be on the trail that we frequented was if they were making merit, making up for something bad they had done, to make their karma better. I wonder what kind of heinous crime the monks imagined we'd done while they watched us running back and forth like chickens.

Already after a few weeks our team was making speed records. We had so many fun memories of our early morning treks that I felt that even if Shan State got its freedom before our team got there, the training for the trip would've been worth it. Shaune went on to become fitness mama and the Shan's answer to Mother Teresa. Greg was able to speed-walk part of the way and with much less water than he thought he'd need. I think he memorized the posts on our budget in order to stay focused. Craig once brought his teenage daughter to do the hike with him, and he was pleased to announce that he smoked her, and I'm pretty sure that there was no cussing.

The trek to Shan State was eventful and dramatic and worthy of another chapter in my book. Suffice it to say, there were tales of people getting lost, of walking in utter blackness, and of sliding down hills into the darkness.

I didn't get to go on the trip and was unbelievably envious. When they came back down from their otherworldly adventure, however, I had them over for cinnamon rolls and coffee and got to hear the stories. Craig gesticulated the most and had stories more incredible than Lemuel Gulliver. The rest of the team just said it had been great and they wanted to go again. Which all of them did.

MARVELOUS MARV

At the Partners office we all eat lunch together at noon. We pull out the woven straw mats and we sit on the floor eating our rice or noodles from environmentally-destructive Styrofoam boxes. (In Thailand it's impossible to get your lunch served in anything but plastic bags or Styrofoam. It's one of the stressful things about living there.) My personal favorite is a bag of sticky rice and a plate of freshly made Som Tam, a salad made from grated unripe papaya, three cayenne peppers, peanuts, tomatoes, loads of raw garlic, palm sugar, and fish sauce. I think I could eat that for lunch for the rest of my days and still be content. The Som Tam is sweet, sour, and spicy. "And, please, no raw field crabs," I tell Bom before she heads off to get our lunch orders.

Bom has worked with us pretty much since Partners came into being. She is a Thai lady in her late forties and is as much of a fixture in our office as our desks and computers. I think that if she disappeared, Partners would cease to exist. She came to our office years ago looking for work. Steve came home that afternoon and said he'd hired her. "She was so cute and I didn't have the heart to reject her," was his reason for employing her. "We don't have the money to pay her," he admitted," and I'm not really sure what we'll have her do, but I'll think of something." These were the early days of Partners where it was a privilege just to have a desk. We got exasperated with employees who expected Partners to pay for their ballpoint pens. A salary was a rare benefit.

Bom started out by cleaning the office and doing other odd jobs. We paid her almost nothing, and that gave us a bad conscience. One day Steve found her a job as an assistant teacher at an international school. She would be earning loads, and she would get to do something more fun than cleaning toilets. She used to be a teacher, so this would be a dream job. When he announced the good news to Bom, she cried. "I don't care about the money and the new job," she said. "What I want to do is to work here with Khun Steve (Mr. Steve) and Partners forever." So she stayed. Later, after we had given her some English lessons, she confirmed her commitment to us by writing us a note that said, "I want to work with you infinity."

Over the years her responsibilities have increased, and her salary has gone up to where it should be. She still cleans the office, but now she also is the person who goes to get us our lunch every day. Plus she spends hours and hours stuffing envelopes and sending out all the thousands of pieces of literature we produce. Not many people in the world have stuffed as many envelopes as Bom has. But she makes the job a culinary experience together with all the other Thais and Karen who usually join her doing it. They sit together on the floor chatting, putting pieces of paper into envelopes, and snacking on deep-fried beetles or fried pork rinds.

At around eleven o'clock she will show up by each of our desks with a piece of paper and a pen. With the cutest smile in the world, she walks from desk to desk saying in English, "Lunch?" We tell her if we want Kaw Man Gai, Phat Pak Ruam, Khaw Soi, or other Thai dishes that cost us about fifty cents each. Then she gets on her little motorbike and drives off to markets and restaurants getting us exactly what we ordered. Is it any wonder that we love her?

The fact that Bom works with us proves she is a risk-taker. So does the fact that she has gone rock climbing with our tribe. When we had a staff day at the newly-opened ice-skating rink in Chiang Mai, Bom had the most fun dancing tango with a chair the whole time. (The rink only stayed open some months then they ran out of money to pay the power bills.) At our staff retreats she goes all the way out with her costumes. On our last retreat she came dressed up as a rich man from Bangkok. She wore a pink suit, sunglasses, and had her hair combed back in a lazy style. She acted in a play where she wanted to marry the poor peasant girl.

We rarely see Bom not smiling. It looks like she must have a good life. It's not so easy, however. She lives in a small village about forty-five minutes away from our office. She drives her motorbike that entire way every morning. You may think that sounds like a refreshing way to start the day, but the reality is that it's like trying to get yourself killed every day. At seven in the morning it appears that all the people behind wheels are on speed, and that half the country decided to hit the road at the same time.

Her husband had an accident some years ago and was unable to work any more. Recently he passed away, leaving Bom to provide for her family by herself. Her mother-in-law also stays at her home, and, though I have never met her, I think she may be in the class of "not the best-mother-in-law-in-the-world". With her meager salary, Bom provides for her daughter, and mother-in-law. It's a good thing, Bom says, that she has her dog Frank. He understands her and listens to her when she's down. And when she's at the office and has a break, she sings one of her favorite songs with Dorothy: *Que Sera Sera*. The two of them make a fine duo, but not as fine as Bom and Dorothy's husband, Marv were. In the early morning hours, before the cockroaches had gone into their hiding places, Marv and Bom would practice tap dancing. This would be before Marv pulled out the day's Bangkok Post and started reading out loud from the news.

Marv made a game of the news. He read them to the Thais and made every event exciting by exchanging all the names with Chiang Mai. It's amazing all the things that took place in Chiang Mai during the course of a day.

Marv had to take many breaks during the day because he had cancer and he was in his mid-seventies. He would lie down on the couch at the office and take a nap sometimes before he walked all the steps up to his office, which we often referred to as The Laboratory. Marv stayed away from computers. He liked to be hands-on with stuff, whether it was people, plants, or pigs. Actually, Marv's first claim to fame was by introducing soap-making technologies to our staff, and, little by little, to Thailand and Burma. It seems like a small thing—soap. But not when you put it together with Marv. Then you got the feeling that simply producing the right kind of soap could solve all the world's problems.

Marv and his wife Dorothy were some of our longest-lasting friends, and some days I think of them as an extra set of parents. We had met them more than twenty years ago and my first memory of them is when they showed up at the parking lot in the apartment building we lived at in Las Vegas (Yes, Las Vegas) with the biggest camper you've ever seen. I think it was a hundred years old and it drank gasoline like an elephant drinks water at the water hole. The camper was a gift from them because they'd heard we were too poor to buy a car, and this was Vegas. Steve and I tried getting around town on our bicycles, which was possibly more dangerous than Bom riding her motorbike through town early in the morning. Dorothy and Marv also wanted to bless us with some furniture. They had filled the camper with the humongousest set of couches and recliners I had ever seen. It confirmed my childhood beliefs that everything in America was enormously huge. Steve and I, newly married and penni-less, but still with a certain taste when it came to interior design, looked at the furniture and gulped. "It won't fit," was all Steve said and Dorothy and Marv got the message.

From that day on they continued to shower us with blessings. These blessings came in the form of carrot muffins and tea, houseplants and baby clothes, toddler clothes and big-girl clothes, books, music, art supplies, toys, uncountable meals, money, and art from Japan.

During some of the hardest years while we had small kids, little money, too much work and too many problems, going to stay with them at their nutty place in Utah was like an oasis where we just drank in their hospitality and friendliness. We poured our hearts out as if they were the Catholic priests in the confession booth and we were about to die. I actually think they saved our lives on more than one occasion.

Then Marv got cancer and it was as if the world was not real. It simply couldn't be that Marv would die, now when we'd given him grandchildren and all. (Dorothy and Marv never had any kids. They gave birth to twins at about the same time that Steve was born, but, sadly, they died. They never had more children.) The doctors didn't give Marv much of a chance to sur-vive beyond a few years—I think four at the most. He was driving around on the lawn mower with Naomi on his lap and they were having such a fun time and I thought about how sad it would be to lose him.

Both had jobs back then. They've always been working below their pay grade because I think they believe it's more important to make an impact in people's lives than to earn a lot of money. Marv was actually a genius. I'm not kidding. He used to work in a chemical lab forever ago, and you could tell that he knew his stuff when he got going on chemistry. (I started thinking about cake recipes because I couldn't follow his talk at all.) There was a problem at the lab though. Marv's partner had secretly been making LSD instead of medicine like Marv thought. That ended their friendship. Marv lost his business and a lot of money and never really got back into chemistry after that, not until he started making Marv's Marvelous Soap.

When Marv got cancer, he and Dorothy took a serious look at each other and their lives. Marv was facing the end of his life. How did he want to spend those last years—on his recliner watching Discovery channel?

In Marv's own words, he wanted to leave this world with a bang. So they decided to pack up their home, quit their jobs and move to Thailand and join our tribe. I have to be honest and tell you that at first I thought they were joking. How many people do you know in their sixties (They were both in their mid and late sixties when they joined Partners) and with cancer that move to a totally new culture and work with a group of people who all are slightly loopy? Morphy and Darv did it. They made the big leap to the great unknown of Partners' world. Not unexpectedly our whole family fell in love with them the way we had.

Dorothy, you know, drives me crazy on occasion. The reason is that she always acts like Jesus and it makes me feel like the dirty rag I sometimes am. I'm not joking about this. She's so committed to doing the right thing and to giving everybody else the best that I know that if I comment on her nice shirt, she'll take it off right there and give it to me. It's just how she is. She is by far the most generous person I have ever met. She ended up doing the finances at Partners (poor lady). It's a big job and she thinks that this is why she comes to work every day. The rest of us know that she's there to be everybody's mother and the shoulder we all cry on. She's the person who makes sure justice happens to all, and if we don't take care of somebody she'll personally meet the need. Do you have any idea how many meals she and Marv provided for lost souls, and how many nights a week somebody was sleeping over at their house? They all thought they were the most special ones in Dorothy and Marv's lives because that's how they treated everybody.

The Thai and the Karen staff in particular took a liking to Dorothy and Marv. They thought they were amazing. The most astounding thing was that they could do so many things at such an advanced age—driving a car, for example. They still think it's quite impressive that Dorothy wears pants, drives a truck, and that she even still has teeth in her mouth.

Marv started making soap and training people from Burma and Thailand to do the same. He was not one to brag about his accomplishments, Marv. He was just there doing his thing while the rest of us were proclaiming our achievements to all. One day he'd do training for an MP or some influential businessperson. The next day he would be at the woman's prison training young single mothers in the art of soap-making. In Shan State and Karen State and in the villages of Northern Thailand they're now making soap the way that Marv taught them. It's improving hygiene and creating sustainable jobs. The Thais named him *Ajarn Sabuu*—a very impressive title that means Professor Soap. None of us has a title like that. We were simply just the Ajarn's friends.

Then Marv discovered Moringa. This is a leaf that's been around for thousands of years. Moringa works like magic: it can rebuild weak bones, enrich anemic blood, and enable a malnourished mother to nurse her starving baby. One ounce of Moringa has the same amount of calcium as four glasses of milk, as much Vitamin C as seven oranges, and the potassium of three bananas. If you put some of it in dirty water, it turns the water drinkable. What other plant on earth has the same qualities? The Moringa is a tree, and because of Marv and his companion Boonsong, a Thai Karen, we now have thousands of them at the Partners farm. The verdant leaves will provide essential nutrition for thousands of people in Burma.

There was a lot of talk about Moringa at our office. One day Marv declared that he could pee straight and had gotten darker hair since eating the leaf three times a day. He even whispered in Bom's ear that perhaps Dorothy was pregnant at sixty-five. We were served Moringa tea whether we wanted it or not. Soon we will be the healthiest and the prettiest charity in the world—all because of Marv and the miraculous Moringa.

"There are no little people in Partners," Steve says regularly. It's true. There are only giants working with us. If they weren't, they wouldn't stick around. Marv stayed with us, serving and loving us, listening to us, and making us laugh until the cancer took him away. He had no living relatives when he died, yet he was surrounded by people who loved him, people who called him father, daddy, grandpa, mentor, and friend. He didn't teach Bom to dance, but he taught us all how to live a little more, to love a little more, and to laugh because life is short.

EXCUSE ME, MADAM, BUT WHAT ARE YOU DOING HERE?

Part of my job consists of speaking. This is a great benefit in my life. I love to speak, and the fact that I get to go to places (like New Zealand), speaking to people from all kinds of weird, beautiful, and interesting backgrounds is not unappealing. One of the most wonderful things about Partners is that we're a big, global family, and on my speaking tours I get to meet the people who make our work in Burma possible. And I get to encourage people to join the family. There have been times when I've driven for seven hours just to have four people show up. That can be disheartening. But mostly I enjoy it, even if it is a small group in somebody's living room. That's where I've had some of my best talks.

Sometimes though, I get to go to huge buildings, speaking to people with huge influence. Those are the times when I question my own IQ and abilities to retain facts and logical thoughts. Yes, and of course I wonder if there was a mess-up and they sent the wrong person.

Once I was going to London to speak about Partners, Burma and the refugees. One of the places I was going to was the Parliament. I had been rehearsing for weeks.

Between getting my family ready for my absence by writing lists for my husband, I'd read the documents sent to me by my very intelligent friend John, who seemed to spend a good portion of his life at the Parliament. I tried to understand the new vocabulary that included such words as *repugnance*. This ended up being a very useful word that described my feelings exactly about the regime in Burma, and apparently some politicians felt a lot of repugnance as well. This was reassuring.

When not reading challenging documents or preparing my family for my absence, we also spent a bit of time discussing how I was going to transport my luggage all over London and other places I was going. I'd be doing all my traveling on the train and it needed to be easy to get my stuff on and off and from one station to another. We settled for a rather large backpack. In it I could fit all my clothes, my computer, and all the Partners literature that I needed to take with me to my meetings. I dug out all my warm clothes from my closet that mainly had warm weather outfits, and I was off for the jungles of London.

I soon discovered something very important about Londoners: like me, most of them did all their travels on the train and subways, but none of them wore a green Marmot rain jacket, a hand-knitted red and black wool sweater and a backpack the size of their own body. They wore long black coats and carried their luggage in designer-made roll-on suitcases that were just the right size. I stuck out considerably. Obviously I didn't belong in this jungle and somebody could easily eat me. For days I criss-crossed the country, and saw landscapes that reminded me of Postman Pat's world as well as Dickens' descriptions of English landscape. Stone fences looked a hundred years old, and behind the antique windows everybody must have been having their afternoon tea. I was an outsider watching an exhibition.

Reality always struck when I had to get off and start figuring out where I was on a map that looked like an illustration of lots of yarn in different colors. I needed to find which color yarn I had arrived on, and which color I was getting on next. Then I joined the other millions who were running to catch their trains, looking super-stressed, all the while looking at my watch. Would I make it on this one or would I have to wait for the whole two minutes it'd take until the next train arrived? I was proud of myself until I saw my image in a store window: a short person with bushy hair wearing a green jacket and a knitted sweater, carrying a backpack that was too big. I looked like a Norwegian mountain woman who had accidentally ended up in the big city. And when I thought about it, that's exactly what I was.

The day I was going to visit the Parliament started like many other days: by getting on the train early in the morning. The particular raw cold that felt like the ghost of Bloody Mary penetrated me in spite of my wool sweater. I tried forcing my teeth to stop clattering while the scenery zoomed past in route to Gordon Brown's domain. I read through the piles of documents outlining government funding, the government's stand on cross-border aid and the policies that needed to be in place before this and that time. Sanctions were an issue then, as they still are, and there were plenty of good arguments from both camps. I felt dizzy.

Politics has always been a bit of a passion for me. I think I would've made a bad politician though because I lose my temper too often, and I don't pay enough attention to detail. This would've been my death. But still I often imagine myself articulating my arguments in such a way that the only outcome is victory. Over the years I have interacted with a number of professional politicians, and I've observed that for many, their passion seems to be more to enrich their own career than to do what is morally right. I wonder if that is how I would've become had I chosen the way of legislation and policy.

My documents were full of important and meaningful content, but they were still just words. As the delicate flower gardens of rural England gave way to industrial chimneys I had to remind myself that this trip was not about me speaking eloquently and having memorized the facts and the different positions. This was about speaking for people who are alive and who are afraid that soon they won't be. Their stories had been given to me and it was my job to make them heard.

I met John at the station and he was going to be my guide and protector for the day. John is very English, and although I'm not actually able to distinguish Oxford English, I'm sure that's what he speaks. He sounds so smart that no matter what he says, the rest of us who have the other accents, agree. He couldn't miss me. This morning, as all other mornings, I alone was wearing a backpack. John was probably looking at the newsstand behind me, but to me it looked like his eyes moved from my pack to my green jacket and the wool sweater that stuck out under it. He just said "Hi" in his usual friendly manner, but what I heard was, "Oh, God! Am I to take *her* to the Parliament? We'll be lucky if they even let us in." I was experiencing what is called extreme insecurity.

There was a long line in front of the sacred building. These were all the tourists from afar who had come to see one of London's many attractions. I wondered if they knew that I wasn't one of them, but that I actually had meetings set up inside. I walked past the hundreds, following John and trying to look important.

The guard took one quick look at me. "She cannot go inside without first standing in line." I knew what he was thinking too. "That lady looks like she's going on a hike in our halls. I don't believe she has any meetings scheduled." John resorted to using all his charm, his diplomatic skills, his Parliament pass with a photo of himself, and his watch. "We have a meeting with John Burkow at 9:00 a.m. for which we cannot be late. You may call him to confirm. I come here all the time. Please be so kind."

With a deep sigh and a look that approved of John (but not of me), the guard let us through.

Now we were inside the building and it filled me with awe and jealousy. Here people in suits and high heels ran to and fro with important looks on their faces. There were people talking with loud hand and arm gestures, while others were having a cup of coffee whilst reading important documents. The people here were running a nation and also influencing the world. Me, I was an unprofessional aid worker without the right degree, with too little money to actually make any headlines, working with one of the smallest charities in the world. To confirm my low class I carried a backpack with me all day—like a yoke, and I wore a rain jacket. I wondered how I had ended up here.

While John took a small detour to the bathroom I enjoyed the sights: art on the walls, vaulted ceilings, famous people. "Excuse me, madam, but what are you doing here? May I have a look at your pass?" A guard in uniform and a hat was talking to me. I woke up from daydreaming and asked him to repeat his question. "Well, you don't look like you belong here and I would like to see your pass and take a security check on you." I must have looked doomed.

"You see, nobody has ever come here carrying such a big backpack and it looks a little suspicious." I totally agreed with him, but would he understand if I told him I had traveled from Bristol on the train this morning and I was going to Sheffield the same evening? Of all the other things I carried with me, I had two pounds of icing for Sonya's wedding cake in my backpack, because she couldn't get icing in Mae Sot, Thailand. She was going to marry a Karen resistance leader and she really wanted a white cake on her special day. I had nowhere to put my stuff because there are no lockers in London. And I was here to speak for IDPs who are displaced in the jungles of Burma, and if nobody helps them then they'll die. Luckily John came just in time to prevent me from getting thrown out of Parliament. He used his charm again, and the guard gave me—or maybe it was John—a look of pity before letting us head for the MP's office.

Mr. John Burkow's office was a beehive of activity. There were little bees running in all directions, making photocopies and this and that. It was like Mr. Burkow's own world up there on the fourth floor where his office was. The world was overlooking Big Ben, and I thought that he must be one of the more important MPs in the building since he had the office with a view of one of London's big treasures.

The room fell silent as I entered. I knew it! It was the backpack again. They don't carry them in London and especially not where I was now. For some seconds I could hear a pin drop. "Hi, is it okay if I move in with you?" I asked bravely. People smiled and went back to their photocopying.

John Burkow himself came and shook hands with us, ordered us some espresso and took us to his nook, a friendly room with the best view of Big Ben. "So, tell me what's on your heart," he said while leaning back in his office chair. He appeared to have all the time in the world. I got the feeling that I was talking to a friend, not somebody who spent his days making laws. I forgot all the difficult words from the documents I had been reading, and told the story of Partners instead. I talked about the people we wanted to help, and how hard it is to do so without money. I talked about the need for help in the areas where big aid organization don't dare to go, but we do. Of course, I mentioned that we only dared to go because we did so with our big and tough brothers and sisters from FBR. This he had no problem understanding. He knew FBR, and now he knew me. I think that was all he needed to know. This man had such an intoxicating sense of humor that soon we were laughing at his jokes, and he added some new words to my limited English vocabulary. Then he shared about his time with the refugees and his own feelings about the people of Burma. "You have to excuse me," he said and wiped tears from his face. He was a real person. Those tears made me confident that when he spoke on behalf of the people of Burma, he would do so, not for his own gain, but because he is a politician who believes that he has to do what is right because it's the right thing to do.

When our meeting was over, he thanked us for coming and we thanked him for giving us of his time. I walked away lighter in my head although my backpack weighed just as much as ever.

I think that I also need to add that after most of my meetings in England were done, and I'd shared my stories a million times, meeting people who gave me hope that there's love in the world, and getting lost a few times, I had an afternoon off. I knew exactly how I wanted to spend it.

I got on the train and headed for the nearest H&M. There I went straight for the coat section and without a twinge of conscience, purchased the coolest black long coat for fifty dollars. It was a little sad that my time was almost over when I got my coat, but I knew I'd be back in London one day, and then I'd be prepared. If only I could get some Samsonite roll-on luggage too.

WORKING WITH POLITICIANS IS
A BIT LIKE RAISING CHILDREN

A while back, I also stole some valuable minutes with the Foreign Minister of Norway. He is a well-liked, well-respected, and absolutely above-average kind of guy. In fact, there has been some talk in Norway about how he may be *too* perfect. Politicians need to have some vices too, and it appears he has none. Anyhow, my meeting with him and his deputy had resulted in a trip to Oslo for me.

Downtown Oslo is a bustle of activity that you wouldn't think possible in Norway. Carl Johan, the capital's busiest and most interesting shopping street, is far removed from the postcard photos of fjords and snow-covered mountaintops. At its end is the Palace of the King and the Queen, and before getting there, you also pass the Parliament. Cafés and boutiques line the street, musicians and artists entertain, and social activists try to get you to agree with their causes. "Grandmothers for Peace" were particularly active on the day I strolled up and down the boulevard.

I was as far removed from my comfort zone as Carl Johan was removed from the natural wonders of Norway. Again I had gotten myself into the political scene, and again I wondered why *I* needed to do this. I had a meeting scheduled with the Foreign Ministry and my job was to inform them about the situation for the ethnic peoples in Burma, about the lack of concern the world seems to have for the atrocities going on there, about Partners' work, and about a report we were about to publish which would highlight the military junta's aggressive abuse against children in particular.

There was a light drizzle that warned the musicians to take cover, then the drizzle turned into November rain and with the rain came a wind that took hold of my cheap umbrella and turned it inside out like a sausage skin. I carried my briefcase with my Mac and documents I needed for the meeting. I had tried to do some Christmas shopping for my girls and carried a paper bag of goodies that was now in great danger of water damage.

There are times when I've wished that I worked for an organization less idealistic and more affluent than Partners. On this day I did. If I'd worked for the UN, for example, I probably would've taken the plane to Oslo, checked into a downtown hotel, taken a shower and dressed in my business attire, before taking a taxi to the meeting place just in time for the appointment.

The Partners way was to stay with friends and take the bus. I had rented a locker at the train station where I kept my suitcase since I'd be taking the train to another destination later in the day. Now I was walking up the street on my way to the political meeting. My hair was getting wet and my mascara was not waterproof. My shoulder was sore from carrying a heavy briefcase for some hours and I wondered if I knew enough numbers about Eastern Burma. I took a break at one of the many cafés just to gather my thoughts and to get a brief hiatus from the unfriendly weather.

Earlier in the day I had panicked when thinking about my lack of political skill. I knew what I knew, but my fear was that I wouldn't be able to articulate it well enough, that I wouldn't know the details well enough, and that I'd say something politically incorrect, which is not unusual for me. I called Steve and asked him a lot of questions about infant mortality, measles deaths and names of places. That I asked Steve about that proved that I was in a distressed state of mind. Steve is detail-challenged. He still doesn't remember his mother's birthday or the year Burma gained its independence. He's a big-picture kind of guy in the truest sense. So when I asked for facts, he just agreed with all my numbers, and said, "Yeah, that sounds about right. You'll do great, honey." He then suggested I call Dave in the jungle. Dave is like an ATM machine for facts and details. Just punch in the code, and out comes all the information you can ever ask for.

"What you need to say is quite simple," said Dave on the satellite phone, his voice slurring like it always does when the sound has to go all the way to a satellite in outer space before getting to the person on the other end. "First you describe the situation—and you know the situation. Innocent people are getting killed. They have no security, no food, no shelter, or medicine. Then you tell them what the local people along with Partners and FBR do to help. And then lastly you tell them that the real problem is the unchecked power of the dictators. You can tell them that apart from Partners and FBR, no outside group—not even the UN—is providing any assistance in the conflict areas. None. No protection is given to the civilians in this area. You can say that they should feel ashamed of themselves and ask them what they'd do if what happens to the civilians here happened to their daughters."

After I had finished the phone calls I felt a little like I had been sent out on a mission. The desire to fight for righteousness was bigger than the fear of failure or death. My muscles were unimpressive and my weapons primeval, but I had a cause to fight for that was worth the battle.

Walking into the Foreign Ministry building I realized that my appearance was not much better now than it had been when I'd been to the Parliament in England a year back. I carried a broken umbrella, a man's briefcase, a paper bag full of small toys for my kids, and a plastic bag of books I had accidentally bought when I passed a great English bookstore. My hair was wet from the rain and I hadn't seen a mirror for a while.

My hosts were friendly and interested. They didn't seem to care about my messy exterior and listened with interest and empathy about what I had come there to speak about. "What will Norway do to help these millions who receive no assistance?" I asked after I'd spoken for a while. Professional as they were, they made no promises and said nothing that could be used against them. They were diplomatic in the way they condemned the dictators and justified the lack of help from lofty charities by saying things like policy, dialogue, and national security. They had probably heard some of what I said before, and some was new. Some things made an impression and even challenged them. And I'm sure there were things I said that made them scratch their heads when I was gone and ask, "Who *is* this woman?" But I left the meeting feeling like I'd done my duty and I hadn't messed up too much. Whether my effort would make a difference for the people of Burma was impossible to tell though.

Working with politicians is a bit like raising children. You keep doing what is right, you keep teaching them the good values and then hope that one day, when they have to make their own choices, they'll choose honorably because of what you taught them all these years. It's like asking your kids to pick up their socks for eleven years, and then one day, they actually do it. That's what I felt walking out of the meeting. Perhaps the next time policy is made, the stories of Burma will come to mind, and they'll vote for what brings justice.

I walked back to the train station with a bounce in my steps. Now I needed to get my luggage full of mostly Partners literature and my clean clothes for the next day, and be off to a small town three hours away where I'd meet with some Karen who had become Norwegian. They called themselves *Norwegians for Karen Freedom*, and I was looking forward to meeting a band of revolutionaries.

With a suitcase, a briefcase, a couple of shopping bags and a sandwich that I had just bought for the ride, I headed for platform seventeen. I was looking forward to eating my five o'clock lunch and reading a book that was not a Burma paper. A confused lost-looking individual was standing on the platform. He turned to me and asked in broken English if I could help him find his car. It's the kind of thing you say yes to. I looked at his ticket and asked a train person to show us where to go. He pointed us in the right direction, which, it turned out, was practically right in front of us. Coincidentally, the lost guy and I appeared to be going to the same train car. As we started walking up the steps, his friend appeared from inside the train to meet us. I figured he had gotten there earlier and now came to let his friend know where he was sitting. He offered to lift my suitcase and we walked into my car. I thought it was nice that men can be gentlemen from time to time and fell down on my seat exhausted.

A minute later I was going to get my ticket from my wallet and noticed that the wallet was gone. It only took seconds to realize that the whole scene I had just experienced had been a planned robbery. My wallet was gone along with the two Eastern European men whom I thought I had befriended and helped. In panic I called Steve to close all my credit cards and then I talked to the conductor (when he asked to see my ticket) in a much less composed way than I had spoken to the politicians an hour earlier. Then for the next couple of hours I was talking to credit card and bank officials in between calling Steve and trying not to cry. The robbers had apparently followed me for a while and had been able to see my pin code when I'd paid for something. Within minutes of the robbery they had emptied my bank account and taken out a few thousand dollars on my credit card. My cash was gone, my driver's license, and a lot more. I'm a person whose wallet is big and full of memories and stuff, kind of like my desk. For example, all the passport photos of the girls over the years were gone.

My chicken tikka sandwich didn't taste as good as I had hoped. The taste of salt tears didn't go well with it. My book remained unopened. All I could think of was how stupid I had been to walk right into their trap and that now I was on a train far from home without so much as a dime to my name. Some important-looking men were sitting across from me with their laptops and suits. They had heard my entire emotional story and they looked at me with pity and then back to their important documents. I wanted to tell them to either get lost, or to at least give me some money to get home. But they just walked off the train after a while and probably told their wives about the poor lady they saw on the train. "Gullible," they probably said.

Soon I was among friends. The Karen of Gjovik welcomed me with their handshakes and smiles. The house of Saw Wai and family was more like a Karen house in Burma than I would have thought possible in Norway. On top of the bookshelf loomed a giant stuffed tiger, and on the walls photos of family members and important people were taped to the paneling. There were piles of paper in neat and not-so-neat stacks, and the smell of cooking filled their house. The odd thing was that they had furniture and they now sat on chairs and sofas. For an instant I missed squatting down on the hard floor around a low, round table.

We exchanged personal information and found that we knew a lot of the same people in Thailand and Burma. Then they wanted to hear my story about Partners, so I told them who we were and what we did and why. We watched a couple of our videos and there were tears on their faces. "You must not forget who you are, and that you have a calling to fight for your people here also," I told them and they nodded. They knew. "But it's so hard for us Karen in Norway to be taken seriously," they said, referring to the fact that they spoke Norwegian with varying degrees of thick accents. While talking I let my mind take a detour to explore the surreal scene I was in. Women can do this—think about two things simultaneously. It wasn't a scene I could have envisioned: to sit in the home of warm and friendly Karen whom I may even have spent time with in Thailand, to hear them speak to me in Norwegian, and to drink strong *norsk* coffee while it snowed outside.

The night concluded with Abraham, the most outgoing and forceful spokesman, declaring that Partners and *Norwegians for Karen Freedom* were now married. They had told me, when the meeting started, that one of their goals was to go to visit the king and tell him about their people. Now Abraham, with the approval of the others said, "I have a better idea. You go to visit the king and tell him about us, and we, the Karen, will go with you and be your cheerleaders." Then we took the obligatory group picture where we all lined up and looked solemn. My new friends had to head back to their homes. Work, school, and finals were waiting for them the next morning.

Before going to sleep that night I received a phone call from Lucky. She'd been the only lady in the group. She was one of those sharp and kind women of which there are so many in Karen State. They're the ones who should run the world, with wisdom and compassion.

Lucky called and told me that after going home that night, she and her dad had talked about the meeting and about me losing my wallet. Her dad wanted to give me five hundred Norwegian kroner before I left the next morning.

Every time I tell people this story, I start to cry. And even now, while writing it, my vision blurs because I tear up the way I do when I watch *Cinderella* or *Sleepless in Seattle*. The gift I received from Lucky's dad kind of closed the circle for me. The wealthy businessmen who had watched me after I was robbed hadn't offered to help; rather, the people who had been robbed of their homeland and the right to exist where they were born, they had helped. They understood what I needed. They were refugees in one of the richest countries in the world but that didn't leave them with a lot of cash to spare, yet they still gave because it was the right thing to do. I kept the five hundred kroner in my pocket and we bought groceries with it when I got home. For many days we had no money at all since our account had been emptied and all our credit cards closed. It felt strange to think that it was the generosity of my Karen friend who got us through that week.

THE DRUMS IN YOUR HEAD

Mostly, however, it's neither to the Parliament nor the Foreign Service that I go. Normally I go to speak to people not so unlike myself. They may appear different on the outside, but the more I interact with people the more I see this: we are quite similar in our fears, longings, and dreams.

I think Spencer had been given two tickets already that day. Spencer was our fearless American director of Partners who was blessed with an ability that many Partners staff have: if there isn't enough excitement already, they'll make some happen. He (accidentally) drove through a tollbooth without paying, made a couple of illegal U-turns, and ran a few almost-red lights. The trickiest time was when he ran the red light with a cop on the other side of the road, and then shortly thereafter did the U-turn. It was a good cop. He must have sensed that here was a poor charity worker who was very hungry for an *In-N-Out* burger. I kept thinking that Spencer is made for Partners. He drives just like Steve.

"Tell me again about this church we're going to tonight." "Well, it's kind of a branch-off from another church that started as a Bible study for young people. Many of them are kids with real different backgrounds. There will be a lot of tattoos and piercings. They don't want to meet in a church building, but in a home. They meet in a large home because they are quite a few. Should be interesting."

I felt nervous and excited at the same time.

It was easy to spot the house church. There were lines of cars down the entire street—and the next street. Young people were decorating the sidewalks and the tidy front yard of the home. None of them seemed to take notice of me. I suddenly felt very self-conscious of my age and wondered if any of them thought I was their mother. I noticed a man who was three times as big as the others. He looked Hawaiian. Ornate tattoos decorated his sumo-wrestler leg and I noticed his silver earrings.. His voice matched his size and he headed straight for me. "Hi, there! Is it Audrey? Oh, Oddly. Hi. It's so good to have you here. We're going to have a great time tonight. I'm Eric, and I'm one of the leaders of this little group of people." He talked on, and I started liking him. "So you're the pastor here?"

I asked. "Well, yes, kind of. It's my part time job. My other job is living with drug addicts and trying to help them out."

Inside it was buzzing with life. One girl was curled up in a chair sleeping. Others were sitting on the sofa chatting. The kitchen was crowded with volunteers who were setting up the communion table on the kitchen island. There were paper cups with juice and stale bread from 7-11 that you could walk up and partake of whenever you felt like it. That was the communion.

The service was about to start. Only twenty minutes late. Wes was going to lead worship. Wes loved his music and his guitar. On a low chair in front of the crowd of forty or fifty colorful youth he scrunched up, let his knit-hat slide down his forehead and played music. "God, it's a screwed-up world. Please help us," he prayed before he started. The songs were filled with soul and passion, and the music from the guitar was raw emotion given to God. Nobody sang along, however, because nobody knew any of the songs. Somehow it didn't seem to matter. I closed my eyes and sighed. I felt like I was in a Christian pub and I desperately wanted a beer.

Then I thought, *Oh, Jesus, please help me out a little here. What exactly shall I share that will be relevant to these kids?"* I was thinking while Wes kept the tunes flowing. I had been thinking about the Elie Wiesel sermon, and the Martin Luther King Jr. ideas. But, holy cow, these kids wouldn't know who that was, or at least they wouldn't find it very relevant. *Crap, is that a grey hair on my shirt?* I wondered. *Come on, Oddny. You're going to have to get them excited about Burma and Partners. Yeah, right.*

Wes was done. I wanted his CD. Then Matt jumped up. His green T-shirt said: *The drums in your head.* He had written a poem about love. He was like a dancer with words. English sounds became a ballet in our ears, leaving us slightly breathless. Eric took over. He said, "We want to go on a houseboat together next week. We'll have a great time together, so you should sign up if you want to go. Oh, we don't actually know where we're going yet, but we'll go somewhere, that's for sure." He gave a short introduction about me and about loving your neighbor, and then it was my turn.

I had no tattoos, no hat, I couldn't sing or compose, and my poetry sucks. How was this going to end? I decided to follow my gut and not my logic and started sharing my swim story from Karen State. It wasn't strictly focused on Partners , but it felt right. As soon as I started talking I felt like I connected with the group in front of me. I rambled on for thirty minutes instead of fifteen, and it felt like we were on a boat together and we were going to a place with dangerous monsters. Now I had to convince them that together we could fight the monsters. "Don't let your fear control you, but decide to do what is right," I said, and I said it to myself. The talk was over and Buzz, the other leader of the group came up. Buzz had no hair and a kind face. You didn't think of a pastor when you saw him, but of a person you'd like to be friends with. Buzz had been moved by the stories. He wanted to give and to pray.

"We don't often take up offerings here," he said, "but sometimes we do. Sometimes these guys give a lot, and then we get huge offerings, as much as three bucks." He then addressed the group: "Guys, I want us to give tonight. I want you to give more than three bucks. The KFC buckets are in the back there, on that antique thingy. You can put your money there when you leave. And I want us to pray now." So we prayed. Buzz prayed for the relief teams, that they'd be brave. He prayed for their group, that they'd remember to pray for the relief teams on a regular basis. He prayed for security. Then Wes continued, "God, we hear a lot about suffering, but tonight was different. We heard it from the horse's mouth … uh … hmm …. a very pretty horse…"

The meeting was over after Spencer invited them to get our literature and to sign up for our mailing list and stay with us forever.

Spencer and I picked a group each, and a couple of hours later we were still talking. "I want my life to matter," said Kevin. He had a flannel shirt and spiked hair. "I'm thinking that I could get a degree in agriculture so that I can do better development," said Brianna. "I'll be there," bubbled Michelle. "You just watch! One day I'm going to work with you!" I had so many talks, and the recurring theme was, "I want to do the right thing. Can you help me see what that is?"

At midnight the house was empty. A VONS plastic grocery bag was handed to us. It was the offering. The bag was full, and I suspected that there was more than three bucks in it. Spencer was a little reluctant. "What do you think a cop will say if he pulls us over and sees this bag full of cash?" The inside of the car already looked a bit like a home of the homeless: boxes and bags full of Partners literature, shirts, and paraphernalia filled the trunk and the back seat. We decided to live dangerously, so we set the bag of cash in the back seat and headed off for Redlands.

When we added up the crumbled dollar bills the next morning, we had $2,600. No more than fifty college kids and young adults with low income had been moved to not just show God's love with words, but with actions. It made me cry and filled me with hope.

I thought to end this story here, but recently I received this email:

Dear Steve and Oddny,

I hope this letter finds you well and I hope you are encouraged.

It was a warm evening as are most in Southern California and I received a phone call from a friend of mine, Eric Bothello, who told me if I was in town I should really come check out the Sanctuary service that evening that would be taking place at a house. He went on to tell me that there was going to be a guest speaker who is "right up my alley." I was volunteering at the time with a junior high ministry and preparing for a long-term documentary trip but was available that night. I showed up with little expectation and feeling comfortable in a plush chair, I sank down and cleared my mind.

Years later I cannot recall what was spoken but I do remember watching a short film. I remember the conviction in which I heard Oddny speak and was brought to silent tears from my seat. I remember feeling overwhelmed that I did not know where Burma was. I remember feeling worthless that I did not have any cash in my wallet. I grieved that night but came away feeling empowered. Empowered by the film and the visual and a personal vision that was affirmed that night for me.

I am hoping to document the repercussions and suffering communities of both the Christian Church and ethnic Burmese minorities in Thailand and surrounding countries as well as the jungles of the ethnic Burmese states. I am writing you this letter to offer my services to you and your organization. I hope to provide assistance to NGOs such as yours, utilizing my skillset of photo, video, and web storytelling for no charge and no credit. I would love to share more of my mission with you and would love to ask you some questions as well.

I believe citizens of other countries need to see more of what is happening there. I believe video to be a powerful tool that must be

*claimed for the glory of the Kingdom. Thank you for awakening my
heart with your words and your efforts. I pray blessing for your organization and safety over you. Be well and be encouraged, that night my life
was changed.*

Sincerely,
Ryan

Ryan and his wife, Leah, did what they said they would do and moved to
Thailand where they joined our tribe. Already Ryan is busy making movies,
and taking award-winning photos. I'm sure you will see them one day.
Never underestimate the power of a living room church service!

NORMAL IS OVER

One thing that has been the story of my life is that as soon as it gets easier, it gets harder. As soon as one baby is potty trained, along comes another. As soon as all the babies are potty trained, along comes a puppy. I have wondered if this is a dysfunctional condition with Steve and me. It seems as if we attract crises like magnets. And if the crises don't come to us, we go looking for them.

One of the Partners most popular taglines, our version of Nike's *Just do it*, is *Normal is Over*. Steve came up with the idea while listening to Bruce Cockburn's *Trouble with Normal*. Our *Normal is Over* T-shirts are our best-selling Partners products. They sell so much better than the toiletries bags and the chopstick holders.

Steve has a sermon, or a talk, where he challenges the listeners to think about why they're living, and what they want to have lived for at the end of their lives. Who among us wants to say, when we're at the old folks' home, "I sure was good at keeping up with the Joneses"? "What do we live for?" Steve asks. "Do we live for what really matters or for what the world has labeled normal, sensible, and safe? Is it time to say goodbye to normal and take a leap of faith into the unknown?"

This is, of course, a very simplified version of a very good sermon, a sermon that has caused pastors and other influential persons to contact Steve and ask if they can make this line their own, if it can be the title of their book, and a lot of other things that could potentially make them rich and famous.

While I couldn't agree more with Steve and his message, there are days when I think the Jones family got a good deal. They live in their cul-de-sac and will have paid their mortgage off in seven and a half years and they have the college savings for their children in the bank with the best interest rate. Mrs. Jones knows which casserole to make for the church potluck Friday and today she'll drive down to Wal-Mart and get new patio furniture. This she will do right before her children get home from school, carrying with them their A+ report cards. They'll sit down to dinner (I think it was chicken-pot-pie today) before heading off to T-ball practice, followed by a PTA meeting. Some days this sounds like a life I'd like. So predictable and mellow. Those are the days when I think about launching a new item at the Partners store, a T-shirt that says: *I Want Normal back.*

Our lives are so unpredictable that our friends and relatives have completely given up on planning anything around our schedules. I tell people who ask if we're free for dinner next Sunday that that's so far in the future that I have no idea. For all I know we may be in a different country then. When working with victims of war who constantly need food to survive, in an organization that's under-staffed, under-funded, and under-organized, predictability becomes a challenge and crisis is the norm.

There have been many days that I just want to quit. I am so tired of the whole *help-the-refugees-and-change-the-world-in-the-process game.* Some days I'd rather work at a supermarket dusting cereal boxes and rear-ranging pop tarts. You may have been reading my account of life the way I see it and thought, *Wow! What a fun life. So much adventure and great challenges. She must never be bored. Wish it were me.* Let me tell you a secret: while all the stories I share are true, I have left some stories out. For example, I haven't written much about unanswered emails filling my inbox, about days inside an office trying to meet marketing deadlines, about budget meetings and databases, or about running out of money while buying groceries for our family on more than one occasion.

I haven't told you about the constant hunt for money to pay for our projects and about the big and so-called professional organizations not wanting to have anything to do with us because in their mind we're like a mouse trying to approach a well-trained doberman pinscher. Some of them laugh at us and say things like, "Do you *really* think you're making a difference? *You?*" Others will avoid relating to us and say things like, "You have *no* idea how *busy* we are." (This implies, of course, that they're too busy for mice like us.) Most of them don't even bother answering our emails. Some of them have stolen our stuff and taken the credit for it.

I could've written some stories about churches not allowing us to speak for reasons that were so lame that I think they must have made them up on the spot too. Here are a handful of commonly-used excuses: (1.) We don't quote enough Bible verses when we speak. (2.) They had been plan-ning to watch a homemade video of the pastor's wife doing a Bible study that night. (3.) I am a woman. (4.) They support missions already. (5.) They don't like people to share at their church who they haven't met before. (6.) They're in a building program and don't have any (meaning nothing, zero, nil, zilch) money to spare. (7.) They're afraid we'll ask for money from the pulpit. (Apparently there's a verse in the Bible that says: "You shall not ever ask the congregation for money unless you're the pastor and know what to ask for.") (8.) They think we don't know the church's doctrine well enough. (9.) They only support projects among unreached people groups (I guess it's worse for *them* to be hungry and sick than the people groups who have heard the Gospel already). (10.) The pastor is the only one who can share from the pulpit except for two Sundays a year, and those two Sundays happen to have been taken by others already.

When talking about the church, I feel like I'm talking about my family, and I don't appreciate how they behave sometimes. It's upsetting and embarrassing, like if my brother was caught drunk driving. Once when I was on my way to share at a ladies' Bible study at a large church and the leader for the group called and said she wanted to give me some guidelines for my talk. They were as follows:

1. I couldn't even mention money in my talk. (Shoot. I was going to share about Doh Say carrying *money* through the jungle to give to teachers in the war zones.)

2. I couldn't hand out any literature that mentioned money. (Hard, since the point of our literature is to inform about our work and to raise money for the people we help. Why did this lady think I was going to share at her group again? To make her ladies feel fuzzy and warm?)

3. *If*, for some weird reason, somebody came to me and (a) handed me some money or (b) asked if they could give me some money, I would have to quickly tell them it was *not* okay until they went to speak to the pastor and asked his permission to give to Partners. In that way they'd know that they didn't do anything wrong by giving to us. (This pastor, whom I've never met, must be very close to God. How else would he know so much? Like how all his several thousand members ought to spend their money?)

I haven't written about conflicts we've had with staff and coworkers, that have left us (and them) bruised and wounded, and relationships broken. I can handle the lack of money and at times lack of sleep. I can even get over rejection from the professionals and the church, but nothing, nothing, nothing hurts more than relationship conflicts. I can say I learned some lessons, but the pain will always be there—a little duller over the years, but still a constant reminder of something that really stung.

So some days I want to say out loud, "I quit!" There are obviously Christians, aid workers, administrators, fund raisers, mothers, writers, and designers that can do this better than me, so why don't I let them?

I sit and stew by my desk or on the couch or wherever and feel so sorry for myself that I cry. My life is the pits and I'm fed up with everybody who is better than me and who has more money. I'm especially fed up with organizations that spend a hundred times more on just their marketing campaigns than we spend on all our projects included. It's easy to get the bucks when you have the bucks to spend to get them.

Sometimes there is a voice trying to get through all the noise in my head. I think that voice is always there, but I only hear it when I am really desperate. The voice simply asks, For *whom are you working?* I know the answer immediately.

If I take the time to really think about my mission instead of filling my head with bitterness and jealousy, I know exactly why I am where I am, doing what I'm doing. It has nothing to do with being invited into the club of prestigious organizations or churches. It has nothing to do with my retirement savings, or if my boots are in style this season. I'm not living the way I do so that people will look at me and say, "Oh, my God! I wish I were like her!" (Although, you have to admit, it would be nice if that *were* the case.)

I take a deep sigh and admit: God, I'm doing this for You and I'm sorry that I'm such a screwball. I'm sorry that I get the plot wrong over and over again. I'm sorry that I'm looking for affirmation and acceptance in all the wrong places, and that I try to fix all the problems myself. I should know by now that me fixing *anything* mostly ends in disaster.

All these things I say while I try to believe that they're true. I'm not sure if this is the case with all people, but I have a tendency to rationalize everything, and also to help God figure things out when I feel like He takes too much time. So in the same breath as I'm saying that I trust Him, I also produce small worry farts: we're a few thousand short of budget this month, You know. Did You *see* what that lady did to me? My kids may get into drugs.

I'm slow at learning, and I have a suspicion that when I'm eighty-five and walking with a cane, that you'll still find me arguing with God, and actually thinking that I have a good case that I may win. It's amazing that God doesn't just throw His arms up in the air and with an exasperated shout say, "Okay, then, just do it your way if you know everything so much better!"

He doesn't. He is as patient and forgiving as the Bible says He is. And again and again He proves that He is right. Gently, He points me in the right direction.

The things I learn are so banal that it borders on embarrassing. I should've graduated from these subjects during early years at Sunday school. But while they may be unimaginative issues, they're still the hardest to learn, at least for me.

God loves me no matter what, I realize. It's not the results or the fame or the successes that determines His love for messed-up me. It's the fact that He really, really loves me in spite of all my shortcomings. It's freeing to see, with my heart, that even if Partners one day became as professional as World Vision God won't love me any more than He does now. And *if* I—and this is even more unlikely that the World Vision idea—manage to empty my inbox on my computer, His love will still will be the same as it is now at 478 unanswered emails. Just like I won't love my kids any more than I do now even if they become the President of the United States of America. (Which Naomi aspired to become when she was six. I don't think she stands much of a chance with us as her parents, but I was proud of her ambitious goals.)

Childrearing experts talk a lot about the affection children need growing up—from their dads especially. They need lots of cuddles, hugs, and just hours and hours of lap time. Add positive reinforcements to the cuddles (loads of encouragement and affirmation) and you have yourself a recipe for success. Children, girls in particular, who don't get this will go looking for the affection and the affirmation elsewhere. It's so much like God and us. The difference is that while parents often are the ones who fail to give the children what they need simply because we're blind and lack wisdom, when it comes to God, it's us, the children, who fail to go to Him to get what we need. We go to places like the fridge, the arms of a man, or the plastic surgeon instead. Some of us, believe it or not, go to the office.

I'm living my life for Him, is my second realization. My life is a love offering to God, not a Broadway show to dazzle the world. I think that puts things in perspective, at least for me. Kristin, I must say, is one of the worst English-spellers in the world. She's also one of the kindest and most affectionate children I have ever met. (Okay, so I'm biased. She's my kid. But did you notice I said she was a bad speller?) Her tank empties very fast if she's not able to hug, touch, and feel us. While Elise and Naomi are getting ready for school by eating breakfast and making lunches, Kristin is getting ready by sitting on my lap getting kisses and hugs. I have a suspicion she'll be doing this well into her teenage years. This is what Kristin does: almost every night after we have said good night she will write us a note and put it on our bed. The other night she'd gotten herself in a bit of trouble and we had a long talk that didn't end so well for Kristin. When I went to bed, I found a note that said: "Hi. I am kreeing my hed off. I love u. God Nit. I love u. Kristin." (If you couldn't interpret this, it means: *Hi, I am crying my head off. Good night.*) How could a parent *not* love that and forgive her all her trespasses?

These notes are some of my most prized possessions. One of the reasons I love them so much is because of the way she writes: hardly one word is spelled correctly. Still, the intention is impossible to miss. The notes are declarations of devotion from a little girl who wants us to know that she loves us. I think our offerings to God can be like Kristin's love notes—imperfect, but sincere.

Look around you, is the third lesson. You're so focused on the weeds that you don't even see the lilies, I hear the voice saying. So I start looking and counting. First I look at the people whose lives have been affected by the work Partners (and that includes me) has done. There are hundreds of thousands. Last time we counted there were half a million who had been helped by Partners in just one year. Do my life's choices matter to them? I guess they do. These hundreds of thousands of people may not know that there are charities around the world who develop better websites than Partners does, but they do know that they were fed when they were starving and that they received medicine and care when they were sick or dying. Half a million people, Oddny! Is that worth a few tears and frustrations? The blisters life has given me become mere bagatelles when compared to lives saved, enriched, strengthened, and set free.

Then I ask myself, How did we get here? I'm still listening to the voice speaking in my head. Lists as long as the Pan American Highway with names of people who have faithfully supported our work for years. Who are they? Mostly Christians, individuals and churches. There is a small prick in my heart as I realize this, because while I've been criticizing my brothers and sisters, they've been busy paying our bills. Without them there simply would not have been any Partners. I start thinking about some of the churches I know who have rallied behind us through all kinds of rough weather. Many of them have given sacrificially of their resources and time. They have been there for us when we have needed it the most. Many of them are people Steve has called on numerous occasions when we just had no money to pay for unexpected (as well as expected needs.) "Tell us what you need," they've answered, and within days we'd have money. I'm not even going to guess how many prayers have been offered on our behalf, but I think it's safe to say that quite a few battles have been won by men and women interceding for us.

So some churches act with immaturity and lack wisdom at times. So some of them decide to watch a DVD of the absent pastor's wife instead of listening to me. So there are some sour apples out there. But, can't I, for a moment, focus on the masses that are the pillars of our work and our lives? Where would I be without them?

Some years ago we were getting pretty close to the edge. We had been in crisis mode a little too long, and the challenges had been a little too many. Getting out of bed in the mornings was the worst part of the day, because we knew that the days would be as intense as an Olympic sprint, and we were tired already before the race started. Out of the blue came a church team (actually I think they came from New Mexico). And out of the blue they handed us a generous check. There was one instruction attached: *Take a vacation!* Every time I tell people about this I start to cry—again, because I recall the fatigue I felt before heading off to that amazing vacation. I start crying because I'm reminded that God loved us so much and cared so much about our souls that He told a group of people from New Mexico to go to Thailand to help us take a break. And I cry because I'm so thankful that those particular people were so much better at listening to God than I am and that's why they knew that we needed a break.

Look around you, and look behind you! There are people every-where who have some part of God's plan in my life. Why do I ever think that I'm alone?

Lastly I ask myself: what did God say? Didn't He say to do this? Understanding God's voice—or rather, knowing what is God's voice—is one of life's hard challenges. To distinguish whether what I think I hear is God, or simply me wanting something so badly that I make myself sound like God, is tricky. I know that others have the same issues. I've been the victim of people who've had some hearing problems on more than one occasion. Some of those people have said that God told them to marry my husband. I think it's safe to assume that was not God.

I'm not always able to say what God is up to and getting a straight answer from Him can be difficult. I attended a Bible school many years ago, and I remember this lady teaching us about how to hear the voice of God. For a week we learned so many principles about this subject that I thought that it'd all be straightforward from now on. It'd be almost as easy as palm reading or looking into a glass ball. But—it turns out—God doesn't fit into a box or a formula. It's when we think we have Him figured out that we're in real difficulties. I'm not a specialist on the subject, but it seems to me that the best way to hear God is to quiet myself and to listen to my heart. The other trick is to listen to the advice of others. I think those two things can get us at least *close* to where God wants us to be.

And no matter how hard things have been at Partners and in my personal life, it always comes back to this: I'm doing this job because I feel this is what God called me to do, and any other job at this point in my life would be running away from what I know I need to do. It's totally clear in my heart. When I imagine myself in any other job, I know it's wrong.

When in desolation, Ignatius wrote, don't make life-changing deci-sions, and don't go back on a decision that you took during a period of consolation.[20] When you haven't slept for several nights because your baby is colicky, and he just threw up all over you, it's not the time to decide that you actually don't think that parenting is for you anyhow. When people we thought were our friends backstab us, when there are more bills than there is money, when there is more work than there are hours in

---

20 Margaret Silf, *Inner Compass* (Loyola Press 1999)

the day, when there are more emails than I can count and when there's no more coffee in the pot, it's not the time to decide to quit. In essence that's what Ignatius is saying in plain English.

In her book, *Inner Compass*, Margret Silf, says this: *If you turn a forty-foot boat around in a tunnel, you will cause a thorough shipwreck. Your life, and your journey with God are on board that boat. Don't risk sinking them forever in the depths of that dark tunnel. Nor is backpedaling a realistic alternative: it doesn't work, because it robs you of your steering control. Difficult enough to reverse safely in a car, but try walking backwards in a straight line with your eyes closed for any distance. At best you may get back to where you began, albeit with bumps and scars and gashes from your blind collisions on the reverse journey. But is that really where you want to be—back where you began?*[21]

I don't want to be where I began. I don't want to spend my life keeping up with the Joneses. Life is too short for that.

---

21   Ibid

Epilogue

EPILOGUE

The day is as hot and stuffy as only a day in Thailand during the monsoon season can be. I'm covering my body with a fragrant blend of sunscreen and mosquito repellent then passing it on to the girls with an admonition to follow my example. It's dengue fever season, and it's better to take precautions. As I approach the simple structure over by the pigpens, the duck-pond and the Moringa orchard I hear excited chatter and see lots of movement, like a giant anthill. The girls take off, running ahead of me, catching up with their friends and the latest on the movie and fashion scene. It's a surreal reality—being surrounded by tropical frogs and trees, listening to several languages spoken, smelling a mixture of barbecued chicken, jasmine flowers, and mud, and hearing references to a trendy shoe shop at the same time as discussions about strategies for development projects.

It's a staff picnic at the Partners farm in Northern Thailand. There are mango trees as far as I can see. The mangos are gone now, eaten or sold at markets. Many simply fell to the ground, bringing sweet nutrition to the soil. In the distance we can see hills.

I walk over to a small house by the corner of the property. Squatting on the ground at the back of the house, picking up food with their fingers, are my friends. They're eating as eagerly as they're talking. Food is spread on plastic plates on the ground: pieces of chicken, spicy sauces, local sausages (filled with meat, ginger, chili peppers and rice), sticky rice, and *Som Tam* (unripe papaya salad). Everybody is taking a little with their fingers, making perfect bite-size balls of sticky rice.

The occasion for the picnic is two-fold. Zingh and his family have just finished the house we helped them build. They are from the Pa-Oh people group and escaped from the harassment of the Burma Army three years ago. Now they help run the Partners training farm and their lives have acquired new meaning. They get to make things grow. They'll make it possible for others to come from Burma and learn how to grow things too. Not only that, they'll learn how to raise frogs, fish, pigs, ducks, and other creatures that will provide food and nutrition. They'll learn about composting, and about how to grow things that help other things grow.

Boonsong is one of our Karen workers and is the brain behind much of what we do at the farm. He is a man who I doubt has ever been mad. I believe that he smiles as long as the sun is up. He is mightily impressed with Zingh. "At first we ask him help us day by day," says Boonsong. "But then we can ask him to work for us. It is the significant turning point for us because we pursue to have him as our fulltime farm worker. From that day until today he is our hero for he is the one who makes every practical activities become real. It is a essential prove that God be with Partners."

And today Zingh, his wife Wan, and their little son Prathan can move into their new house. It's a reason to celebrate.

The other reason we have the picnic is that we were able to purchase a water pump at last. Now we can get water up from the pond with all the fish and frogs to the fields with all the tomatoes, lemongrass, and chili peppers. Bia, Bom, Dara, Boonsong, Niew, Sombat, and Nit Noi have practiced a song they want to sing for us. It's an English song that they've learned during their weekly English class, and then there is one more song in Thai.

Afterwards the conversation resumes until the afternoon sun makes us so snoozy that we either need to take a nap or go back to work.

That night I call Steve, who is on the other side of the world, speaking about Partners to people who want to hear. "I'm with my family here," I tell him. "This isn't just our work. This is our life."

APPENDIX

Their enemies thought they were *pusillanimous*

A very brief history lesson on Burma

I often talk to children in schools about Burma and Partners. I explain some of the issues like this:

Burma is a country full of diversity and beauty. It's a fruit cocktail of different people groups, all with their own cultures, costumes, languages, history, and traditions. They're all unique and part of what makes Burma so colorful. Think of the map of Burma as a jigsaw puzzle with each piece being the territory of one particular people group. Some of these people groups used to be their own countries in the past. They had their own rulers and governments. In 1886 Burma became a colony of England, and all the ethnic groups were included in the package. One of these people groups was the Karen. After a while the Karen got the feeling that if the British stopped ruling Burma, the ethnic groups in the country would suffer more. They were concerned that the dominant Burmese population wouldn't give the ethnics their rights and their land back. So when the British promised the Karen their own independent state if they'd just fight with them, the Karen thought that was a good option. They fought together with the Brits against the Burmese, and many died.

The British ruled the country until it became an independent nation in 1948. But when they left, they conveniently forgot all about the promise they had given to the Karen. The Karen who had given their lives in the battle weren't rewarded with as much as a plot of land to grow their pumpkins.

After independence the country was named the Union of Burma since all these different people groups were included. This, of course, made it pretty difficult to rule the nation. Everybody had their own opinion about what was important and what was right, so while the new rulers of the country probably tried their best to make everybody happy, they did have some issues and didn't exactly succeed in making it a united nation.

There was a man who perhaps *would* have been able to do this better than the ones who eventually ended up in power. His name was Aung San. He had dedicated his life to the freedom of Burma, and was the first prime minister. He helped write a constitution for the country, and put together a cabinet that consisted of the best-qualified men in the country at that time.

Very sadly, some of his rivals secretly entered the Parliament building and killed Aung San and six members of his cabinet in 1947. Imagine what a tragedy that was for the country! So many good people shot dead. Some people were charged with this crime; but the one held responsible was a man named U Saw. He was later executed for what he did. However, many people believe that he wasn't the main person responsible. I don't think we'll ever know the whole story.

Jump ahead to 1962 and another big and tragic event happened that shaped the history of Burma. Like I said, the new rulers struggled to hold things together. You know how we all know how something should be done until we're put in charge ourselves? Then we realize that it's a lot easier to talk about how to run things right than to actually run it. I think that is how Prime Minister U Nu and his guys felt. Their enemies thought they were *pusillanimous*. (For younger kids we can use the word chicken, or wimpy.)

A man with ambitions, General Ne Win On, came onstage at this point. He had earlier been asked to help the government fix the country, so to say, and in 1962 he decided to take matters in his own hands. He staged a military coup and arrested the Prime Minister and other important leaders. There was never a trial, so they weren't told why they had been arrested, and didn't get to defend themselves. This would become a common practice over the next fifty years and beyond. Then Ne Win dissolved the parliament, which is a nice way to say he kicked out the rest of the political leaders. While he was at it, he also suspended the Constitution that Aung San and his team had written in 1947. By suspend, Ne Win meant that for the time being, until further notice, they didn't live and act by the Constitution. Then, as the icing on the cake, General Ne Win got his handpicked advisors (The Revolutionary Council) to give him a new title. It was an impressive one: "Supreme legislative, executive, and judicial authority."[22] This title will, of course, not fit on any business card. In plain English we say *Dictator*.

---

22   Barbara Victor, *The Lady* (Faber and Faber, Inc.) pg 78

At this point of my speech we move on to talk about what a dictator is, and what the difference between a dictatorship and a democracy is. When I speak with first and second graders, I make it even simpler than this. We talk about the good guys and the bad guys, just to avoid confusion. And then they tell me about the bad guys they know. I love to hear about them. But this is beside the point. The point here is that what *could* have become Southeast Asia's most prosperous nation took a dive, hit the bottom, and has still not come up.

One of the first assignments Ne Win gave himself after becoming Supreme legislative, executive, and judicial authority was to visit one of Burma's neighbors, China. What he observed in China so inspired Ne Win that he decided to create his own ideology: *The Burmese way to socialism.* The ideology was, of course, not a belief system the way we think of it. It was a euphemism for xenophobia and superstition. (Okay, so I'm forgetting that I'm talking to children here, using words that may not be in their spelling bees.)

The Revolutionary Council, which served as Ne Win's advisors, promised to establish "mass and class organizations" based "primarily on the strength of peasants and other working masses that form the great majority of the nation."[23]

These were some of the grand promises. The real story took an entirely different form. Within a couple of years Burma had fallen into desperate poverty. The country—once called Asia's rice bowl—soon was one of the poorest nations in the world.

Here we have to take a break and explain difficult words such as *revenue* and *natural resources*. Revenue, of course, means all the money you get from something you sell, stuff or services (selling lemonade or helping dad wash the car). In Burma, they have lots of teak, precious stones such as emeralds and diamonds, oil, and gas. All this we call natural resources. It happens to be the kind of resources the world desires and thinks it needs. In fact, many are willing to kill to get it. These resources can be sold for millions. The government in Burma could easily have built schools and hospitals for the whole population with the money (revenue) they made from their natural resources; they could have built roads and

---

23   Ibid

made art galleries; they could have given people grants and started research centers. But instead they spent most of the money on weapons and nice houses for the generals and their children.

As local communities and ethnic groups fell into deeper poverty, they became less and less impressed with Ne Win and the junta. Their land was stolen, their people killed, their children lacked everything from food to medicine and schools. Not surprisingly, insurgency groups popped up. (Insurgency is the same as organized rebellion aimed at overthrowing a government, using weapons or subversion. Children sometimes form insurgency groups to overthrow parents' bedtime or dishwashing rules.) Wouldn't you have joined one if you had the chance? How were the people supposed to make a change if not by working against the government?

And this is where we take our recess while I finish the rest of the story in my head.

My country, Norway, was occupied by the Nazis during WWII. One morning in 1940 the people of Norway woke up to find out that Germany had invaded our country. The Nazis destroyed our towns, stole our food, moved into our houses, forced our king to flee, killed our innocent men, made children starve, took away our rights to listen to the radio, read the news, wave our flag, sing our songs, and to make our own decisions.

We weren't about to put up with such treatment. All over our countrymen risked their lives to fight the enemy. They crossed mountains and plains on skis under difficult conditions; they fought ice-cold waves in row boats; they traveled on foot through the countrysides and on bikes in towns. Our bravest men and women fought the enemy by sabotaging their equipment, stealing their information, blowing up their boats, informing the civilians, bringing supplies, printing leaflets, and passively or aggressively combating the intruders. Did they use weapons in their efforts? Of course! If they owned them. They carried their rifles on their backs, ready to shoot if need be.

These men and women are our country's greatest heroes. We credit them for our freedom. We write books and make movies about them, we learn about them at school, we have given them medals and honor. Nothing less would suffice for such bravery, laying down their lives to fight an evil regime.

While I've never met a single person who would question the ethics of what my countrymen and women did, I often meet people who have question the resistance movements of the Karen and the other ethnic groups. People will ask me, "Do they carry weapons? Are they *guerrillas*?" When they ask, they say the word *guerrilla* the way they would say *communist*, which is the same way they would say *Nazi* or *terrorist*.

And I have to wonder: why shouldn't they be allowed to defend themselves, their people, their children, their land and their homes? What are they supposed to do when armed criminals enter their homes, raping, killing, torturing, stealing and destroying? What would we do under such circumstances?

I'm not for the death penalty, and I used to be a pacifist. I think we spend too much money on weapons, and I would never be able to shoot somebody. But after spending time with Karen and other resistance fighters who spend their lives defending their country, I must say that I don't understand why we should deny them that right. Our countries invest a lot (more than strictly necessary, some of us would argue) on military this and that. This, we argue, is necessary to protect our nations. And this most of us do without even having an enemy that threatens to come and burn our homes and rape our children. Why, then, should the Karen not be able to do the same? Their resistance army defends the civilian populations, using outdated WWII weapons, relying on strategy, skill and determination. Often they're outnumbered ten to one, and frequently their old guns jam during battles.

By now, whether you're in the school class I am teaching or in an adult meeting where I'm speaking on the plight of the people of Burma, you may raise your hand and say, "Excuse me, Mrs. Gumaer, but isn't what you're talking about old news? I thought democratic elections were held in Burma not so long ago, and the nation is no longer a military dictatorship, but well on the way to becoming a democracy. Free elections and the release of opposition leader Aung San Suu Kyi should prove that."

I will then take a deep breath and say, "I sure wish it was that simple. But it isn't."

This is why:

The worst natural disaster that Burma has ever experienced happened in 2008. Typhoon Nargis devastated large portions of the country, killing more than 100,000 people and leaving many more homeless. It was a terrible disaster. From the Irrawaddy River delta, where the cyclone did the most damage, we received photos of corpses floating, of people dressed in rags looking through the rubble, searching for their relatives and their belongings. We received firsthand accounts of the government blocking aid destined for the victims, of soldiers forcing refugees back to their destroyed villages, and of orphans being kidnapped by government agents.

One week after this disaster the junta held a referendum. People were asked to go the ballots to vote *Yes* or *No* to the Constitution the junta had drafted. With no input from any opposition or ethnic groups they had penned a Constitution the way they thought it should be.

Not only was the referendum held while the country was still in shock after the disaster, but the rest of the circumstances around the event were suspicious as well. Soldiers went door to door forcing people to vote *yes*; threats were common and family members disappeared; and ballots, already filled out, were given to the people who showed up to vote. In some villages no polling stations were set up, in others they closed early. In others the mayors cast the ballots for the entire village. Not surprisingly, the Constitution was approved by an overwhelming YES. And what did the Constitution say?

I am no student of law, and find it hard enough to understand the traffic rules sometimes. But I do understand that there is a problem with a Constitution that states these things:

Rather than giving power to the people, it reserves almost absolute power for the military. By law (the Constitution) the Army is to be given 25% of the seats in Parliament. There would be a huge outrage in my country if the army tried to take 25% of the seats of our Parliament, making decisions on finances and laws. It would be like letting my husband plan the family menu—a disaster. In Burma, however, this has now become an accepted practice.

By law (the Constitution) the Ministry of Defense can work independent from the rest of the Parliament, which means that while the rest have to abide by certain rules, the military can make their own rules without anybody interfering.

The law also states that in order to make changes to the Constitution, there needs to be the approval of more than 75% of the Parliament.

This means, of course, that the military effectively has veto power over any attempts to change the Constitution. Add to this bizarre mix that the Commander-in Chief is the one who prepares a list from which the President must choose several of his ministers.

Jared Genser who is a Lecturer in Law at the University of Pennsylvania Law School and facilitator of the European Burma Network, whom I heard at a conference recently said this: "*The Constitution also effectively legalizes military coups. When the President declares a state of emergency, fundamental rights are suspended and the Commander-in-Chief assumes power over all branches of government. And in the shadows of the official branches of government, the Constitution establishes a National Defense and Security Council, whose powers and responsibilities remain vague, suggesting it is merely the latest incarnation of the State Peace and Development Council, the junta's official title.*"

So there you go. Even if the so-called democratic elections in 2010 *had* been free and fair (which they weren't), the Constitution still gives the military pretty much exactly the same power and influence as before. The clothes of the people in power may have changed. Their methods have not.

As I am writing this in 2011, I am receiving reports about positive changes in Burma. Media and politicians are saying that the new leaders in Burma are moving in the right direction. This may be true in some areas of the country. But at the same time as I am receiving these reports, I am also receiving daily reports of attacks in the ethnic areas, of abuse, famine and death. Not much has changed, and I dare to predict that it will take a while before Burma is free and the children can live their lives to the fullest.

THANK YOU

No man is an island entire of itself; every man is a piece of the continent, a part of the main, said John Donne almost five hundred years ago.

Oddny did not write this book entirely by herself, is what I want to say today. The book you have just read could only be written because of the people who have been a part of my life.

Thank you to all my friends from Burma who have willingly shared your stories with me, who have put up with me scribbling frantically in my notebook while you talked, who have answered all my questions about your lives—questions that at times must have sounded unnecessarily personal. Thank you especially to *Arthur, Clasper, Doh Say, Paw Htoo, Raykaw, Rose* and *June Rose.*

Thank you to all Partners staff. You are more than co-workers. You are more than staff. You are my friends, my heroes and my inspiration. You are the dream team— people who have given up your own ambitions, your own careers, your own comfort and safety to serve and bring life. How lucky am I to be on your team! And how boring would my life, and this book, be without you! I am sorry I didn't write a story about every single one of you.

Thank you to all of you who have encouraged me to write, to those of you who had to plough through my first couple of drafts, so full of inappropriate words, statements that were childish, too personal, and full of mistakes. *Linda, Lynn, Chris* and *Ruth, Ben, Dave* and *Karen, Brad* and *Joyce,* I hope it wasn't too traumatic.

I had an editor who was perfect for me. *Ed Strauss* corrected grammar, fixed spelling and rewrote unintelligible sentences. He was very sensitive in the way he suggested that I keep some opinions to myself, thereby perhaps saving me from a lawsuit. The best thing he did, however, was to encourage me and tell me that my writing was good. To be a writer and hear that from an editor is like hearing Pavarotti if you like opera.

Sacha, thank you for being born! The world sure is a more beautiful place with you in it! This book has become a piece of art because of you. I want to become like you one day. Teach me your Illustrator, Photoshop and InDesign secrets, please!

Thank you to the STEPS foundation for making the publication of this book possible.

Without my family there would have been no book. Thank you *Elise*, *Naomi* and *Kristin* for being such goofballs, such troopers, and such brats at times. Thank you for hugging me and making me feel loved and for challenging me in ways I thought I never would be. You have made my life worth living and given me years of material to write about!

Lastly thank you to my best friend, my lover, and my hero above all heroes, *Steve*. With you I believe I can do almost anything, even change the world.

BIBLIOGRAPHY

These are some books you should read if you want to know more about Burma, Partners, how to care for kids of war, and how to get closer to Jesus. It's not a comprehensive list of everything I have read. Just some books I have enjoyed and learned heaps from.

BURMA

The Trouser People, Andrew Marshall, Penguin Books, 2002

Land Without Evil, Ben Rogers, Monarch Books, 2004

Little Daughter, Zoya Phan, Pocket books, 2010

The Land of Green Ghosts, Pascal Khoo Thwe, Flamingo, New Ed Edition, 2003

For us Surrender is Out of the Question, Mac McClelland, Shoemaker & Hoard, Div of Avalon Publishing Group Inc, 2010

Finding George Orwell in Burma, Emma Larkin, Granta Books, 2011

Twilight over Burma: My life as a Shan Princess, Inge Sargent, University of Hawaii Press, 1995

Living Silence in Burma: Surviving Under Military Rule, Christina Fink, Zed Books Ltd; 2nd Revised edition, 2009

The Lady: Aung San Suu Kyi: Nobel Laureate and Burma's Prisoner, Barbara Victor, Faber and Faber; illustrated edition, 1998

Perfect Hostage, Justin Wintle, Arrow, 2008

Than Shwe: Unmasking Burma's Tyrant, Ben Rogers, Silkworm Books, 13 July 2010

The Burma Road, Donovan Webster, Farrar, Straus and Giroux; 1st edition (October 13, 2003)

FAITH

Divine Compass, Margaret Silf, Loyola Press, 1999

Traveling Mercies: Some Thoughts on Faith, Anne Lamott, Anchor Books, 2000

Bird by Bird: Instructions on Writing and Life, Anne Lamott, Anchor, 1995
Blue like Jazz, Donald Miller, Thomas Nelson, 2003
Million Miles in a Thousand Years, Donald Miller, Thomas Nelson, 2009
The Way to Love, Anthony De Mello, Bantam Doubleday Dell, 2000
The Irresistible Revolution, Shane Claiborne, Zondervan 2006

GENERAL INTEREST

The Soul of Money, Lynn Twist, W. W. Norton & Co, 2006
Healing the Children of War, Phyllis Kilbourn, Marc Pubns, 1995

NOVELS

The Other Hand, Chris Cleave, Sceptre, 2009
The Poisonwood Bible, Barbara Kingsolver, Faber and Faber, 2000
What is the What, Dave Eggers, McSweeney's, 2006
Shantaram, Gregory David Roberts, St. Martin's Press, 2004
The Help, Kathryn Stockett, Penguin Books, 2009
The Power of one, Bruce Courtenay, Ballantine Books, 1989
Cry, the Beloved Country, Alan Paton, Scribners, 1948

CHILDREN'S BOOKS WITH A MESSAGE

We are Going on a Bear Hunt, Michael Rosen, Walker Books Ltd, 1997
The BFG, Roald Dahl, Puffin, 2007
Momo, Michael Ende, Puffin Books, 1973

VISIT THESE WEBSITES

www.partnersworld.org
www.fbr.org
www.mizzima.com
www.irrawaddy.com
www.burmacampaign.org.uk

www.csw.org.uk
www.hrw.org
www.uscampaignforburma.org
www.dvb.no

Oddny Gumaer

Oddny Gumaer from Norway founded Partners Relief & Development (PRAD) together with her Alaskan husband Steve. The organization helps hundreds of thousands of displaced people and refugees from Burma every year. For sixteen years she and her family lived and worked at their PRAD base in Thailand— leading the work from there. Oddny is the mother of three daughters who say they sometimes wonder what their nationality is. She and her family currently live in Norway, although their work still is with the people of Burma. When not busy working for Partners, taking care of her kids, her husband and their Labradoodle, Bob Marley, Oddny likes to go for runs, hikes, cross-country ski trips and she dreams of owning a kayak one day.

If you want to follow her, visit her blog at *www.oddnygumaer.com*